ISBN: 0-87973-878-2

Library of Congress Catalog Card Number: 74-177999

The author owes particular thanks to Robert Lockwood
and Ronald Altenhof of the OSV staff, who aided in
putting all of this material together.

Cover Design by James E. McIlrath
                  National Geographic Photo,
                  George F. Mobley. Courtesy
                  U.S. Capitol Historical Society

Published, printed and bound in the U.S.A. by
OUR SUNDAY VISITOR, INC.
Noll Plaza, Huntington, Indiana 46750

OUR AMERICAN CATHOLIC HERITAGE

Father Albert J. Nevins, M.M.

OUR SUNDAY VISITOR, INC.
Huntington, Ind. 46750

CONTENTS

I. THE AGE OF EXPLORERS

II. THE TIME FOR PIONEERS

III. THE CHURCH COMES OF AGE

Old Mission Church, Taos N.M.

America's Catholic Birthright

S OMEONE once remarked, "Scratch the soil of any part of America, and you will find roots set down by Catholics." It is one of the aims of this book to find out whether this is true.

There are other aims. Perhaps, in these days of intensified ecumenism it may at first seem strange that a book should be written on the contributions of any one religious group. But it is also a purpose of this book to show all Americans what one particular group did to help build the greatness of the United States, hoping that this will create greater understanding and more ready cooperation.

Finally, in revealing to Catholics what their fellow co-religionists did in building America, they may take new pride in their own citizenship and re-dedicate their own efforts to the fulfillment of the American dream which entailed great privation and sacrifice on the part of so many others.

Many nations and peoples have contributed to the greatness of the United States, but it was the English who had the most influence. As it will be seen, the United States could have been French or Spanish. But through circumstance and historic timing, the English were in the right places at the right time. As a result, we Americans received our language, our system of education, our respect for law, our traditions of justice and equality, all from our English heritage.

Unfortunately, because of our Anglo-Saxon culture and language, our thinking and even our history books have often been influenced to ignore, or at best to play down, the roles of non-Anglo-Saxon peoples in developing the United States. This was not the result of deliberate conspiracy but the result of many contributing factors.

It must be remembered that England, France and Spain were not only rivals, but at times bitter enemies. Only fifteen years before the first English settlement in the New World, the English had defeated the Spanish Armada. Much of the early history of the American colonies included war between French and English.

Another important factor was the bitter feeling that existed in Europe between Protestants and Catholics, resulting from the chaos of the Protestant Reformation. The English represented Protestantism, and the Spanish and French represented Catholicism. Since the English culture became dominant in the United States, some of this feeling was transferred here and the contributions made by Catholics were sometimes distorted or more often entirely overlooked.

I can remember that, as a boy, I believed the Pilgrims were the first settlers in what is now the United States. I am sure now that no teacher actually said that this was so; but the historical emphasis put on the *Mayflower*, the Pilgrims, and the first Thanksgiving, led me to conclude that American history began with the landing of the Pilgrims on Plymouth Rock in 1620. It was a great surprise when I learned later that the Spanish had founded the city of St. Augustine in Florida, in 1565, and had contributed much to the development of our country.

It is regretted that national and religious ri-

NEW MEXICO STATE DEPARTMENT OF DEVELOPMENT

valries that existed in Europe were transferred to America, because sometimes they caused distortions that changed the development of America. Father Isaac Jogues, a French Jesuit of whom we shall hear more later, discovered a beautiful lake in New York State, which he named "Lake of the Blessed Sacrament." Later the English changed the name to "Lake George" in honor of the English king, and it is this second name that endures. However, the people of New York State have partly rectified this error by erecting an impressive statue of Jogues, which looks down on the lovely lake he discovered and mapped.

One of the greatest injustices was the nationalistic and religious bigotry shown towards the Acadians, a French people who lived in what is now Nova Scotia. The Acadians were simple folk who minded their own business, desiring only to be left in peace to tend their well-kept farms and practice their Catholic religion.

Then one day without warning, English soldiers rounded up the Acadians and put them aboard ships, which carried them to southern colonies. Some Acadians died; many children were separated from their parents and never found them again; and the displaced people were left homeless and penniless. Some Acadians reached Louisiana, where their descendants, now called "Cajuns," still live. You can read the tragic story in Longfellow's poem, *Evangeline*.

Because the Spanish and French explorers were Catholics, they brought many priests and missioners with them to the New World. Thus the Catholic Church came early and played an important role in the founding of the American nations. This book will tell something of the contribution Catholics made to the United States.

ALBERT J. NEVINS

Lief Ericson discovers Vinland in 1000 A.D. Viking ruins have been found in Newfoundland (Vinland).

I. THE AGE OF EXPLORERS

The Forgotten Norsemen

ONE of the great mysteries of history is who really discovered America.

He might have been an Irishman, or a Chinese, or a Norwegian, or an Egyptian. No one knows. One thing is sure, however: Christopher Columbus wasn't the first man here. Columbus came upon America by accident while looking for the East Indies. His contribution was that, when he returned home and told of his discovery, he focused the attention of the European powers on the New World, powers which were at that moment ripe for trade and external expansion. But all evidence indicates that other explorers were in the New World before him.

Actually, America was "discovered" at least three times, and probably many times more. The first discoverers were those ancestors of our Indians who about twenty thousand years ago crossed over from Siberia. Some scientists think that there was then a land bridge connecting Asia and America, and that this bridge disappeared ten thousand years ago when the great Canadian ice sheet melted.

Among the early records of the Chinese, there is the story of one Hoei-Sin, a man who sailed four thousand miles east of Japan to discover a land called "Fusang," where he saw animals with branching horns and men who painted their bodies

9

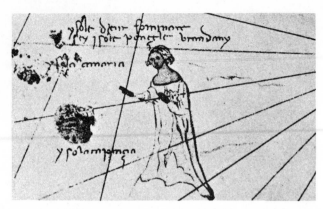

Saint Brendan's Island is shown in 1367 Italian map.

with many colors. There are Irish legends that tell of voyages out onto the Atlantic Ocean and the discovery of new lands. Saint Brendan is reported to have gone on a seven-year voyage, seeking a "mysterious land" far over the sea. There are even legends, for example among the Mayas and Aztecs, of "foreign" visitors to their peoples.

None of these legends can be confirmed. The accounts are mixed up with so many imagined and miraculous happenings that the truth is almost impossible to sift out. This is not so, however, with the sagas of the daring Norwegian sailors, known as Norsemen or Vikings. Their records establish the fact that they did venture far out on the sea and discovered Iceland and Greenland.

The Norsemen began their journeys in this way. In the latter part of the ninth century, King Harold gained control of all Norway. Many Norsemen, particularly the lesser chiefs, did not wish to submit to his rule. Those men gathered their families and embarked from Norway in great, open, sail-driven boats, some as long as eighty feet. Some Norsemen went to England; others to France; and still others to serve the Byzantine emperors, on the Mediterranean Sea.

There was one group of Norsemen, however, who loved the cold, high-running seas of the north. In the year 874, those hardy seafarers sailed westward, beyond Scotland, until they reached a land where there was much ice. They named their discovery "Iceland," and there they settled. In due time they built stone houses, raised livestock, and carried on trade with Europe.

About that time there was a man by the name of Thorvald, who lived with his son, Eric, in the Orkney Islands. Thorvald and Eric were accused of manslaughter, and they left the Orkneys for Ice-land. There Eric prospered, was nicknamed "the Red," married, and had three sons: Thorvald, Thorstein, Leif. A feud broke out between Eric and a neighbor; and in the course of it, a number of men were killed. To escape prosecution, Eric decided to take his ship and search for a land to the west, which had been reported years before by a Norseman who had been driven off course to Iceland by a storm.

Eric sailed west and reached that new country. It had great rocky bays and fjords, as had Norway. There was much ice. There were no trees, but the slopes of the hillsides were covered with grass. Eric immediately saw the possibility of colonizing that land, so he called it "Greenland" because, he said, "men would be the more readily persuaded thither if the land had a good name."

For three years Eric explored Greenland. The ruins of his stone houses can still be seen today. Then he returned to Iceland, made peace with the family with whom he had been feuding, and organized an expedition to settle Greenland. Twenty-five Viking ships set out for the new land, but fourteen were lost on the way—an indication of the perils of travel in those days. The survivors founded the colony; other settlers followed from Iceland; and trade was begun with Iceland and Europe.

For one such trading mission, Eric chose his son Leif as leader. Leif sailed to Norway without going by way of Iceland. This was considered a great feat of navigation, because the Norsemen used no maps or charts or compasses. Leif was something of a hero when he arrived in Norway. He was received by King Olaf. Norway by that time had been converted to Christianity, and King Olaf explained this religion to Leif, as he did to all heathen visitors.

Leif asked to be baptized a Catholic, along with his crew. This was done. Then the zealous ruler charged Leif to return to Greenland.

"Thither thou shalt go on my errand," said King Olaf, "to proclaim Christianity there."

Leif returned home and, as the saga tells us, "proclaimed Christianity throughout the land." Leif's mother ordered built a church, where the people gathered to say prayers in common. Leif's father, Eric, was slow to embrace the new religion, but finally he was baptized. It was not long before the people in Greenland were asking to have their own priests and bishop.

One day a man whose name was Bjarne arrived in Greenland to visit his father. Bjarne told

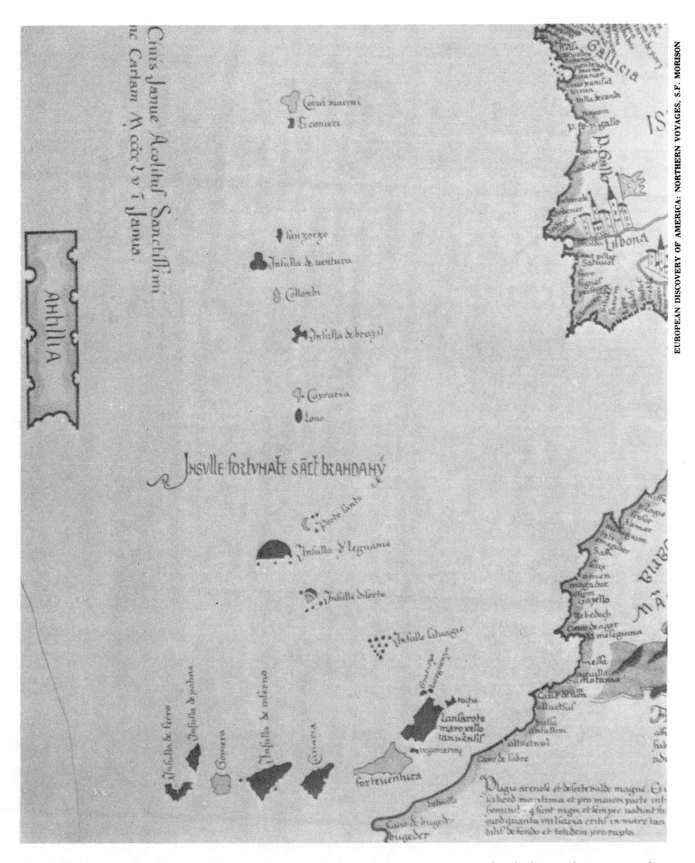

EUROPEAN DISCOVERY OF AMERICA: NORTHERN VOYAGES, S.F. MORISON

The real and the imaginary make up this map of the Atlantic, interpreting the findings of Saint Brendan.

11

Vikings raid a French seacoast

of how, after leaving Iceland, his ship had become lost in a heavy fog. He had kept sailing westward, and when the sun came out, he saw land. As he drew near, he saw that it was not a treeless region, as was Greenland. There were no mountains, but only gentle hills with forests that came down to the ocean.

"This is not the land I seek," the unimaginative Bjarne then concluded.

Bjarne's crew wanted to land to take on wood and water, but he ordered the ship back to sea. A gale arose, and all hands forgot the new land in an effort to ride out the storm. At last the ship reached Greenland. The hardy Greenlanders were vexed with Bjarne for not having made an effort to learn more about the land he had seen. They were particularly excited about the forests because wood was at a great premium in treeless Greenland.

When Leif Ericson heard the story of Bjarne, his imagination was immediately stirred. He bought Bjarne's ship, recruited a crew of thirty-five men, and set sail for the west. The explorers finally sighted land, and this was in the year A.D. 1000. The land was flat rock, beyond which was ice reaching up to snow-covered mountains. Leif named it "Helluland"; that is, "Place of Flat Stones."

Leif did not linger in that inhospitable place —which may have been Labrador. He sailed to the south and came to a new land where there were broad beaches of white sand behind which thick forests spread as far as the eye could see. Leif named his discovery "Markland"—"Land of Forests." No one is sure where that land was, but a good guess would be Nova Scotia proper, or Cape Breton Island.

Once more Leif put to sea. Again he sailed to the south, with a strong wind behind him. The Norse saga tells what happened:

"They came to an island, which lay to the north side of the land. There they went ashore and looked about them. They observed that there was dew on the grass, and it so happened that they touched the dew with their hands, and touched their hands to their mouths, and it seemed to them that they had never before tasted anything so sweet as this."

The saga goes on to tell how Leif took his ship to the mainland and up a river. The story continues:

"They resolved to put things in order for wintering there, and they accordingly built a large house. They did not want for salmon; and they thought the salmon larger than any they had seen before. The country thereabouts was possessed of such good quality that cattle there would need no fodder in winter. . . . Day and night were more equal than in Iceland or Greenland."

Leif and his men explored the countryside. One day a German crewman, named Tryker, who was so close to Leif that the Norseman thought of him as a foster father, returned to camp with some grapes he had found growing wild. Leif immediately named the country "Vinland." Just where Vinland was, we do not know. Some historians believe that it was in Nova Scotia; others that it was part of New England—perhaps Massachusetts. A strong argument can be made for the latter belief, but the final answer remains one of the mysteries of history.

Leif and his companions spent the winter in Vinland. They kept themselves busy cutting down trees and loading their ship with timber. In the spring the explorers sailed for home. On the way back to Greenland, Leif found fifteen men shipwrecked on a rocky island. He rescued them and took them to Greenland. Because of his discovery and the rescue, Leif was given the added name, "the Lucky." From that time to this day, he has been known as Leif the Lucky.

Leif's discovery and his cargo of timber caused much excitement in Greenland. His brother, Thorvald, was challenged by the news. He asked Leif if he might borrow the ship and go to Vinland. Leif gave his brother permission. Thorvald was well respected in Greenland, and it was not difficult for him to recruit a crew of thirty men. They reached Vinland without incident and spent a quiet winter there.

In the spring, Thorvald and his companions began an exploration of the coast. They found the country rich and beautiful. On an island they came upon a rough, wooden building used for storing grain; and for the first time, they realized that the land was inhabited. In a storm, Thorvald's ship was damaged, and it had to be beached for repairs. The place where the repairs were made, Thorvald named "Keelness."

Keelness was a beautiful spot. There was a good anchorage, and the nearby forest was luxuriant.

"It is a fair region here," Thorvald told his companions, "and here I should like to make my home."

Before Thorvald could build his house, the

Viking fighting ship and a typical warrior at sea

party encountered some savages, probably Indians, who had bows and arrows and used skin boats. The Norsemen captured most of the savages but one escaped and roused his tribe. The savages attacked the Norsemen, and the latter took refuge behind the war boards on their ship. The attackers were finally driven off, but Thorvald was mortally wounded when an arrow struck him in an armpit. He asked his men to bury him on the headland where he had wished to build his home.

"Place a cross at my head, and another at my feet, and call the place 'Crossness' for ever after!" Thorvald requested.

The Norsemen followed their leader's wish, and thus was performed the first recorded burial of a white man in continental North America. In 1831, a skeleton was dug up near Fall River, Massachusetts. The skeleton wore a rusted breastplate, a portion of which many years later was analyzed by a Swedish metallurgist who said that its composition was similar to metals used by the Norsemen. Possibly the skeleton was that of Thorvald Ericson.

Two years after the burial, one Thorfinn Karlsvene sailed his ship to Greenland. He made his home with Leif Ericson and soon set his heart on the beautiful and clever Gudrid, the widow of Leif's dead brother, Thorvald. Leif approved the marriage, and it took place that winter. In the spring of 1007, Thorfinn sailed from Greenland with sixty-five men and women and various kinds of cattle, to set up a permanent settlement in Vinland. At first the colony prospered, trading with the Indians and growing an abundance of food. Gudrid gave birth to a son, Snorre, the first European child born in the New World. However, after four years, because of quarrels, the colony was abandoned. The settlers returned to Greenland, rich with grapes, furs and lumber. After Thorfinn's death, Gudrid became a nun and spent the remainder of her life in prayer and fasting.

Three bishops are numbered among her grandchildren and great-grandchildren.

There were other attempts to colonize Vinland. Bishop Eric Upsi is recorded as having gone there in 1121, to do missionary work; if he did reach Vinland, he was the first missioner to the New World. For a reason as yet unknown, the Vinland colony disappeared. Some historians believe that it may have been given up because of the Black Plague, which raced over Europe. Another cause may have been destruction of the Greenland colony by barbarians (perhaps Eskimos or hostile Indians); after the loss of the mother colony, Vinland was abandoned.

One additional puzzle remains. In 1898 in Minnesota, a stone was unearthed in the west central part of the state on which was carved an inscription in Runic, the language of the Norsemen. The slab, 30x16x6 inches in size, weighs over two hundred pounds. The inscription is made up of 206 Runes, three Latin letters (AVM—Ave Maria) and twelve numerals. The message on the stone was this:

"We are an exploring party of eight Swedes and twenty-two Norwegians, traveling from Vinland through the west. A day's journey north of this stone, we camped by a lake containing two rocky islands. Here some of us went fishing for the day. When we came back to camp, we found ten of our men dead and covered with blood. Hail Mary! Save us from evil! We left ten of our men by the sea to look after our ships, fourteen days from this island. A.D. 1362."

Some scholars say that the Kensington Stone is authentic; others, that it is a hoax. Those who believe it to be a relic of the Norsemen—and many good historians and archeologists do—conjecture that a Viking expedition may have sailed through Hudson Bay, down the Nelson River into Manitoba, and then into Minnesota. At any rate, the stone is one more mystery related to the Catholic Norsemen.

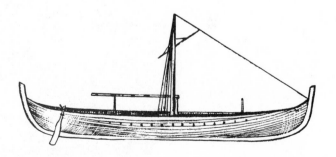

The Age of Discovery

THE discoveries by the Norsemen began no rush of Europeans to develop the New World. There were a number of reasons for this. First, they themselves lived on the fringe of the known world. Then, the Norse findings were not properly understood or evaluated in Europe; at best they were thought of as a few islands somewhere across the North Sea. Finally, the countries of Europe were in the process of their own development. Italy was a confusion of city states; Spain, a series of disjointed kingdoms; and William the Conqueror had not yet begun his unification of England. Because there were no strong nations, national rivalries did not yet drive one country to seek commer-

cial advantages over another; commerce itself was still in its infancy.

Five centuries later, that picture had completely changed. Mighty nations had come into being, each seeking to extend its power. The great commercial houses in Portugal, Spain, France, England, and Italy competed for the fine silks and the exotic spices of the East. The journal of Marco Polo, which appeared about the year 1300, excited the imagination of men, with its stories of fabulous wealth that could be obtained in Cipango and Cathay.

Then, in 1453, Constantinople fell to the Moslem Turks, the bitterly anti-Christian followers of

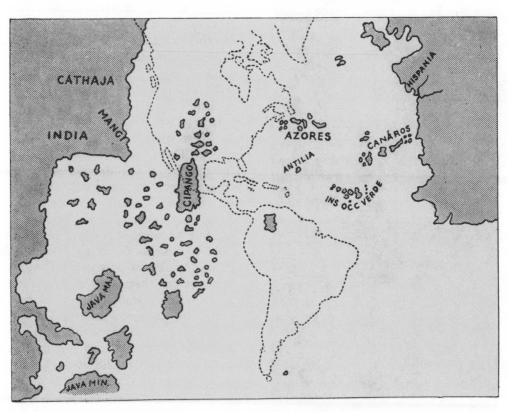

Section of Martin Behaim's globe (1492). Dotted lines show unknown America.

Mohammed. With Constantinople in their power, the Turks effectively controlled all of the Near East. This meant that the land routes to the Far East were blocked to European traders and their caravans. When businessmen find their profit threatened, they become inventive. A new route had to be found to Asia. Was it possible to go around Africa? Was there any other way?

Some wise men believed that there was another way. Most people in that time held the opinion that the world was flat—something like a saucer floating through space. If a person got to the edge of the saucer, he could easily slip over the edge and be lost in space forever! But there were a few people who did not hold this theory. Those men knew that the sun appeared to rise in the east in the morning and set in the west at night, only to reappear in the east the next day. They observed that stars moved in large circles, some of them disappearing beyond the horizon at certain times of the year, and that the appearance of the heavens varied according to seasons.

Their observation of natural phenomena led those men to the conclusion that the earth was not flat, but was really a sphere. When there was night on one side of the sphere, there was day on the other. And if the earth was a sphere, it should be possible to sail westward and reach Asia. It should even be possible to start westward and reach the point where the voyage had begun!

But where was there a man with sufficient courage to risk his life to prove such a theory? No one knew what terrible dangers lay beyond the horizon. The seas were uncharted and unknown. There might be terrible whirlpools, areas of devastating storms, and dangers that surpassed the capability of the imagination. Perhaps there was a region of perpetual darkness, where a voyager would soon lose his way; or a windless area, where a ship would become becalmed and remain to rot. Just as our own explorers in space did not know exactly what awaited them, the men of those days knew even less about what lay beyond the known horizons of the sea. Yet whenever there is a great challenge, there is always some daring soul who will accept it. This is true in our own time with the challenge of space, and so it was with the challenge of the unknown seas. A small, courageous group of men dreamed of finding an answer to the problem. To them, the quest for knowledge, the possibility of a solution, outweighed the risks and dangers. One of those men was a studious, Italian mariner—Christopher Columbus.

The Admiral of the Ocean Seas

Christopher Columbus

COURTESY CHICAGO HISTORICAL SOCIETY

Columbus appears before Queen Isabella of Spain seeking her help. For five years his hopes were in vain.

The Admiral of the Ocean Seas

CHRISTOPHER Columbus was a self-made man. He was born in Genoa, about 1451, the son of a wool weaver and tavern keeper. He had very little formal education; but by reading and reflection, he made himself a scientist and scholar. In a letter to the King and Queen of Spain, he not-too-humbly described himself in this way:

"My intercourse and conversation centered around people of wisdom, religious as well as secular scholars, Latins, Greeks, Indians, and Moors, and many others of various professions and nationalities . . . (God) made of me an expert in navigation: He gave me enough astronomy, geometry, and arithmetic. He gave me an ingenious mind, and hands capable of designing the earthly sphere . . . I have seen, and endeavor to see, all the books on cosmography, history, philosophy, and other sciences."

Another indication of the scholarship of Chris-

topher Columbus is found in his papers, in which he gave the reasons for his belief that a western route to Asia existed. He summarized his reasons in three parts: first, deductions drawn from scientific research as found in the works of ancient geographers such as Ptolemy, Strabo, and Marinus of Tyre; second, a similar opinion expressed by such authorities as Aristotle, Seneca, Marco Polo, Cardinal d'Ailly, and Paolo Toscanelli; third, unconfirmed but separated reports of land to the west, given by storm-fleeing sailors over many centuries.

Books belonging to Columbus still exist, and they are full of marginal notes that he wrote. Three of those books—*Travels* by Marco Polo, *The Image of the World* by Cardinal d'Ailly, and *Cosmography* by Pope Pius II—had great influence on his thinking if we can judge by the number and kind of notes he wrote in their margins. Columbus was also a student of the Bible.

When Columbus was born, Genoa was one of the greatest seaports and commercial centers of the world. Into its harbors sailed caravels loaded with treasures of the then-known world. It is not surprising that the boy Christopher was drawn to seafaring, rather than to his father's mercantile business. Columbus first went to sea at the age of fourteen. His voyages took him about the Mediterranean, along the west coast of Africa, to England and Iceland. In the latter country, he probably heard the stories of distant lands, as preserved in the saga of Leif the Lucky.

Between voyages, for a reason not known to us (perhaps because his brother, Diego, had a small business there or to make sure he escaped his father's business), Columbus made his home in Lisbon. When he was not at sea, the mariner drew maps to support himself. He married a Portuguese woman of noble birth, who died shortly after his son, Diego, was born.

Always in the back of his dreamer's mind was the challenge of a westward voyage. Columbus was convinced that there was a westward route to Asia. He even calculated the distance at about 2,500 miles. He knew that someday someone would make that voyage, and he resolved that he was to be that man. But the costs involved in outfitting a fleet for exploration were more than any one man could meet: the project had to have the backing of a powerful nation.

Finally Columbus proposed his scheme to King John II of Portugal. But that ruler's advisers reported that the idea was ridiculous, and it was turned down. Columbus then approached officials of the City of Genoa, but the city fathers had no confidence in an absentee native son and he was refused. England was his next hope—and King Henry VII was not interested. Running out of countries and as a last recourse, Columbus took his small son and left Portugal for Spain.

During the next five years, Columbus had his hopes alternately raised and dashed in Spain. At first Queen Isabella received him kindly and turned him over to the royal commissioners, her hard-headed protectors. Through the years, the commissioners made a number of studies of Columbus' proposals; sometimes they seemed ready to accept the scheme but each time the final decision was negative. There were various reasons: lack of money in the royal treasury, lack of confidence in the idea, the concentration of the Spanish on the war against the Moors. Finally, after

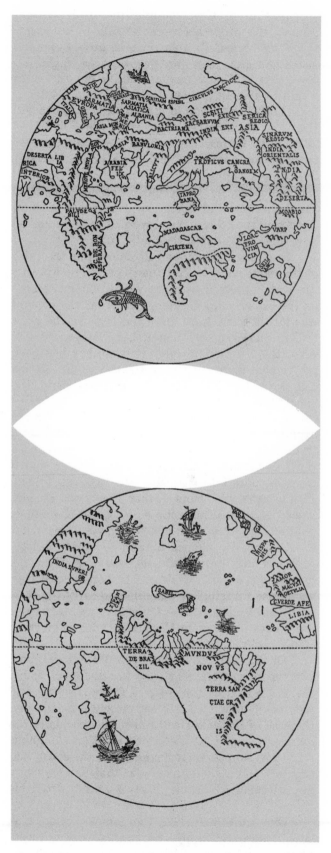

The world as it appeared in 1510 on the Lenox Globe.

the capture of Granada and the defeat of the Moors, the proposals were restudied. But again they were rejected—this time because Columbus asked too great a reward for what he might discover. He was only risking his life but the court would be risking money!

Disillusioned and despondent, Columbus left Granada. He intended to go to Cordova and then possibly to France. He and his young son traveled on foot, too poor even to have a horse. Towards dusk one evening, they were passing the Franciscan monastery of La Rabida. Columbus went to the monastery and asked the doorkeeper to allow his young son to rest there overnight. He explained how tired and hungry the boy was.

Standing near by and listening, was the prior of the monastery, Father Juan Perez. The Franciscan was impressed with the way Columbus pleaded for his son, and he recognized that the pleader was far different from the usual beggar. The prior told the doorkeeper to admit both father and son. After the visitors had eaten and the boy had been put to bed, Father Perez invited Columbus into his cell, in order to satisfy his curiosity about the background of his unusual guest.

Columbus was so wrapped up in his dream of exploration that he readily poured out his story. Father Perez listened carefully. He soon realized that Columbus had given this matter much thought. Late into the night, the two men talked. It was not long before Father Perez was as convinced and as enthusiastic as his guest. Columbus pointed out what such discoveries could mean for the Church. He likened himself to Saint Christopher, wading through the sea with a staff in one hand and the Christ Child on his shoulders. So God would use Christopher Columbus to carry the Gospel to the Indies. (Later Columbus was to have a representation of Saint Christopher drawn on some of his papers.)

On the next day, the convinced Father Perez left the monastery and went to the royal court. He had served as confessor to Queen Isabella and was readily admitted into her presence. He pleaded the case of Columbus and rallied his friends to the mariner's support. Isabella ordered that Columbus should be summoned immediately to the court, and she sent him a gift of money so that he might buy new clothing and come in style that befitted his claims.

On April 30, 1492, the famous "Capitulations" were signed by the Spanish court, meeting the conditions set by Columbus. He was to be

FROM The Journal of Christopher Columbus

As Ferdinand and Isabella bid him farewell, Columbus departs for the New World. This 1621 engraving probably is of the second voyage, 1493, or third, 1498.

given the title, "Admiral of the Ocean Seas," governorship of any lands he might find, and a tenth of all profits resulting from the expedition. Also, he was to be provided with three ships, in which to carry his expedition; these would be outfitted at the expense of Spain.

The ships were these: the *Santa Maria*, ninety feet long and in poor condition; the *Pinta*, about forty-five feet long; and the *Nina*, even smaller. Columbus set to work repairing and making ready the boats and gathering crews. The latter was no easy task, as few men cared to risk the unknown waters. Columbus begged, cajoled, and even had prisoners released from jail; but in the end he could get only ninety men to sail the three ships.

On the morning of August 3, 1492, Columbus sailed out from the port of Palos. He had to put into the Canary Islands for repairs of both the *Nina* and *Pinta*. Then he sailed off to the unknown seas. As the days continued to pass without sight of land, his crew became more and more worried. Soon the men begged Columbus to turn back. His only reply was: "Sail on! Sail on!" He confided in his journal that he never had any thought of turning back, because he "had sailed to go to the Indies and would continue until, with the Lord's help," he should find them!

Conditions became worse. Water turned bad, and food was running out. On October 10, some of the sailors wanted to mutiny and throw Columbus overboard. Fearlessly, Columbus faced the frightened men. He told them that God had taken care of them thus far and He would continue to watch over them. Finally his captains agreed to go on for three days more before turning back. Columbus said nothing regarding this new threat.

The next day, October 11, was full of hope. A green reed was found floating in the sea—then some cane—a small board—and finally a branch covered with berries. Admiral Columbus believed surely that land was near, and he ordered a careful watch. But dusk fell, and no land had been sighted. At ten o'clock that night, Columbus was on the high poop and believed he saw a light flickering in the distance. He called one of his officers, who confirmed the light. The vindicated leader then led his men in singing the "Hail, Holy Queen," and afterwards he told them to watch well for land.

At two o'clock on the morning of October 12, a sailor aboard the *Pinta* saw the moonlight brightly reflected by the white sand of a beach some miles ahead of the ship. Immediately the cry of "Land! Land!" was echoing throughout the little fleet. Columbus ordered the ships to stand by until morning.

When daylight came, Admiral Columbus went ashore on the island, took possession of it in the names of King Ferdinand and Queen Isabella, and called it "San Salvador." It was one of the Bahama Islands; probably the one now known as "Watling."

There were many people on the island. With them, Columbus made friends by giving gifts because, as he said, "they were a people who could be more easily freed and converted to our holy Faith by love than by force." Columbus in one of the great mistakes of history called the people

Columbus as he is leaving from La Rabida Monastery

"Indians" because he thought he had landed on an island off the coast of India.

However, he was anxious to move on, for he wrote, "In order not to lose time, I intend to go and see if I can find the island of Cipango." Cipango was Marco Polo's name for Japan. So Columbus set sail to continue his search. He discovered Cuba and Haiti. On Christmas Eve the *Santa Maria* ran aground and split her timbers, becoming a useless wreck. Columbus decided to leave most of his crew on the island to form a colony, but he himself returned home on the *Nina*.

When he reached Spain, Admiral Columbus was given a hero's welcome, because everyone believed he had found a new route to Asia. Then the Spanish sovereigns decided that a second expedition should be immediately organized to colonize, convert the Indians, and seek gold. On September 24, 1493, Columbus sailed with seventeen ships and 1,200 men, a sure sign of success and big expectations. On that voyage he discovered other islands, including Puerto Rico. To all the islands in that region, he gave the name "Indies"; and that name is still in use. He set up a colony in what is now the Dominican Republic, and appoint-

Columbus in irons. He died believing in his cause.

ed his brother, Diego, as governor. From that colony, some of the Spanish were to move into Central and South America.

Columbus made two more voyages to the New World, always hoping to reach Asia. In 1498 he discovered Trinidad and sighted the coast of South America. In 1502 he explored the Central American coast, still seeking a passage to India and Japan. After storms, shipwreck, mutiny, and many other hardships, he returned to Spain in 1504.

His benefactress, Queen Isabella died shortly after his return. Columbus was out of favor in the royal court because his promises of gold and wealth had not materialized. Ill and exhausted from his explorations, poor from having invested his own money in search for the Indies, humiliated by the Spanish Government, Columbus died a disappointed man. That was in the year 1506. Thirty-six years later his remains were taken to the New World, as he had requested, and were interred in the Cathedral of Santo Domingo (Dominican Republic), on the island he had named "Hispaniola."

The great discoverer never believed that he had failed. "I have opened the gates that others will enter," he said shortly before his death. Others did enter those gates and built great nations. But because it was Christopher Columbus who opened the gates, his name will be immortalized as long as those nations exist.

"Wherefore Your Highnesses . . . determined to send me, Cristóbal Colón, to the said parts of India . . . and ordered that I should not go by land to the East, as the custom was, but by way of the West, by a course which no man, to our certain knowledge, has taken until this day."

—Columbus' journal

The Man Who Gave a Hemisphere His Name

Portrait of Amerigo Vespucci by an unknown artist. Vespucci was a respected astronomer and geographer.

IT is one of the ironies of history that, although Christopher Columbus pioneered the way to the New World from Europe, the goal of his explorations bears the name of another Italian astronomer. One South American country, a Canadian province, a river in the Northwest and a few cities in North America, have been named after the Admiral of the Ocean Seas. Also, the United States has been given his name unofficially, in a national song: "Columbia the Gem of the Ocean." But the Western Hemisphere, the eastern fringe of which had been discovered by Columbus, was named "America"—after Amerigo Vespucci, whose Latinized name is Americus Vespuccious.

Amerigo Vespucci was born in Florence. He was employed as a commercial clerk in the house of the Medici, a wealthy and powerful family of Florence. He had a hobby of collecting globes, charts and maps, and studying geography and astronomy. In time he became a leading astronomer and was called the greatest expert of his day in calculating longitude and latitude.

Sometime near the year 1490, Vespucci went to Spain as a representative of the Medici business. He became connected with a large, Spanish, commercial house that outfitted Columbus' second voyage. Later he took part in four voyages to the New World. He described those voyages in two letters written to friends in Florence. One of those letters was printed and widely circulated. That printed letter told how Vespucci's ship traveled from what is now Cape Honduras in Central America, to Cape Kennedy in Florida. And Vespucci remarked that, because the coastline was so long, he had felt that he was sailing, not along an island, but along a continent.

In the Medici letter, Vespucci described another voyage, made in 1501-1502. Then he had sailed along the Brazilian coast. He called that region *"Mundus Novus"*—the Latin for "New World," a name that remains in use for the Western Hemisphere to this day. He concluded that the land he had seen was not part of Asia, but was a region unknown to ancient geographers.

At about the same time, a young German geographer published a book called *Introduction to Geography*, and a large map of the world. Both in the book and on the map, he placed in large letters the name "America" on the continental areas about which Vespucci had written. Other geographers picked up the name; and gradually it was applied to the two continents—North and South America. When we call ourselves "Americans," we honor a Florentine merchant who found geography and exploration more challenging than a life in a counting house.

The Bristol Voyages

The type of craft used by merchants in Cabot's time

HENRY VII, King of England, was a disgruntled man. He realized that he had been shortsighted in not listening to the proposals of Columbus. Opportunity had come to him, and he had let it pass by. As a result, Spain had gained a foothold in the New World, and England had not. True, Henry had married his son to the daughter of King Ferdinand and Queen Isabella of Spain, and had joined two Catholic monarchies (and thus had laid the foundation for England's withdrawal from the Catholic Church when the Pope later refused the son, Henry VIII, permission to divorce his wife) but the marriage was not going to bring gain to the royal treasury as new lands might.

Henry VII was resolved that he would not make the same mistake again. He had before him a petition from a group of merchants in the city of Bristol, requesting a royal license for one John Cabot to make a journey of discovery. Henry would grant this license, but specify that the exploration should not be done in areas already ex-

plored by the Spanish and Portuguese. Since the costs of the voyage were to be born by the Bristol merchants (this suited their sovereign's nature), any trade that would result from the Cabot voyage would belong solely to the port of Bristol.

Bristol at that time was England's second-most-important port, exceeded only by London. The city had grown rich with trade to Iceland and Northern Europe. Bristol was also the codfish center for England; Catholic England observed the days of abstinence, and fish was in great demand. But the Bristol merchants wanted to extend their trade, and they had already sent out expeditions seeking new lands, but without success.

There was living in Bristol an Italian sea captain and geographer, one Giovanni Caboto, who had Anglicized his name to "John Cabot." Born in Genoa, a citizen of Venice, he had been a resident of Bristol for some years. Like Columbus,

The Ptolomeic map of the world

Cabot was obsessed with the idea of finding a western sea route to Asia. His idea found ready acceptance among the trade-hungry Bristol merchants.

On May 2, 1497, John Cabot with his three sons—Lewis, Sebastian, Santius—and a crew of eighteen other men, sailed out of Bristol harbor aboard a small ship, the *Matthew*. Rounding the coast of Ireland, Cabot set his course west into the unknown. After fifty-two days at sea, the lookout sighted land. Cabot went ashore, planted a large cross, and took possesson of the territory for the King of England. He named the country he had discovered "New Found Land."

Cabot returned to England and great acclaim. "Vast honor is paid him," wrote one man of that

time. "He dresses in silk, and the English run after him like mad people!" Another writer, who spoke to Cabot and his crew, observed: "They affirm that the sea is covered with fishes . . . that they will bring so many fishes that this kingdom will no longer have need of Iceland, from which country there comes a very great store of fish."

But John Cabot had his mind set on something greater than fish trade—Japan. He was planning a new expedition, which would "go farther on to the East from that place already occupied, hugging the shore, until he shall be over against an island called Cipango, where he thinks all the spices of the world, and also the precious stones, originate." Cabot planned his second journey carefully and with great expectations. He made lavish promises to his backers; one friend was to be governor of an island, and several Italian priests were to be bishops.

In May of 1498, Cabot sailed from Bristol. His fleet consisted of six ships, manned by a crew of 300. Despite the fact that he had said he was going to colonize and trade, Cabot set a northwest course, hoping to find the long-desired passage to Asia. His crew became confused by the almost continual daylight. At last the bitter cold and the bleakness of the land made him turn south.

For weeks Cabot probed the North American coastline. His son, Sebastian, later said that the fleet journeyed as far south as the latitude of Gibraltar, in Europe. If true, this means that Cabot's ship was opposite the Carolinas. Reluctantly and with great disappointment, John Cabot gave the order to return to England. For that return, late in 1498, no hero's welcome awaited him. His backer's dreams of profit, colonization and a share in the fabulous wealth of the East had vanished.

Broken in spirit and health, John Cabot died shortly after his return. But his discoveries had given England a claim to North America. And although the riches of the East had escaped his grasp, his pioneering exploration opened a way for the English to claim what has become the greatest nation in the world.

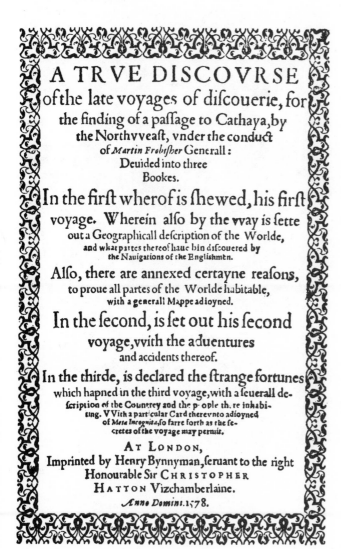

A TRVE DISCOVRSE of the late voyages of difcouerie, for the finding of a paffage to Cathaya, by the Northvveaſt, vnder the conduct of *Martin Frobifher* Generall: Deuided into three Bookes.

In the firſt wherof is ſhewed, his firſt voyage. Wherein alfo by the vvay is ſette out a Geographicall defcription of the Worlde, and whatpartes thereof haue bin difcouered by the Nauigations of the Englishmen.

Alfo, there are annexed certayne reafons, to proue all partes of the Worlde habitable, with a generall Mappe adioyned.

In the fecond, is fet out his fecond voyage, vvith the aduentures and accidents thereof.

In the thirde, is declared the ſtrange fortunes which hapned in the third voyage, with a feuerall defcription of the Countrey and the people the inhabiting. Vith a particular Card therevnto adioyned of *Meta Incognita*,fo farre forth as the fecretes of the voyage may permit.

AT LONDON, Imprinted by Henry Bynnyman,feruant to the right Honourable Sir CHRISTOPHER HATTON Vizchamberlaine. *Anno Domini*.1578.

The title page of an early monograph on the voyages

John Cabot and his son Sebastian as they first set foot on North America. Cabot's goal was to reach Japan.

The Spanish Came First

IT was a myth that led to the discovery of Florida. In the folklore of Europe, there was a story of a magic spring that existed somewhere in the world. It was called the "Fountain of Youth." According to the legend, anyone who would drink from that spring would be cured of any sickness and would regain his youth.

The legend first circulated through Europe in the twelfth century when a letter attributed to one Prester John (Priest John, probably John of Montecorvino) made mention of it. For centuries the legend lingered on, kept alive more by the desire of men than by any factual probability. Then somehow after the discovery of the New World, the myth of the Fountain of Youth began to be clothed in new rumors.

Indians are supposed to have told of this magic spring, and even given its location as a place called "Bimini," north of the West Indies. That these rumors reached Spain is certain, because they are mentioned in a book published in 1511. That book even contained a map that showed Bimini as an island.

One man who heard the rumors and was intrigued by them was a Spanish conquistador, Juan Ponce de Leon, a veteran soldier. Ponce de Leon had first come to the New World in the second expedition of Columbus. For a time he served as governor of what is now Haiti. In 1508 he led the expedition that conquered Puerto Rico and for a time was governor of that island, until he was removed by Diego Columbus, son of Christopher and successor to his father. Finding himself "rich and unemployed," Ponce de Leon outfitted two caravels and went in search of the fabulous Bimini. After sailing around for six months, he finally made landfall (March 27, 1512) on what he believed was an island. Since he had first sighted the land on Easter Sunday, which the Spanish call *Pascua Florida* (Flowery Easter), he named his supposed island Florida.

Ponce de Leon was not equipped to colonize so he returned to his base and then proceeded to Spain where he sought and gained permission to

On Easter Sunday in 1512, Ponce de León saw Florida.

colonize his new discovery. The king granted him permission; he equipped three ships in Seville, and returned to Puerto Rico. Some fighting against the Carib Indians delayed his plans and it was not until 1521 that he sailed from Puerto Rico with his three ships to begin his colony. According to an historian of the times, "he took mares and calves and pigs and sheep and goats and all kinds of animals, domestic and useful in the service of men."

Ponce de Leon sailed around the peninsula, almost to Tampa Bay. He made his landing somewhere in the vicinity of the present Fort Myers. But the first attempt to colonize Florida was not successful. The Indians were hostile and

A sixteenth century map showing the Spanish claim in the West (La Florida). Spain later lost all her lands.

put up stiff resistance. In one battle, many of his soldiers were killed and Ponce de Leon was wounded in the thigh with an arrow. He ordered a retreat, and died in Cuba of his wound. He had not found the mythical Fountain of Youth, and he died thinking Florida was an island; but he is the first Spaniard of record to set foot on what is now the United States mainland.

At the time Florida was discovered, another discovery was made that was to have a profound influence on the development of America. A bankrupt businessman, fleeing creditors, heard stories from Indians of a sea on the other side of Central America. He was a Spaniard, by the name of Vasco Nunez de Balboa. With incredible daring and only 190 Spanish followers, supplemented by native carriers, he plunged into the Panamanian jungle. It took twenty days to cover a hundred miles, so difficult was the traveling. Swamps, snakes, scorpions, polluted water and hostile Indians caused the deaths of half the members of that expedition.

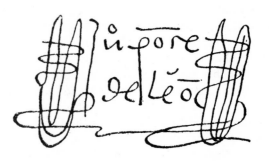

Signature of Juan Ponce de Leon

At last, Balboa and the survivors came out over a hill—and there at their feet was a great, blue sea! Balboa intoned *Te Deum*—a hymn of praise to God—and erected a large, wooden cross on the hilltop. Then he descended and entered the sea, claiming it and all the lands it touched for his patron, the Spanish monarch. He named the water the "Southern Sea." That was in September of 1513.

Balboa made his way back across the Isthmus of Panama and assembled a new expedition. That time, on the backs of hundreds of Indians went parts to make four boats. The fantastic procession fought its way through the jungle again; the boats were assembled; and Balboa became the first westward-bound European to sail on the Pacific Ocean. After his return to the eastern shore of Panama, the intrepid explorer was taken prisoner by enemies and was accused of being disloyal to the King of Spain. On that same day, he was beheaded—strange reward for the successful discoverer of the eastern limits of the Pacific Ocean!

Balboa is commemorated in America's Canal Zone by a town bearing his name, at the Pacific entrance to the canal. His supposed reaction to his great discovery has been commemorated by the poet John Keats; although Keats, being more poet than historian, attributed the discovery to another man! However, the final phrase of the Keats poem is often quoted, in connection with this discovery and also with many other surprises in human lives. The poet's lines follow:

> *He stared at the Pacific, and*
> *all his men*
> *Looked at each other with a*
> *wild surmise,*
> *Silent upon a peak in Darien.*

The year before (1520) Ponce de Leon made his last and fatal expedition to Florida, news was again made in the Pacific; that time by a Portuguese navigator who sailed under the Spanish

NEW MEXICO STATE DEPARTMENT OF DEVELOPMENT

The Spanish Palace of Government in Santa Fe, New Mexico, stands today as evidence of our Spanish heritage.

Primitive Indians of Florida

flag. He was Ferdinand Magellan, a dreamer of the same dream that had possessed Columbus—a westward route to Asia. He knew from Balboa that a western sea existed, and he was determined to find a way onto it. His plan won the support of King Charles of Spain.

In September of 1519, Magellan set sail with five ships, only one of which was to survive and return to Spain. His voyage was a succession of great hardships, attempted mutinies, hunger, thirst, privation. He discovered a way around the southern tip of the New World, through a strait that now bears his name; but it was a fearsome way "where waters are lashed by icy gales, and the rocky land is bleak with eternal cold." When he reached the quiet of the ocean, he was so grateful for the calm that he changed its name form "Southern Sea" to "Pacific Ocean."

Westward, over uncharted wastes, sailed Magellan. Fierce gales blew up and sent two of his ships to the bottom of the sea. Scurvy decimated his men. At long last many islands were reached, and he named them "Philippines" in honor of Prince Philip of Spain. But final triumph was de-

nied Magellan. He died beneath the arrows and clubs of Filipino tribesmen. His lieutenant, Sebastian del Cano, ordered the ships to sea again. Finally, in 1521, the expedition reached the Moluccas, or Spice Islands, a region known to Europeans. Asia and Spain had been joined! Columbus had been proved right—but at a terrible cost. Only one of Magellan's vessels returned to Spain; and of the three hundred men who had set sail, only eighteen survived.

With the conclusion of the Magellan voyage, the Age of Discovery had come to an end and the Age of Explorers began. It was only forty years from the time Columbus sailed from Spain to discover a westward passage, until another "dreamer" circumnavigated the whole world. The Age of Discovery showed how much men were dependent upon one another. Magellan succeeded because he knew from Balboa that the so-called Southern Sea existed; and he knew from various explorers of parts of South America that there was a possible way around that continent.

Columbus was the only one who sailed into the totally unknown. In that remains his greatness.

FERDINAN · MAGELLANVS · SVPERATIS
ANTARCTICI · FRETI · ANGVSTIIS · CLARISS

The great explorer, Magellan

Pánfilo de Narvaez, with Cabeza de Vaca, sailed from Cuba to Florida on an ill-fated expedition early in 1528.

Almost Across a Continent

PANFILO de Narvaez was one of those men for whom things never seemed to go right. He was a tall, strong person with a striking red beard, who had often proved his courage. But he had a streak of imprudence in his character, and it led to hasty action and an ignoring of details. He was also miserly. These weaknesses were to cause a great tragedy and one of the most remarkable journeys ever accomplished by human beings.

Narvaez arrived in the West Indies as a young man, about the year 1500, probably on one of the voyages of Columbus. Like other Spaniards, he had come seeking adventure and wealth. We read of his being in Jamaica in 1510, as a lieutenant to Juan de Esquivel. The following year he took part in the conquest of Cuba under Diego Velasquez. When Velasquez was made governor of Cuba, he rewarded Narvaez with land and slaves.

Narvaez next appears in the pages of history in 1520. Two years earlier, Velasquez had sent Hernando Cortes to trade with the natives of newly discovered Mexico. But as soon as he had set foot on Mexican soil, Cortes announced that he was going to conquer and colonize in his own name,

and had himself elected captain general and chief magistrate. Then with less than 500 men, he set about to overthrow the mighty Aztec empire.

When news of this reached Governor Velasquez, "he was taken with cold sweats as of death." He immediately began planning the destruction of Cortes. The man he selected for the job was his old lieutenant, Panfilo de Narvaez. He raised a fleet of nineteen ships, with 1,400 well-armed men, and put Narvaez in command with one order: "Take Cortes, dead or alive!"

Cortes was one of the most daring military men who ever lived. He was also very shrewd. With only 210 soldiers, he went to meet Narvaez. Cortes chose a rainy night in May to make his attack. Although he was outnumbered five to one, and his enemy had scores of horses and a fortified position, daring and surprise gave Cortes victory. In the battle, Narvaez had one eye put out.

For three years Cortes held Narvaez prisoner. However, when the wife of Narvaez begged her husband's release, Cortes not only agreed but gave his ex-prisoner 2,000 pesos in gold. Narvaez promised to serve Cortes faithfully. He "kept" that promise by going to Spain to appear as a witness against Cortes.

Narvaez had seen the great wealth of Mexico and was bitter because it might have been his. He dreamed of a conquest of his own, and at last petitioned the King of Spain for the right to explore and conquer Florida. In 1526 a royal warrant was issued that gave Narvaez this right. The warrant assigned two priests to accompany the expedition in order to instruct and convert the Indians and protect them against abuses. A man named Nunes Cabeza de Vaca was assigned as royal treasurer.

Cabeza de Vaca came from a family of soldiers, and it was natural that he should follow the same profession. He had fought in Italy and against the French, but his greatest talent lay in administration. He was not a ruthless man, as were many conquistadors; as he later proved, he was a humanitarian who could have made a great missioner. Because of his experience, high character, and honesty, he was put in charge of the Spanish sovereign's share of the Narvaez expedition's expected gains.

On June 17, 1527, the Narvaez party, composed of five caravels with 600 men, set sail from Spain. The first land reached was Santo Domingo. There 145 men deserted because of the poor food on the voyage over; by saving a few pesos, the parsimonious Narvaez thus lost an effective part of his strength. The fleet went on to Cuba to winter. A terrible hurricane struck, and two ships were destroyed and sixty men and twenty horses lost.

It was not until February 22, 1528, that the ill-fated expedition left Cuba for Florida. It was then reduced to 400 men, 80 horses, and four ships. Bad luck continued to plague it. Several ships ran aground, and there were delays getting them afloat again; the winds were bad; two terrible storms were encountered. Finally, on April 7, land was sighted, and two days later (Holy Thursday) the ships anchored close to where Saint Petersburg, Florida, is now located. The next day Narvaez and his party went ashore. They found a village, but it was deserted, the Indians having fled before the invaders. In one hut a soldier discovered a golden rattle. It was all the proof the group needed—gold was to be had for the taking!

Father Juan Juarez, a Franciscan, offered Mass on Easter Sunday, on the shore. Narvaez sent scouting parties, which found several other villages and captured four Indians. Narvaez showed the Indians the gold rattle and asked where it came from. The Indians seemed to understand, because they pointed to the north and said, "Apalachen! Apalachen!" The Spaniards took this to mean a place, when actually the captives were referring to the Apalachee Indians of Georgia.

Narvaez immediately called a meeting of his chief lieutenants. He proposed that the expedition set forth for the interior, while the ships would go north to where the pilot said there was a large bay. The men on land would join the ships there. Father Juarez thought this a good idea, as did most of the other men. But De Vaca objected, saying that they should all go north on the ships until a good anchorage should be found, where a permanent camp could be set up. The treasurer looked upon the scheme as hair-brained. The party had no interpreter, the horses needed time to recover from the sea journey, and Narvaez' idea of living off the land was a gamble no prudent leader should take in so inhospitable a place.

"If you're afraid of going into the interior," said Narvaez, "you can remain with the ships."

The suggestion of cowardice angered De Vaca, but he replied evenly: "I tell you that you will never see those ships again! This is clear from our entering so ill-equipped into a country about which we know nothing. Still, I would rather venture into the danger where you and the others are venturing than take charge of the ships and let people say I was afraid. In short, sir, I will risk my life rather than put my honor to such a pass!"

On May 1, the expedition set forth. There were 300 men and forty horses. At first the way was easy. The Spaniards saw no villages, no human habitations, no Indians, no tilled fields; only a deserted, sandy country. They found nothing to eat, and the two pounds of biscuit and half pound of bacon allotted to each man soon disappeared. Then they came upon the swamps and rivers, the lurking alligators. Finally, on June 25, they reached Apalachen—a settlement of forty miserable huts in southern Georgia. There was no gold. The only booty was some ripe corn and a few deerskins.

By that time the hidden Indians had turned hostile and kept the Spanish party under steady attack. They fired their arrows not openly, but from ambush, and with hit-and-run tactics. There was nothing for the invaders to do but retreat to the sea. The return march was a nightmare, with heat, insects, hunger, and constant attack. Finally the sea was reached and camp made at an abandoned Indian village. Then malaria struck.

Cabeza de Vaca had been right. The ships were not there, and they were never to be seen again. Although no one knew anything about shipbuilding and they had no tools, Narvaez decided to build a number of boats in which the Spaniards might try to escape. Stirrups, spurs, and crossbows were turned into nails, saws, and axes. From the tails and manes of the horses (which were being eaten at the rate of one every three days), ropes were woven for riggings. The skins of the horses' legs were used to make canteens. Men's shirts were made into sails. By hard work and ingenuity, three ships, each thirty-three feet long, were ready for the end of September. And all the time they were under Indian attack!

At last the boats put to sea. The destination was Panuco, the northernmost settlement in Mexico, near the present Tampico. No one knew how far away it was. The castaways hugged the shore. Plagued by hunger, thirst, and sickness, and attacked by Indians, they made a journey that was protracted torture. Slowly they found their way around the edge of the Gulf of Mexico. Cabeza de Vaca saw the Mississippi River and noted its tremendous delta. Death was a frequent visitor. Men disappeared in storms, and died from sickness and starvation. Narvaez himself was lost at sea, swept away in one of the boats during a storm. The survivors finally reached an island off the Texas coast, near the present city of Galveston. By the time winter began, only fifteen were left alive, and they had become slaves of the Indians. The years began to pass. One by one the Spaniards died. Sometimes the survivors were separated, sometimes together. They lived the lives of savages, naked and always hungry. After six years, there were only four Spaniards left: Cabeza de Vaca, Captain Andres Dorantes, Alonso del Castillo, and El Negro Estaban (an African Moor, the first Negro of record in the United States).

Then began one of the greatest adventures, an incredible adventure, in the annals of American history.

The Hike Across America

IN the summer of the castaways' sixth year, the four survivors were together again. At the end of each summer, the Indians gathered to harvest wild figs. The captives took the occasion of their reunion to speak of the future. The Spaniards knew that somewhere to the west was Mexico and other Spaniards; if they ever hoped to see civilization again, now was the time to flee their captors. And so they plotted escape, setting aside figs for food.

At last, in September, the opportunity came and the four men quietly made their way from the Indian camp. At first, they expected pursuit by the Indians but it never came. On their third day's march, the fleeing Spaniards came upon an Indian village. Thirsty and hungry, the weary men debated entering it, fearing a new captivity. Finally, they were persuaded by their physical needs.

To their surprise, the Spaniards were warmly greeted by the Indians, who had heard of them and called them "children of the sun." Cabeza de Vaca was particularly held in honor because while with his Indian captors he had gained a reputation as a healer, and this reputation had gone about the various Indian villages. Cabeza de Vaca undoubtedly had a knowledge of certain European treatments but he tells us that he depended upon God.

"Our method," he reported later, "was to bless the sick, breathing on them, and recite the 'Our Father' and 'Hail Mary,' praying earnestly to God that He would give good health. In His mercy He willed that all those for whom we supplicated should tell the others that they were sound in health, directly after we made the sign of the blessed cross over them."

De Vaca also took the opportunity each time he met Indians to preach to them about God (by this time he was proficient in the Indian dialects), and he records that he baptized many children and sick adults. It is interesting that the first person to preach the Catholic Faith in the United States should be a layman.

Forty-eight years later, Antonio de Espejo, in searching the same area for some missing Franciscan missioners, came upon five Indian pueblos containing about 10,000 people who indicated a knowledge of God. His report stated:

"These people seemed to have some light of our holy Faith. Many of them came to the friar that he might bless them. They made signs of God, looking up towards heaven, and they acknowledged that, from His bountiful hand, they have received their life and being and their worldly goods. The friar asked them from whom they had received knowledge of God, and they answered from three white men and one Negro who had passed that way."

Meanwhile the four survivors gradually made their way westward, passing from tribe to tribe. Despite the fame that went ahead, they were naked and always hungry. Cabeza de Vaca carried smoldering embers with him on his march so that they would always have fire. At night the men would sleep inside four large bonfires. "Like snakes," de Vaca records, "we changed our skins twice a year, and the sun and air caused sores on our chests and backs that gave us great pain."

One day, the Spaniards came to a wide river (the Rio Grande), fording water chest-high. Sometimes they were accompanied by admiring Indians but more often were alone. One day an incident happened that raised their spirits considerably. Castillo saw an Indian wearing around his neck as a charm the buckle of a Spanish sword belt. Despite intense and repeated questioning, the man could not or would not tell how he had obtained this sign of Spanish presence. However, the incident raised the spirits of the unwilling explorers and gave them new incentive to press west.

The exact route that the Spaniards followed is difficult to determine today despite the fact that de Vaca's *Relacion* gives detailed descriptions. Some historians believed they crossed New Mexico although Bancroft and others say their route was to the south of that state. It is also doubtful that they reached California; they probably turned south at either the Colorado River where it prepares to enter the Gulf of Californa or at the Gulf itself. The best retracing of their route takes them across Texas, the Mexican states of Chihuahua and Sonora, and then south through the states of Sonora and Sinaloa to Jalisco, about 2,400 miles as a jet would fly, but only God knows how many twists and turns and round-abouts they actually took.

In one Indian village on the Gulf of California, the inhabitants gave them gifts of coral beads, some turquoises and five emeralds. "Where do these come from?" asked Cabeza de Vaca, indicating the emeralds.

"From the high mountains to the north, where there are populous cities and tall houses," was the reply. "Those people trade us the emeralds for the feathers of our green parrots."

This simple answer, when reported later in Mexico City, was to send two important expeditions into the United States and give rise to the fabled legend of the Seven Cities of Gold. But that is a later story.

Somewhere in the vicinity of the present Hermosillo, the ragged Spaniards began to hear stories of Christians who came and made slaves of the Indians. Cabeza de Vaca records that he and his companions were both made joyous and sad by

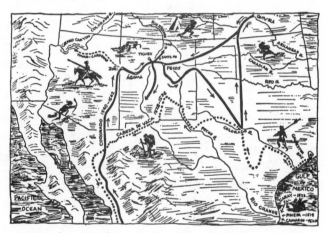

A map showing the route used by de Vaca in the West

this news—joyous because rescue was getting ever nearer, saddened that Christian Spaniards should be carrying off the kind and simple people who had kept them alive and helped them on their long journey. Later when Cabeza de Vaca was made Governor of Rio Plate in South America, he was in charge of many Indians, who, he wrote, "must be given good treatment, for this is the right course, and no other." Those who knew him testified that he practiced what he preached.

At last, one day in March, 1536, more than eight years after they had set sail for Florida, Cabeza de Vaca and his companions broke out of the Mexican scrub to confront four Spaniards on horseback who were frightened at the appearance of these ragged spectres. Explanations were given and Cabeza de Vaca wept as he embraced his countrymen. The terrible journey had come to an end.

The Seven Cities of Gold

Father Marcos mistook a village similar to this Hopi pueblo as the fabled "Seven Cities of Gold" in 1540.

WHENEVER Don Antonio de Mendoza, Viceroy of Mexico, representative of His Catholic Majesty, the King of Spain, had a problem, he was wont to go to the monastery of Zeptharztec and talk the problem over with his good friend, Bishop Juan de Zumarraga. That prelate was a man of considerable holiness and wisdom.

Bishop de Zumarraga, the first bishop of Mexico, worked ceaselessly to develop the Mexican missions, and it was largely because of his direction that the Aztec tribe was quickly converted. He was a great defender of the Indians and constantly brought to the attention of the viceroy the abuses that were reported to him. The King of Spain, at Zumarraga's instigation, had laid down very definite rules (the New Laws) for the kind treatment of the Indians, and the bishop intended to see that the laws were observed, no matter how much that might hurt the pocketbooks of Spanish colonials.

The viceroy's present problem was related to Cabeza de Vaca. The latter's report of "many signs of gold, antimony, iron, copper, and other metals" had set Mexico City buzzing with rumors that de Vaca had been close to the fabled Seven Cities of Gold—about which a legend had long been part of the Spanish tradition. Don Antonio owed it to his sovereign to search for those cities; but an expedition large enough to conquer them would cost an enormous sum of money. Dare he risk the money solely on the basis of a hurricane of talk? Failure would probably cost him his post, for the King of Spain would never forgive him.

Don Antonio took this dilemma to Bishop de Zumarraga. The bishop listened carefully as his friend outlined his problem, and not until the viceroy had finished, did the bishop speak.

"What you need, Don Antonio," said the bishop, "is more information. Why not send out a small party headed by Cabeza de Vaca, or one of the other survivors of the Narvaez expedition? They know the country and the language."

"I thought of that," replied the viceroy. "But de Vaca is to return to Spain and make his report. The others have had enough of wilderness and savages! One can hardly blame them."

"How about Father Marcos de Niza?"

"The Franciscan you brought from Guatemala to tell me about the abuses against the Indians?"

"That is the one," answered the bishop. "Father Marcos has high qualifications. He was with Pizzaro in the conquest of Peru. He knows the art of navigation. He has written books dealing with the Indians of Peru and Quito. Because of his sympathy for the Indians, he would quickly win their confidence and respect."

And so it was decided. Early in 1539, Father Marcos, accompanied by another Franciscan, Father Onorato, and Esteban, the Negro, who survived the Narvaez expedition, departed from Mexico City on foot. On March 7 they departed from the last Spanish outpost, the town of Culiacan. The party had no armed guards, but they were accompanied by some friendly Indians. They followed the coastline northward along the Gulf of California. Father Onorato became sick and was left in an Indian pueblo, with instructions to return to Mexico City.

Whenever Father Marcos met a group of Indians, he showed them the samples of gold and precious stones that he carried. Each time the Indians pointed to the north. Father Marcos sent Esteban ahead with some Indians, to get any information that might bear on their quest. Esteban was to send Indian messengers back whenever he would have anything to report. Four days later an Indian returned with a message. Esteban had learned that thirty days to the north was a land called "Cibola," which had seven large cities whose inhabitants were well clothed and quite wealthy. Father Marcos set out after Esteban.

By that time, the explorers were in what is now Arizona. Father Marcos kept getting reports from Indians about Cibola. He met Indians who had been there, and they described the houses, which rose one on top of another and were reached by means of ladders. Indians told also of other kingdoms—Acoma, Marata, Totonteac. Reports coming back from Esteban were more and more enthusiastic: his escort of friendly Indians had grown to several hundred; he was nearing the borders of Cibola.

Then disaster struck. Father Marcos, enthusiastically hurrying after Esteban, met an Indian staggering back on the trail. The Indian said that when Esteban reached Cibola, the people refused to allow him to enter the city. They put him and some companions in a house on the outskirts. The Indian said that the next morning he had left the house to get water at a nearby river; and while there, he saw Esteban running from the house, and the people of Cibola pursuing him. The Indian immediately fled.

Father Marcos hurried on. When he was a day's journey from Cibola, he met two other Indians who had gone with Esteban. They were

The pueblo of Acoma, New Mexico. This settlement is one of the oldest inhabited areas in the United States.

bloodstained and had many wounds. They reported that Esteban and most of those with him had been killed. They alone survived, having been able to escape. Father Marcos debated whether to return or go on. He finally decided to view Cibola from a distance. Late the next afternoon, he reached the brow of a hill. There across the valley, nestled against another hill, was Cibola!

The white, adobe houses reflected the late afternoon sun, and it was possible to make out their terraces and flat roofs. Having been away from civilization for a long time, and having visited nothing but wretched Indian pueblos, the Franciscan thought Cibola to be a great city, even "larger than the city of Mexico." He gathered a pile of stones, set up a small cross, and claimed possession of Cibola, Acoma, Marata, and Totonteac in the name of the King of Spain. Most historians believe that Cibola was a Zuni pueblo in west-central New Mexico; legends of the murdered Esteban still exist in Zuni tradition.

Father Marcos debated going down to Cibola,

even at the risk of his life. But he finally decided that his first duty was to report this supposed discovery. That report was a sad mistake. The distance and his imagination had turned a small and dirty pueblo into a magnificent city. His confidence in the reports from the friendly Indians, who knew no great city to use as a comparison, led him to believe that the other cities of Cibola were even greater than the one he had seen and magnified. So Father Marcos returned to Mexico City and wrote a detailed account for the viceroy.

That official, Don Antonio, sent the report with a covering letter to the King of Spain, asking that the writer be allowed to send an expedition to secure the rich land Father Marcos had found. Thus was the ground laid for the expedition of Francisco Vasquez de Coronado: an expedition that was to discover the Grand Canyon and pierce the very heartland of the United States, opening one of the richest areas in the world. It was an expedition that was also to have tragic overtones.

Francisco Vasquez de Coronado and his men as they search for the "Seven Cities of Gold" in Arizona.

The Magnificent Failure

THE news of the Franciscan's supposed discovery swept through Mexico like fire. Conquistadors whose swords were rusting from the peace besieged the viceroy to be allowed to join the new expedition of conquest. Youthful adventurers, who had left Spain in the search for fame and fortune, saw in the expedition the chance for a prize even greater than Mexico. The dizziness of opportunity swept the capital like a disease.

At first the viceroy, Don Antonio de Mendoza, thought of appointing himself captain general; but his friends, including Bishop de Zumarraga, reminded him that his first duty was the governing of the colony. The viceroy did not wish to choose any one of the leaders of the many factions in the capital, because he needed a general who would be acceptable to all. He decided on a young protege—Francisco Vasquez de Coronado.

Coronado had come to Mexico in 1535, in the party of the viceroy. Scion of a noble family in Spain, Coronado was a handsome and dashing man. He traveled in the highest social circles and married the daughter of a former royal treasurer. Al-

though he had arrived in Mexico without much money, he had become very wealthy, and he had already contributed 50,000 ducats to the expedition. At the time the expedition was being organized he was governor of the Mexican province of New Galicia, although not yet thirty years of age.

The appointment of Coronado as captain general was well received. When the expedition was finally mustered in Culiacan, it numbered 336 fighting men, of whom 230 possessed horses. There were 1,000 friendly Indians as escort, and 600 beasts of burden to carry supplies, plus a four-footed army of pigs and sheep. At least seven missioners went with the expedition to care for its religious needs and also convert the Indians. One of the priests was Father Marcos de Niza, returning to the scene of his great discovery and due for a rude awakening. Another was Father Juan Padilla, the protomartyr of the United States. A third was Brother Luis de Escalona, who also died later at the hands of Indians.

On March 28, 1540, Coronado led his army

Francisco Vásquez de Coronado

The picturesque beauty of the Grand Canyon

north out of Culiacan. There were several minor skirmishes with the Indians. Because the column was moving too slowly in the Arizona heat, Coronado took fifty horsemen and Father Marcos and went ahead. On July 7, 1540, they reached Cibola; and after a short fight, they conquered the place. In a report sent back to the viceroy, Coronado caustically referred to the claims of Father Marcos. "I can assure you," he wrote, "he has not told the truth in a single thing he said, except the name of the city and the large size of the houses!"

Pedro de Cataneda, one of the chroniclers of the expedition, was more blunt. He described Cibola as a village of about 200 warriors, "little and crowded." He said that, while the houses were several stories high, they were small and dark. Speaking of the soldiers, he remarked that "when they saw the first village, which is Cibola, so many were the curses that some hurled at Friar Marcos, that I pray God may protect him from them!"

Poor Father Marcos! A small settlement seen from a distance, in poor light, and a vivid imagination fed by Indian stories, had caused his report. In fairness to the priest, it must be remembered that he never claimed to have entered Cibola. He had traveled to the area, believing in the Seven Cities of Gold, and he honestly did think he had found them. The Franciscan's imagination had improved upon fact, but the Spaniards excited by the reports added their own improvements and exaggerations as is common with rumors.

When Coronado announced that he was sending a messenger back to the viceroy, Father Marcos asked to be allowed to return. Humiliated and embarrassed, the Franciscan disappeared from the pages of history. He was shortly to be stricken with paralysis and to die a lingering death. A visionary who saw beyond the stolid faces of the Indians, he saw treasures more valuable than gold and precious stones. In a sense, his zeal for God had betrayed him. The treasures that he saw were souls.

Coronado resolved to salvage the expedition. He sent probing parties out to explore the countryside. A troop of horsemen, under Garcia Lopez de Cardenas, crossed the Colorado River and discovered the Grand Canyon. Another group explored the area around present-day Taos, and still another went to the region of Bernalillo. They brought back stories of "humpbacked cows." (The American bison, popularly called buffaloes). Near this latter place, then Tiguex, it was decided to set up winter headquarters, and there an event occurred that heated anew the Spanish fever for gold.

An Indian slave of the local tribe told the Spaniards stories of his homeland. This Indian, named "Turk" by the Spaniards, spoke of regions that were lush in vegetation, far different from the dry, Arizona-New Mexico desert. He described rivers whose banks were lined with wealthy towns and whose fish were "the size of horses." Turk fed the Spaniards stories of gold because he knew that such stories were what they wanted to hear. He told of a king who took his siestas "under a huge tree from whose branches hung golden bells that tinkled in the breeze. He said that the name of this fabulous place was Quivira.

When a harsh winter ended, Coronado started out anew. His destination was Quivira, and his guide was Turk. In that area there were no trees, hills, or other landmarks, and the guides lost their way. Coronado and his companions felt as if they had been swallowed up in a sea of grass. In Texas they saw their first buffaloes—huge herds that stampeded across the prairie. The Spaniards called the buffaloes "woolly, humpbacked cows."

After traveling thirty-seven days, encountering only Apaches and Comanches whose sole wealth was buffalo herds, the explorers became dispirited. Coronado selected thirty horsemen, and Father Juan de Padilla, and sent the remainder of his forces back to the camp where they had wintered. He also kept the lying Turk with him, but that Indian was then in chains.

Into the broiling days of July, the Coronado party marched—at first southeast and later directly north. They forded the Brazos and Red Rivers, crossed Oklahoma, moved on to the very center of Kansas, the geographical center of the United States—and there found Quivira. It was only a camp of buffalo-hide tepees! So another myth was exploded. For his deceit, Turk was put to death on the spot.

Coronado had had enough. After exploring the region around the present Wichita, he ordered a retreat to the base camp in New Mexico. Father Padilla promised the Indians that he would return to Quivira some day. The expedition made its way back to Bernalillo, suffering terrible hardships and hunger on the way. Not long after he reached the base camp, Coronado was thrown from his horse and seriously injured. At first it was feared that he would die. He passed the crisis, but both his spirit and body were broken. After the winter of 1541-42 in Tiguex, he gave up his plan for colonizing and returned to Mexico, leaving behind several friars who had missionary plans.

There were no cheers when the Coronado expedition re-entered Mexico City. The injured leader was received in disgrace, discharged from his job, fined, and for a short time imprisoned. He was blamed for the loss of the money invested in the expedition, and was made the scapegoat for exploded dreams. He was accused of cowardice; and one contemporary writer compared him to Ulysses, who feigned madness to go home to see his wife. The Spanish had an unwritten rule: he who does not settle the land is a failure. Many in Mexico City believed that it would have been better for Coronado to have died in Kansas than return home with empty hands.

Eventually Coronado was reaccepted by Mexican society. He regained his position on the municipal council and obtained new land grants to add to his estate. But when he died in his early forties, twelve years after his return to Mexico City he was still disillusioned and still believed himself a failure. Although he found no gold, Coronado was the equal of any other Spanish explorer. He was as great as Cortes or Pizzaro or Alvarado. Coronado had opened routes into the future United States—routes over which traders and colonists were to travel. His contributions to the development of America were very great.

Signature of Francisco Vazquez de Coronado

America's First Martyr

IN the list of 116 martyrs who met death within the region that became the United States—a list that the American hierarchy has submitted to the Holy See for consideration for canonization—the name of Father Juan de Padilla leads all the rest. Father de Padilla was born in Spain. One of the chroniclers of the Coronado expeditions said that he "had been a fighting man in his youth." He entered the Franciscan order in Spain and became one of the pioneer missioners in Mexico.

Father Padilla accompanied Cortes on an expedition to Colima, near Mexico's Pacific coast; founded new missions around Tulancingo; and later worked with great success in Jalisco and Zapotlan, converting numerous Indians. When Coronado organized his ill-fated exploration, Father de Padilla was one of the seven Franciscans assigned to it. Father de Padilla was a vigorous and energetic man. No sacrifice was too great if he could win souls to God.

When Coronado ordered the majority of his troops back to a winter base in New Mexico and set out for Quivira with a small troop of men, Father Padilla was selected to go as chaplain. After Quivira was reached, the entire party returned to New Mexico. There Coronado decided to give up his search, and he commanded his men to return to Mexico. However, a group of Franciscans decided to remain behind: they had journeyed not in search of worldly treasure, but to plant the Faith in the newly discovered lands.

Father (or Brother) John of the Cross, a Frenchman advanced in age, and Brother Luis Descalona, took up mission work among the Indians in the Bernalillo-Pecos area. Both men had tremendous success, and therefore they gained the enmity of native medicine men. Brother Luis told the Spaniards who had come to bid him goodby that he expected to be killed by the medicine man. Nothing further was heard of either Father John of the Cross or Brother Luis. It is believed that both were put to death by the Indians. No relics of them have been found, and Indian tradition makes no mention of them.

Father Juan de Padilla also remained behind when the Cornado expedition returned to Mexico. He kept with him two young men, who had been raised by the Franciscans and who served as lay Brothers: Lucan and Sebastian. A Portuguese soldier, Andres Docampo, volunteered to stay with the missioners. There were also several Mexican Indians. Father de Padilla had decided to return to Quivira to do mission work. Because of the agricultural potential of their country, the natives of Quivira could become a very important people, if the Spanish conquest should be extended. The Quiviras lived in poverty, in the midst of richness of soil and vegetation, and the Franciscan was determined to help them to a better life.

Father de Padilla made his way back to Kansas in the company of some Indians who had served as guides for Coronado and who were returning home. Only Andres Docampo was mounted; the Franciscans made the journey on foot. At Quivira the returning group was well received. Father de Padilla immediately plunged into his work of conversion and had considerable success. All went well until he decided to move on and begin preaching Christianity to another tribe, enemies of the Quiviras.

The Franciscan had not been among the Quiviras long enough to understand the Indian mind. The Quiviras did not wish their enemies to have the blessings Father de Padilla had given them! They could not understand how he could continue to be their friend if he associated with their enemies. Father de Padilla, who loved everyone with the love of Christ, did not realize the situation.

One day in the autumn of 1542, Father de Padilla and his companions, together with some Indian boys, left Quivira and set out for the village of another tribe. The little group camped that night on the prairie, and in the morning they resumed their journey. Suddenly Quivira Indians sprang from ambush, their war cries rending the morning air.

The priest realized what was happening. "Run! Save yourselves!" he shouted to his companions.

The two Franciscan lay Brothers, the boys, and the Portuguese immediately fled, but not Father de Padilla. He was the person the Indians wanted. He knelt on the Kansas prairie, facing the oncoming enemy. He prayed a prayer of thanksgiving because God had given him the grace that he most ardently desired — martyrdom. An arrow struck him; then another, and another. He slumped to the ground, his blood staining the rich soil of America.

The Indians dragged the dead priest's body to a ravine and rolled it down. Then they piled rocks upon it. Fittingly enough, the place was almost the geographical center of the United States. The great nation that was to rise around that grave was to be his monument.

Father de Padilla's companions eventually reached Mexico safely, after a difficult journey that resembled that of Cabeza de Vaca. They told the story of what had happened, and thus it has been preserved for all time.

Hernando de Soto: Last of the Conquistadors

WHEN Juan Ponce de Leon died of the wound he had received in Florida, and Panfilo de Narvaez disappeared from the face of the earth, it fell to the King of Spain to appoint a new governor. Many Spaniards, some with excellent credentials, sought the post for it presented one of the last great opportunities for exploration and conquest. But when Charles V made his selection, the man chosen was one of the few who had not looked for it. He was Hernando de Soto.

De Soto was born in Extremadura—a rugged, dry, hard corner of Spain that provided so many Conquistadors—on January 1, 1500. He had come to the New World as a youth of nineteen with nothing more than a sword, and a bold and brave character. He joined the forces of Pedrarias Davila, governor of Darien (Panama), and soon won the governor's friendship and admiration by his daring, loyalty and courage. He took part in the conquest of Nicaragua. He became the confidant and right-hand man of the governor and greatly prospered.

When Francisco Pizarro, a fellow Extremadurian, organized his daring expedition for the conquest of Peru and the Inca empire, de Soto joined him, furnishing two well-equipped ships from his own funds. He was in the forefront of action that overthrew the Incas and conquered the west coast of South America and he proved himself a man of honor as well as a great soldier. An outstanding display of horsemanship won him the friendship of the Inca, Atahualpa, and he tried to save the emperor's life when he was later put on trial—but lost to Pizarro's greed. When the conquest was solidified,

50

de Soto wanted no part of the squabbles that arose among the conquerors. He returned to Spain a millionaire, was knighted, married the daughter of Pedrarias Davila, and settled down to enjoy a life of wealth. He was not yet thirty-five years old.

But for one who had led an active and adventurous life, the boredom of idleness and the pettiness of the social whirl were more than the former warrior could endure. After hardly a year of inactivity, de Soto applied to King Charles for the right to explore the South Seas at his own expense. Instead he was appointed governor of Florida and Cuba—Cuba because it would provide a base for exploration, Florida because it was *terra incognita*, unknown land.

De Soto used his own money to organize the expedition. He had no trouble recruiting men, although he did fail to get Cabeza de Vaca to join. That former wanderer knew what lay ahead and wanted no part of it! He repeatedly stated that Florida was a barren land with no treasures, but he was not believed. A large number of Portuguese even crossed over the border to sign on with de Soto. When the young commander finally sailed from Spain in 1538 he had ten ships and some 600 men. Eight diocesan priests, one Franciscan, one Trinitarian and two Dominicans were brought along to preach Christianity to the Indians.

The expedition sailed to Cuba where the final staging was to take place and the expedition was to winter. A scouting party was sent to Florida, and it brought back two Indians to serve as interpreters. On May 18, 1539, leaving his wife behind as acting governor of Cuba, de Soto and nine ships left the

Mission site, St. Augustine, Florida

harbor of Havana. On May 30, the Spaniards entered a wide bay on the west coast of Florida. Since it was Pentecost, de Soto named the bay Espiritu Santo (Holy Spirit). We know it as Tampa Bay. Expectations were high, and no one realized that four years of hunger, danger, hardship, bitter fighting and death lay ahead.

De Soto headed inland and north, wanting to get away from his ships and any thoughts of retreat. There were constant skirmishes with the Florida Indians, who were unmatched in their record of resistance to foreigners; the Indians shot arrows from ambush, set traps, but avoided a head-on clash. In one early battle, taken among the prisoners was Juan Ortiz, a Spanish soldier of the unfortunate Narvaez expedition, who had been enslaved all those years. He was to prove a valuable interpreter. The Spaniards struggled north from one battle to the next. De Soto suffered several wounds in the fighting because, as one historian recorded, "he did not like victories unless he was the main factor in winning them." The expedition traveled a zigzag course which took it the length of Florida, northward across Georgia, and into the Carolinas, Tennessee, Alabama, Mississippi, Louisiana, Arkansas, Oklahoma, and Texas!

The record of that journey is one of heroism, hunger and hurt. At one point the forces of De Soto almost came in contact with those of Coronado, searching for his Seven Cities of Gold. If they had met, many hardships and deaths would have been avoided. But history is full of might-have-beens. Instead, the forces unknowingly passed, and De Soto's conquistadors went on fighting and suffering. The Spaniards had to live off the land which was far from hospitable. They became mired in swamps, succumbing to disease, hunger, and Indian tomahawks. On a rare occasion, the Spaniards encountered a friendly tribe. Then they would halt, regain their strength, and use the respite to explain Christianity to their hosts.

On May 8, 1541, the Spaniards came upon a great river which they called Rio Grande (the Mississippi) because of its greatness, although the Indians referred to it as Meact-Massipi. They built boats and crossed the torrent of waters which European veterans said was even greater than the Danube. Some thought that they were in the vicinity of the Pacific!

A year later they were back at the Mississippi where De Soto hoped to make a permanent settlement. On June 20, 1542, the invincible De Soto took to bed with a fever. "A glutinous fever-blister," one chronicle states, and adds: "Seeing the excessive growth of it, the Governor recognized that his sickness was fatal." First, De Soto wrote his will, almost in code and full of abbreviations, because there was not enough paper. Next, he called a chaplain to whom he confessed his sins and made his peace with God. Thus having taken care of the temporal and spiritual, only the military was left. He called his officers together and announced that Luis Moscoso de Alvarado was to take command. An eyewitness said how "he said he was about to go into the presence of God . . . and since God was pleased to take him away at such a time, when he could recognize the moment of death, he rendered Him hearty thanks." The following day he died.

It was decided to conceal De Soto's death from the Indians because it was feared that the news would give them courage to attack. He was buried at night and horses were run over his grave. But fearful that the body would be found, dug up, quartered and hung on trees, as they had seen the Indians do, the soldiers decided to bury their leader in the "rio grande." The trunk of a thick oak tree was hollowed and the body placed in the space and covered with crude planks. Under the pretense of fishing, the deepest part of the Mississippi was found, the rude coffin weighted, and in darkness confided to the Father of Waters. Thus De Soto's discovery became his tomb.

Moscoso, the new leader, called together the captains and asked what should be done. All agreed to call off the expedition. A few wanted to build boats and follow the river to the sea. The majority voted to go overland to Mexico. They reached the vicinity of Austin, Texas, when the vastness of the land overwhelmed them. The lack of provisions and the fierceness of the Indians were also compelling reasons for retreat. It was finally decided to return to the Mississippi and follow the alternate plan of escape by ship—the only hitch being that they had no ships and were not sure where the river would take them.

It took six months and fantastic ingenuity to build seven boats, but at last the expedition's survivors began their return journey. To their dismay, they were hardly afloat on the Mississippi when forty or fifty large canoes appeared, in some of which there were as many as eighty Indians. The enemy immediately launched an attack. For nineteen days the weaponless Spaniards fought their way down river against frightful odds. Finally they outdistanced the pursuing warriors and reached the mouth of the Father of Waters.

Hugging the shore, the Spaniards sailed westward towards Mexico. They had almost reached safety when a terrible storm arose. Some men had to desert their boats and swim for their lives; others beached their boats. At last they staggered into the Spanish outpost of Panuco, half dead and almost naked. Their bodies were burned black from the sun; their stomachs were empty, and their throats parched. But they did not immediately ask for food, water, or clothing. Instead, in pitiful but brave ranks, they marched to the little adobe church, and there they prayed and gave thanks to God for their preservation.

The curtain had descended on the great age of Spanish exploration. The last of the conquistadors lay at the bottom of the United States' mightiest river. The conquistadors were a special breed of men, which the world never again saw. They were driven on by many motives; pride in Spain, the desire to become rich, and the extension of the kingdom of God. They faced the most arduous perils; risked their lives and even lost them; underwent thirst, hunger, heat, cold; met in battle native fighters who far outnumbered their own small bands. Most of them died in their endeavors. The few conquistadors who succeeded were soon dishonored or assigned to oblivion.

With the passing of De Soto, a different breed appeared. The "new" men were already forming to march into the conquered lands. They carried no swords and wore no armor. They sought no Fountain of Youth — no Seven Cities of Gold. They were the colonists.

The martyrdom of the missionaries of Virginia. The Jesuits were murdered with their leader, Father de Segura.

The Colony That Failed

THE adage, "For want of a nail a kingdom was lost," has many interesting counterparts in American history. One interesting speculation is this: What would the future of our country have been if the Spanish attempt to set up a colony in Virginia had succeeded? Virginia became the mother colony for the English. But if the area had been in possession of the Spanish, our country's history would probably have been vastly different.

On September 10, 1570, thirty-seven years before the first English were to arrive in Virginia, a small Spanish ship entered the Bay of the Mother of God (Chesapeake Bay) and made its way up what is now known as the James River. At a spot somewhere near the present Jamestown, there disembarked a party of nine: two Jesuit priests, three Jesuit Brothers, three novice Brothers, a Spanish youth, and an Indian guide.

The group intended to establish a mission and begin the work of converting the Indians in what is now Virginia. The superior of the group was Father Juan Baptista de Segura, who had been head of his society's mission work in Florida. Originally, the governor of Florida had wanted to send a party of soldiers with the missioners and establish a garrison, but Father de Segura would have none of that plan.

The Jesuit superior protested that soldiers would overshadow the missioners. The whole purpose of the settlement was to spread Christianity. Spanish soldiers often treated Indians harshly, and undid the work of the missioners. It was better, Father de Segura believed, to risk the danger of being unprotected than to be hindered by bad example from soldiers and other officials.

The key to the mission was to be the Indian guide, Don Luis. He had been rescued at sea some ten years earlier by Spanish sailors and taken to Spain, where he was later educated. His home had been in Virginia, and his uncle was a powerful chief there. At first Luis was helpful, but gradually he began to lose the veneer of civilization he had acquired in Spain. Finally he deserted the missioners and went to live among the Indians of his uncle's village, about a day and a half away.

The betrayal by the "educated" Indian had serious consequences. He had assured Father de Segura that they would be able to buy all the food they needed from the Indians, and as a result the Spaniards had carried little with them. The truth was that the Indian villagers hardly grew enough for their own needs, and in addition there was a drought that was causing famine. The missioners had to search for roots and berries to remain alive.

In primitive surroundings, the Jesuits set up religious life. They opened a school for Indian boys. There was daily Mass, and daily spiritual instruction. The three novice Brothers were professed into the Society of Jesus — the first religious profession recorded in the United States.

Soon word reached Father de Segura that Don Luis had completely abandoned Christianity. He had taken several wives, and was leading a dissolute life. Father Segura sent several messages to the renegade, begging him to keep the promises he had made to God and inviting him to rejoin the group of missioners. Finally Father de Segura sent Father Luis Quiros and Brothers Gabriel and Juan to the village where Don Luis lived, in an attempt to persuade him to reform.

The missioners were surprised to be received in a friendly fashion by Don Luis. He welcomed them into his village, listened to what they had to say, and agreed to return with them to the mission. The next morning the three missioners started home, overjoyed because Don Luis had promised that he would soon join them. They did not expect treachery; and when Don Luis, at the head of a band of warriors, sprang on them from ambush, they failed at first to understand what was happening. Father Quiros and Brother Gabriel died immediately. Brother Juan, although wounded, escaped into the forest; but the next morning, the Indians found him and put him to death.

Four days later—February 9, 1571—Don Luis appeared at the mission, at the head of a band of Indians. He told Father de Segura that he had come to help the mission. The Jesuit superior joyfully welcomed back the prodigal. Don Luis offered to cut a supply of wood for the mission, and from the storehouse he passed out axes to his companions. As soon as the Indians had the axes, they gave savage cries and fell on the Jesuits, killing every one of them. Only the youth, Alonso de Olmos, was spared, as it was the custom of the Indians to adopt boy captives into their tribe.

A few months later, a supply ship sailed into the James River, bearing food and other goods to the mission. The captain became suspicious when he saw on shore some Indians dressed in Jesuit cassocks. He steered his ship closer to learn what was going on — and then two boatloads of armed warriors appeared. In the fight that followed, two captives were taken by the Spaniards. From those Indians, it was learned that all the Jesuits were dead, and the boy Alonso was held captive.

In the next year, a punitive expedition was sent from Florida. It was led by the governor himself. The Spanish troops arrested the chief and eleven other Indians. The governor demanded the immediate release of Alonso, and the surrender of Don Luis within five days. That night Alonso escaped from the Indian camp and swam to the ship and safety. When the period for the surrender of Don Luis passed without his appearance, the governor held court on the captive Indians as murderers of the Jesuits. Five were released when judged innocent of the murders, and the seven others were hanged. Thus ended the Spanish attempt to settle in Virginia.

The savage Indians who inhabited the Virginia area

The Forgotten Spanish Gift

THE Spanish explorers, settlers, and missioners bestowed many gifts upon the United States, and their legacy is one in which all of our citizens share. The Spaniards opened up vast areas of our country, penetrating from the Pacific and Atlantic Oceans to the very heart of Kansas. They tamed the wilderness and left behind fine ranches, orchards, vineyards, farms. They developed a network of roads, the routes of which are still used.

The Spaniards gave us lovely sounding place names: Los Angeles, Las Cruces, San Antonio, El Paso, Santa Fe, San Francisco — to mention but a few. They enriched our language with words like rodeo, lariat, mustang, bronco. They taught the Catholic Faith to thousands of American Indians, many of whose descendants still practice it today. Another gift that the Spaniards left us, and one that is often forgotten, played a very important role in the history of our country: it changed the lives of the Plains Indians; it developed our cattle industry. It was responsible for the opening of the West. This was the gift of the horse.

Once long, long ago, the horse was native to North America. Then the breed became extinct and did not return to the New World until the second voyage of Columbus. From the island of Hispaniola (today's Haiti and Dominican Republic), the horse spread to Cuba, Mexico, Peru and the United States. Cortes began his invasion of Mexico with sixteen horses, and it is an historical fact that these horses played a key role in the overthrow of the Aztecs. Coronado and De Soto brought horses into the United States, and undoubtedly some of the animals escaped. But it was from Juan de Onate's settlement in New Mexico that most North American horses came.

At first the Indians looked upon the horse as a welcome addition to their diet. Then they realized the value of the horse in hunting and in warfare. Horses enabled the nomadic tribes to move about quickly and easily; other tribes that formerly lived by farming became hunters. Special bows were developed for shooting from horseback, and the Indians soon discovered that it was much easier to kill bison from horseback than on foot.

The horse brought a whole new culture to the Indians. Horse-stealing from enemy tribes was considered one of the highest feats. Counting *coup* on an enemy from horseback was daring and brought great recognition. The horse gave the Indian soldier, as well as his tribe, a mobility that neither had known before.

Horses spread quickly across the face of America. Wild herds first appeared about the year 1600. Survivors of the La Salle expedition saw horses with Spanish brands in Texas. French trappers reported horses among the Comanches and Pawnees by 1720. In 1757, an agent of Hudson's Bay Company met Blackfeet Indians from Montana who had horses with them; but when he later included this fact in a report, he was discharged for irresponsibility because "everyone knows the Indians do not have horses." By 1800, American adventurers were raiding Texas (then part of Mexico) to capture wild horses.

It is difficult to assay the role the horse played in American history. Certainly, the West could never have been won without it. In the vast deserts and seas of grass, a man without a horse was helpless. It was for this reason that penalties against horse-stealing were very grave. The horse was responsible for the success of the American cattle industry—imagine trying to round up a herd of steers on foot!

Barbed wire and farms brought the end for the roving bands of wild horses. Today the wild horse is found only in remote canyons and hidden valleys of the West. But the horses that are still used on cattle ranches from Florida to Montana, the horses that we see in the rodeo, the quarter horses, and many more, all came from the wiry little steeds introduced by the Spanish — one of the greatest gifts bestowed upon the New World.

The magnificent horse of the American plains could be considered the greatest legacy of the Spanish colonizers.

The First Two American Cities

SEVERAL attempts to colonize Florida failed because of the hostility of the Indians. Apart from military efforts, a number of tries were made by missioners. As early as 1528, a Spanish Franciscan, Father Juan Juarez, was appointed bishop of Florida. The record is not clear what happened to him but it seems he died in Florida that same year with a companion, John de Palos. Death came either from starvation or at the hands of Indians.

Another attempt by missioners in 1549 ended in tragedy. On Ascension Day of that year a group of missioners went ashore, somewhere near Tampa Bay. Within a few days, those men—Fathers Luis Cancer de Barbastro and Diego de Penalosa, and Brother Fuentes, all Dominicans—were savagely butchered by Indians.

In 1565, the extraordinary Admiral Pedro Menendez de Aviles, one of the leading Naval figures of the Spanish empire, was dispatched by Philip II to found a colony in Florida. With him he took twelve Franciscans and four Jesuits to work for the conversion of the Indians. On August 28, 1565, while sailing along the Florida coast, Admiral Menendez saw a peninsula that seemed ideal to defend. He ordered the boats to drop anchor, and on September 8 proclaimed the founding of Saint Augustine—so named because the peninsula had been found on the saint's feast day.

From this center, missioners spread out to convert the hostile Indians. In few other parts of the United States was advancing civilization resisted as much as in Florida. Priest after priest sacrificed his life, but always there was a replacement. Gradually St. Augustine developed, the colony grew, and the countryside became pacified. Missions and monasteries were founded in other parts of Florida. Practically all the Indians north of the Gulf of Mexico and east of the Mississippi River were won to Catholicism.

This does not mean that troubles were over. In place of the Indians, bitterly anti-Catholic French Huguenots appeared. They raided the

Spanish and Catholic Indian settlements, putting to death missioners and their faithful. Sometimes in barbarity they outdid Indian cruelty. Also the British, who had begun colonizing in the north, began raiding Spanish holdings. In 1704, Governor Moore of South Carolina led a raiding party to attack Apalachee Mission, considered the granary of Florida. Three Franciscans were cruelly put to death, along with about 800 Catholic Indians. Another 1,400 Indians were taken into slavery by the English governor.

The Spanish could not continue the unequal war. In 1763, they signed the Treaty of Paris with England, ceding Florida to the British. It was expected that the Catholic Faith would be allowed to remain. However, the English raised all sorts of blocks. The bishop's house was seized and given to the Church of England, the Franciscan monastery was turned into a barracks, the Indian church became a hospital. At the end of the American Revolution, the new government of the United States recognized the injustice and returned Florida to Spanish control until 1821 when Florida was legally purchased and became part of the United States.

Today one can visit Saint Augustine and walk in the spirit of the past. There a tourist can visit the oldest house and the oldest schoolhouse in the United States. He can see the beautiful Bridge of Lions, and sections of the old city wall that had been built to guard against Huguenot and British attacks. And his imagination can picture the army of missioners who once poured from this center to Georgia, Alabama, and Mississippi, seeking only to establish the Kingdom of God in the New World.

The Spanish balanced their eastern colony in Florida with one in the west, although the latter was founded not without difficulty. Several attempts had been made to settle in New Mexico but had not succeeded. In 1595, Don Juan de Onate, a Creole, who had become rich from mines in Zacatecas, Mexico, offered to equip and finance a colonizing expedition at his own expense. The viceroy accepted his offer.

Early in 1598 Onate, accompanied by 400 soldiers and settlers, 10 missioners, 83 supply wagons and carts, and 7,000 head of stock, set out to establish his colony. A settlement was made near a Tewa Indian village and named San Juan (later Saint Gabriel). Here was built the second church in the United States, the first being St. Augustine, Florida. The first winter was filled with many hardships. Food was scarce; the Indians were res-

Hernando de Soto, the Spanish explorer and settler

Signature of Hernando de Soto

An early Spanish map depicting the colony of St. Augustine and the mission of Nombre de Dios in the year 1593

The Fortress of St. Augustine. The settlement founded by Menendez de Aviles is the oldest in the United States.

tive. One incident occurred which is recorded in Spanish annals as a feat equal to the famous leap made by Pedro de Alvarado in the Cortes retreat from Mexico City.

Juan de Zaldivar, Onate's nephew, was leading thirty men to join Onate when he decided to make a halt at Acoma, the spectacular pueblo built on a mesa 357 feet above the New Mexican plains, which is believed to be the oldest inhabited city in the United States. Leaving some soldiers as a rear guard, Zaldivar and seventeen men ascended to the tabletop. The Indians received them warmly and began to show them the city; it was a trick to separate the Spaniards. Once they were apart, the Indians fell upon the strangers. One by one, the soldiers died on the mesa, except for a Sergeant Tabaro and four soldiers who were able to regroup. Slashing with their swords, they hacked a path through the Indians and held their attackers at bay. They were slowly forced to back until they found themselves at the very edge of the mesa which dropped straight down in a precipice. Realizing that they could not continue their defense, and in a moment of both bravery and despair, they leaped out into space. We do not know from just

where they jumped but the minimum drop has to be 160 feet! One soldier was killed in the leap, but the other four almost miraculously survived with only bruises; they landed in some sand which the wind had blown up against the foot of the mesa.

To punish Acoma, Onate sent another nephew, Vicente, brother of the dead Juan de Zaldivar, and a force of seventy men to capture the pueblo and punish the murderers. It was another example of Spanish confidence and elan for the Indians, whose warriors outnumbering the Spaniards ten to one, seemed impregnable in their sky-top fortress. The soldiers took with them a small mortar, more for psychological effect than anything it could do. One day towards the end of January, 1599, the siege began. While the main force feinted an attack at an invulnerable side, twelve men dragged the stone-mortar up an undefended rocky outcrop, separated from Acoma by a deep gully. That night other soldiers dragging pine logs, joined the mortar crew, and dropped the logs as a bridge across the gully. At daybreak they began to cross to the pueblo. When the Indians realized what was happening, they came charging at the Spaniards. At the same moment some soldier let go of a rope

Re-creation of the founding of St. Augustine on the fourth centennial celebration of the landing of de Aviles.

holding the bridge, stranding twelve companions on the Acoma mesa. An officer realizing the situation took a running Olympic-size leap and landed on the other side of the chasm. He pulled the bridge back into position and soldiers dashed across to aid their companions who were already doing battle. The mortar, which would have been useless against stone walls, was able to blast holes in the adobe walls. After three days of furious fighting, the Indians asked for peace. Zaldivar accepted the surrender and ordered that no further punishment be leveled against Acoma since half the town was in ruins and the chiefs who had ordered his brother killed and their Navajo allies had died in the siege.

The story of Acoma is related at length because it is indicative of what the Spaniards had to endure in their conquest. Meanwhile, while he had troops protecting his base, Onate explored as far away as Wichita, Kansas, and California. On this latter journey he reached what he called the "South Sea." It could have been the Pacific Ocean but most believe it was the Gulf of California. On the return journey from there, the Spaniards had to eat their horses to keep from starving. One evening they reached a huge sandstone peak rising some two hundred feet from the valley floor. It was a landmark used also by Coronado, Antonio de Espejo and Father Francisco Beltran. At its foot melted snow and rain collected, a precious treasure to the thirsty traveler. It was here on another journey that Onate learned of the original treachery at Acoma. Now he paused to rest and cut into the sandstone wall a message: "Here passed by Adelantado Don Juan de Onate, from the discovery of the South Sea, April 16, 1605." Future travelers were to see that inscription and carve their own—other explorers, U.S. soldiers, emigrants bound for California, gold seekers. A guidepost on the trail west, it became known as Inscription Rock, and most Americans have seen it at one time or another in a Western movie. Today, it is under government protection with its original name — El Morro National Monument, New Mexico. It is the first American public billboard.

All of this exploring cost money and Onate was becoming disillusioned with the lack of return. The Viceroy of New Spain was unhappy with the slowness of development. New Mexico was an economic drain, not an asset; moreover, there was continual fighting with the Apache, Navajo and Comanche Indians and the result was a lack of colonization. Onate resigned as commander and Pedro de Peralta was assigned there with orders to build a new capital and colonize. This Peralta did (about 1609) selecting a site which he named Royal City of the Holy Faith of Saint Francis, or as simply known to us, Santa Fe (Holy Faith).

Peralta laid out the new city, centered about a plaza. On the northern side, he built a long one story palace of adobe brick and log beams. This Governor's Place stands to this day, the oldest public building in the United States. It has been the residence of Spanish, Mexican and American governors and for a short period was held by Indians who drove the Spanish out until Diego de Vargas subjugated them in 1692. It was the residence of governors until 1909, and today it is operated by the Museum of New Mexico.

Despite Peralta's optimism, colonists were slow in coming to Santa Fe. Instead, the city was mainly a Spanish military base and the center for mission activity. From here, missioners went out to the Indian pueblos, planting the Faith, often at the cost of their own lives. By 1617, eleven churches, or missions, had been established around Santa Fe. By 1625, there were 43 missions and 34,000 Christian Indians.

Acoma, scene of an earlier revolt, remained hostile to the Spaniards. In 1629, Father Juan Ramirez, a Franciscan, refusing the offer of a military guard, set out alone and on foot to found a mission at Acoma. After many days, across the burning desert, he reached the island rock. As soon as the Indians saw him, they began shooting arrows at him. Without flinching and with peculiar confidence in God so markedly Spanish, Father Juan began climbing the steep steps hewed into the cliff, even though some arrows pierced the cloth of his grey habit. As he climbed, a small girl, watching at the brink of the mesa, lost her balance and toppled over the edge. Providentially, after falling a few yards, she landed on a ledge. Father Juan picked her off the ledge and carried her to the top. The Indians, thinking she had fallen the whole height of the cliff, believed the priest had worked a miracle. They received him kindly.

Father Juan dwelt in Acoma for twenty years. When he died, the people of the sky-city knew their catechism, and many were able to read and write Spanish. He directed the Indians in building a large church (Saint Stephen the King), but it was later damaged in the Pueblo War of 1680 when the resident Franciscan, Father Lucas Maldonado, was martyred. Today, the church—one of the largest and least altered of New Mexico mis-

Little is changed in the way of life in some of the areas where the Spanish explored in the sixteen hundreds.

sions—is used only during the Acoma fiesta because the handful of Indians left no longer justifies a resident priest. But thousands of tourists visit it each year. They also climb the hewn stairway used by Father Juan to enter the pueblo and the Acoma Indians still call it *El Camino del Padre* (The Path of the Father).

The world seems to have passed by these natives of Acoma, N.M., as they cling to their old ways.

NEW MEXICO STATE DEPARTMENT OF DEVELOPMENT

An aerial view of the Acoma, New Mexico, Indian town. The pueblo is situated on a mesa 400 feet high and has consequently been referred to as the "Sky City."

The remnants of the mission of Pecos, New Mexico. A 1680 Indian raid destroyed most of the structure.

The Mission San Xavier del Bac, the mission is the legacy of the great Jesuit, Father Eusebio Kino (Page 65).

The Further Beyond

NOT far from Tucson, Arizona, is a gem of a mission that today, although a national monument, is still the parish church for the Pima Indians. Its simple beauty — twin towers, dome, baroque facade — has long been a favorite for photographers. Its history, particularly its survival through Apache attacks, has made it a popular visiting place for tourists. It is Mission San Xavier del Bac. Once it was the heart of thriving Pima Indian life, surrounded by rich farms and herds of fat cattle. The founder of this mission was one of the greatest pioneers our country has known and the father of the modern cattle industry.

He was the Jesuit Father Francisco Eusebio Kino, who although he worked under the Spanish crown and in Spanish territory, was an Austrian from the Italian Tyrol (Trent). His real name was Kuehne or Kühn, although the Spanish form is the one under which he is known. Early in life he determined to be a missioner—but in Asia, not America. He took as his model St. Francis Xavier, the Apostle of the Indies. He prepared to go to the Asian missions as a mathematician, something in the pattern of a fellow Jesuit, the great Matteo Ricci. But at the last minute, he lost out when there was not enough space on a ship, and this extraordinary man came to Mexico instead, where he proceeded to learn agronomy and animal hus-

65

The portal of the Mission San Xavier del Bac, the Church was designed by Father Kino.

bandry along with Spanish.

Professor Herbert Bolton, of the University of California, an authority on Kino, called the Jesuit "the most picturesque missionary pioneer of all North America—explorer, astronomer, cartographer, mission builder, ranchman, cattle king, and defender of the frontier." Kino's field of labor was Pimeria Alta (the Upper Pima Country) which now embraces the Mexican state of Sonora and our own southern Arizona. No one has ever estimated the thousands of miles Padre Kino traveled on horseback but he was ever on the move. When he was elected to National Statuary Hall, Bolton hoped he would be represented on horseback, but he is shown standing erect.

Father Kino's maps were the most accurate of the time and brought him fame in Europe. It was he who declared that Baja California is a peninsula and he was the first cartographer to draw it this way. Scores of towns and cities that exist today were begun by Father Kino. He founded nineteen stock ranches. Over a vast area, it was he who introduced European cereals and fruits that today bring agricultural riches. Wheat culture in California began with a handful of seed he sent across a desert to a Yuma chief who had once befriended him.

Kino was a master builder. His San Xavier del Bac is called the finest example of Spanish Renaissance architecture in the United States—a fitting monument to his heavenly patron. Kino so won the hearts of the Pima Indians that they defended San Xavier with their lives against fierce Apache attacks. After the expulsion of the Jesuits, the mission was turned over to the Franciscans. Another mission established by Kino in the United States is Tumacacori, also a national monument. A description of the mission in 1698 tells of its "fields of wheat, herds of cattle, sheep and goats." This mission also came into the possession of the Franciscans who did much building there. In 1848, it was abandoned and many of its ecclesiastical appurtenances were moved to San Xavier del Bac.

Whenever Father Kino spoke a certain term kept cropping up in his conversation It was *mas alla*—which can best be translated as "the further beyond." Like the indefatigable Saint Francis Xavier, Kino thirsted for the souls that were always beyond the next hill or horizon. He was ever on the go and averaged two extensive mission journeys a year, some of more than a thousand miles. He was tireless in the saddle, traveling thirty to forty miles a day, including halts to preach and baptize. He

opened trails that are roads today. He kept journals of his travels and observations, and his papers are preserved in the Huntington Library, San Marino, California.

Kino's only failure—and it can't really be called a failure because he never had the opportunity to try, but it bothered him—was that the Apache Indians were not converted. Those indomitable warriors stood between Arizona and New Mexico. If they could be won to friendship and the Faith, the way beyond would be open—to the Pacific, and to New France (Canada). With Kino it was always the *mas alla*—the vision of new conquests for Christ. While some missioners are suspected of being Spaniards first and priests second, Kino, because of his antecedents, gives the lie to the priority. He was interested only in the expansion of the Kingdom of God and the human welfare of the people he served.

At the age of sixty-six, Father Kino was still in the saddle. He rode out from his mission center in Dolores, northern Mexico, to dedicate a chapel at Magdalena, again named in honor of his favorite saint, Francis Xavier. While singing the Dedication Mass, he became ill. He died as he had lived, in great poverty. His death bed was on a dirt floor—two calfskins for a mattress, two blankets for cover, and his pack saddle for a pillow. There he passed away, a few minutes after midnight on March 15, 1711, the missioner who was truly a great American pioneer.

The Jesuit, Father Eusebio Francisco Kino

The Forgotten Missions

An example of the missions of Father Antonio Margil

FOR some reason the missions of Texas and the Spanish efforts there have never received the attention in American history that they deserve. Texas was the field of labor of Father Antonio Margil whose cause for canonization has been introduced and one of his beautiful mission foundations, near San Antonio, is a still used parish church and a National Historic Site of both the state and nation. The Franciscans from their missionary center at Zacatecas, Mexico, developed a chain of thirty-eight missions. Perhaps the historical oversight is due to the fact that Texas was late in joining the United States, or that many Texans were not proud of the state's Mexican beginnings, or the emphasis given to the Alamo in American history, or the Texan preference for men from the north—

NC PHOTO

Fr. Antonio Margil, priest, scholar and missionary

Davy Crockett, Sam Houston, and other Anglo-Saxons of their repute.

Nevertheless, the University of Texas is one of the major sources for Hispanic history in the Americas. The University has an outstanding collection of early manuscripts, among them twenty-five letters written by Junipero Serra. A half million pages of documents form the Bejar Archives at the University, a gold mine of early Texan history. Other collections, such as the twenty-five thousand volumes from Jenaro Garcia, make this source one of the largest and richest for the Hispanic student.

Texas was the scene of competition between Spain and France. Although the Spanish were there first, the French through the Mississippi River reached the state from Canada. LaSalle was responsible for building Fort Prudhomme in Tipton County and Fort St. Louis in Victoria County; in fact, it was during an exploration to Texas that LaSalle was murdered by mutineers. To counter the French thrust, the Spaniards founded San Antonio de Bexar Mission (the present San Antonio) and made it the seat of government and center for mission activity. Other missions such as San Saba and San Luis and San Francisco de los Tejas (whose site is lost) were also part of the chain.

Perhaps a short history of San José de Aguayo Mission will indicate what was developed in Texas. San José is interesting because it is one of the finest surviving missions in the United States and it was founded by the already mentioned Fray Margil, who ranks with Kino and Serra as the greatest of Spanish missioners.

A Spanish mission was not merely a church and a residence for priests. It was an entirely self-sufficient community, including farms and cattle ranches; homes for Indian converts who worked at the mission, and for teachers, nurses and guards; there were schools, hospitals, and guard posts for protection from Apache and Comanche attacks. One governor who visited San José described the "84 flat roofed houses of stone, arranged according to a plan with parapets and battlements" that housed 281 Indian workers. The mission had a carpenter shop where all furniture was made, a textile shop to weave cotton and wool cloth, a tailor shop that made clothing and blankets, and a granary that could hold 4,000 bushels of corn. Adjoining all this was an irrigated farm that produced principally beans and corn.

That same governor (Jacinto Barrios y Jáuregui) described how the Indians were trained in self defense and to take sentry duty at night. He commented that the Indians loved the mission which was proven by the fact that none of them ever deserted it.

Another visitor, some years later, commented on the transformation worked in the Indians. After speaking of the various occupations which the Indians had learned, he commented on their singing and musical skills, all taught by the missioners. Then he added: "These Indians are so polite, so well-mannered, and so refined that one might imagine that they had been civilized and living at the mission for a long time." This same visitor reported that in addition to the corn and beans, the mission farm was then growing "lentils, melons, peaches weighing as much as a pound each, other fruits, potatoes, sugar cane and various kinds of vegetables." To the original shops had been added a brick kiln, a smithy and a new granary. All the visitors who left a record commented upon the wells and irrigation which were necessary for so large a project.

But the early support of the Spanish crown finally was no longer available. The first blow came when a governor made all the unbranded cattle the property of the government. In 1793 the mission

Depicted in these sketches are the activities of the missioner, Fr. Kino, the "Padre on Horseback."

was suppressed by the government and secularized. Missioners were limited to religious duties. In 1824 the new Mexican government took over the missions completely and the Franciscans had to leave. The golden age had come to an end. With the passing of years, the mission, including the church, fell into neglect, walls collapsed, and in 1874 the roof and dome of the beautiful church crashed to the floor. Vandalism completed the damage.

In 1912, the Archdiocese of San Antonio began a restoration program with funds from local people. In the period 1934-37 tremendous strides were made in bringing the mission back to its former beauty which had given it the title "Queen of the Missions." In 1941 an agreement was worked out between the Archbishop of San Antonio, the Texas State Parks Board and the National Park Service after which the entire property was designated a National Historic Site and thus preserved for future generations of Americans.

The Mission San Jose, the beauty of this structure earned it the name "Queen of the Missions."

The Middle Colonies

Henry Hudson's ship the "Half Moon" which he used to explore the New York Bay and Hudson River region.

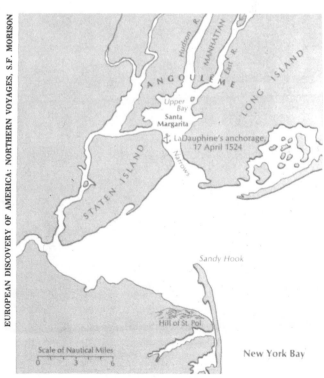

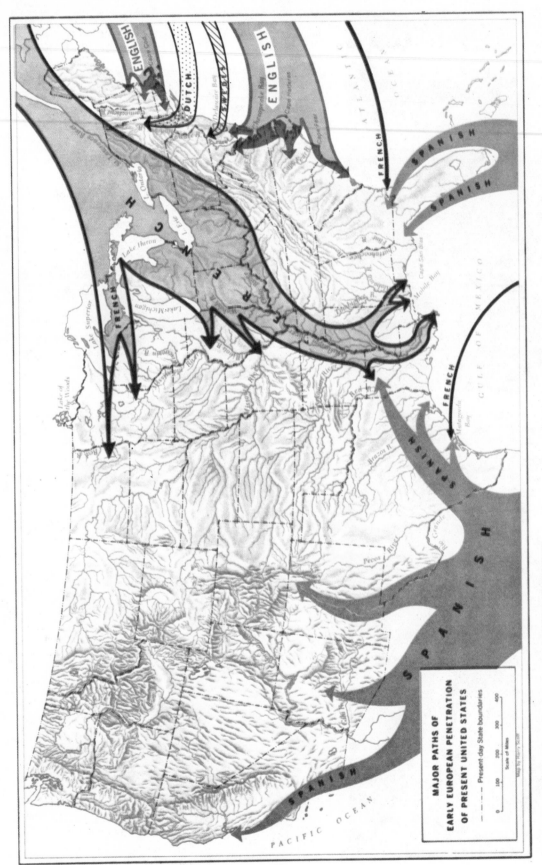

EUROPEAN DISCOVERY OF AMERICA: NORTHERN VOYAGES, S.F. MORISON

The United States Begins to Develop

Builder of the Royal Highway

Junipero Serra, a humble Franciscan, hangs his mission bells in California.

FOR the Statuary Hall of our nation's capital, each state is allowed to nominate a very limited number of its famous citizens to be commemorated there. One statue is that of a humble Franciscan priest. He is represented standing erect, holding a church in his left hand, while his right is lifted high holding a cross. The statue gives the sense of motion and challenge. On the pedestal is the simple legend: *Junipero Serra, California.*

At the unveiling of the monument, the senior senator from California described its significance in this way: "This man, whose memory is indis-

Typical old mission library at San Fernando, Calif. That of Father Serra is at Misión San Carlos in Carmel.

solubly one with the epic of California, was great in his humility; he triumphed by his courage, when everything would have appeared bound to discourage him and beat him down; he is one who is worthy of first place among the immortal heroes who created our nation; so his memory will never die, and his name will be blessed from generation to generation."

Father Junipero Serra, a short stocky man of quick smile and sparkling eyes, arrived in the harbor of Veracruz, Mexico, on December 6, 1749, as part of a group of Franciscan missioners who had been assigned to evangelize the Indians of northern Mexico. He was then thirty-six years old, a man of scholastic reputation. Accompanying him was his faithful friend over the years, Father Francis Palou, also destined to be his biographer. The Franciscans were particularly welcome in the New World missions because they had the reputation for devoted mission work with a minimum of politicizing. "They are the ones who preach the doctrine with the greatest care and example, and the least avarice," the Viceroy of Peru wrote to King Philip II. Of no Franciscan could this be

more true than Junipero Serra.

He was born on November 24, 1713, in Petra, Majorca, and baptized Miguel Jose Serra the same day. His father was a farmer who worked also in a nearby quarry to supplement his income. The father persuaded some Franciscan friends of his to instruct his son in Latin and the humanities. The boy was so taken by these humble gray robed men that, when he was sixteen, he asked to join them. A year later he took his first vows and the new name of Junipero, after Saint Francis' humble companion. The Franciscans were not taking any great risk in accepting the Petran; they had long observed his brilliance.

The years passed. Father Junipero was known throughout the region for his oratory. He was esteemed among scholars for his keen philosophical mind. The Franciscan was a man who already had it made in Majorca, and his future was undoubtedly anything he wanted it to be. Then like a bolt from the blue, he gave up his honors, his missions, his professorship at the Lulian University, Palma. He asked to be assigned to the missions of Mexico. His stunned colleagues asked to know the reason.

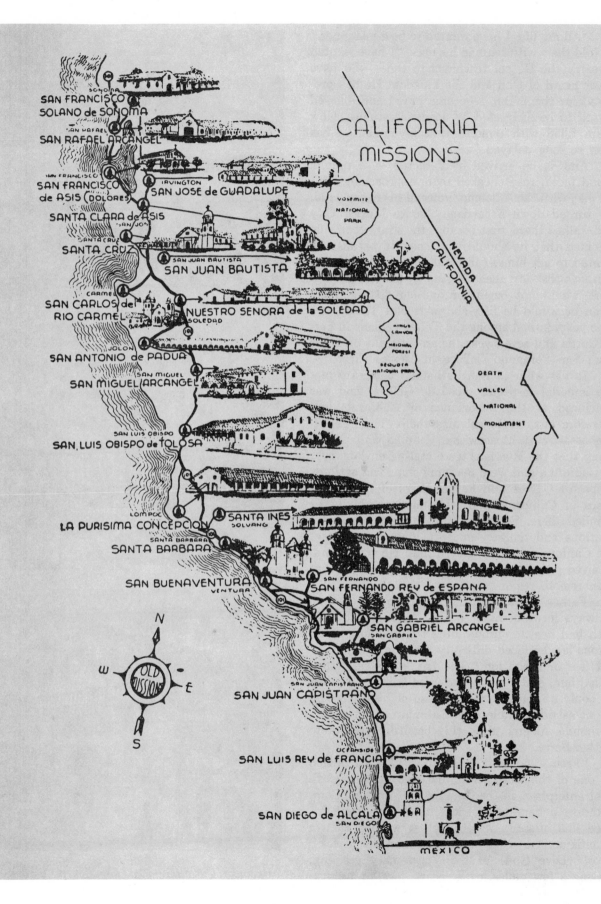

CALIFORNIA
MISSIONS

SAN FRANCISCO
SOLANO de SONOMA

SAN RAFAEL ARCANGEL

SAN FRANCISCO
de ASIS (DOLORES)

SAN JOSE de GUADALUPE

SANTA CLARA de ASIS

SANTA CRUZ

SAN JUAN BAUTISTA

SAN CARLOS del
RIO CARMEL

NUESTRO SENORA de la SOLEDAD

SAN ANTONIO de PADUA

SAN MIGUEL ARCANGEL

SAN LUIS OBISPO de TOLOSA

LA PURISIMA CONCEPCION

SANTA INES

SANTA BARBARA

SAN BUENAVENTURA

SAN FERNANDO REY de ESPANA

SAN GABRIEL ARCANGEL

SAN JUAN CAPISTRANO

SAN LUIS REY de FRANCIA

SAN DIEGO de ALCALA

NEVADA
CALIFORNIA

YOSEMITE
NATIONAL
PARK

DEATH
VALLEY
NATIONAL
MONUMENT

MEXICO

OLD MISSIONS

75

"All my life, I have wanted to be a missioner," he told them with tears in his eyes. "I have wanted to carry the Gospel teachings to those who have never heard of God and the kingdom He has prepared for them. But I became proud and allowed myself to be distracted by academic studies. Now I am filled with remorse that my ambition has been so long delayed."

And so he arrived in Veracruz — a plump, round faced, rosy cheeked man, approaching middle age, with the soft tenor voice of his native land. He turned down a carriage ride to Mexico City and walked there, first because the Franciscan rule enjoined that he should walk, second because he wanted to get himself in condition for the mission journeys that lay ahead. Actually, his real mission work would not begin for another sixteen years when he would be fifty-six years old! There were nine years buried among the Toltec Indians in Serra Gorda and seven years as an itinerant preacher from San Fernando College in Mexico City.

It was while at San Fernando that Serra met the imperial inspector, José de Galvez, who was convinced of the importance of California and therefore anxious to colonize there. The Spanish Ambassador at Moscow had learned and passed along that the Russians were casting envious eyes at California and were readying ships and settlers. Inspector Galvez told Father Serra of the importance of California and why missions should be founded there. Serra was not interested in fortifications and military outposts but the needs of the California Indians moved him. He sought and received permission to begin mission work in that then remote region.

Father Serra had as his motto the phrase, "Always forward, never back." Although afflicted with bad health, chronic lung trouble, and an ulcerous leg, he faced difficulty after difficulty without fear or hesitation. "The Lord's Walker," they called him, and it was a deserved title. Only when he could no longer walk because of his leg would he sit astride a mule. The Latin American writer, Fernando Alegria gives this beautiful tribute to Father Serra.

"From 1750 until his death in 1784, he carried on one of the most heroic and historically significant enterprises in the Conquest of America. Commanding a handful of friars humble and enlightened like himself—with no other weapon than a crucifix and no other watchword than the 'Amar a Dios' (Love God) of their customary greeting; driving a few mules, cows, goats, pigs, and chick-

Missions of California as foreseen by Father Serra.

ens; replying to poisoned arrows with the apostolic blessing; struggling without rebellion against the abuse of unscrupulous military chiefs—Father Serra converted the solitudes of California into a true earthly paradise. Where before, the law of the jungle had reigned, and the Indian tribes had annihilated each other in cannibalistic battles, Father Serra's Franciscans established, in less than half a century, a kind of communal republic that filled the civilized world of the eighteenth century with admiration."

Father Serra founded nine important missions in California, and his successors founded twelve more. It was about these missions that the great cities of California grew. Father Serra's own missions—San Diego, Carmel, San Gabriel, Santa Clara, San Luis Obispo, Ventura, Capistrano, San Francisco—were keys to the colonization and development of California.

Father Serra's whole life was a testimony of his love of God and his fellow man. He had practical knowledge that man is a creature of both soul and body. It was not enough to convert the Indians to Christianity: he had to lead them also to a better life. Under the hot California sun, he showed his friends how to sow and harvest. He turned battlefields into rich farmlands. With his own hands, he built forges and mills, slaughterhouses and wine presses. He was never at one place for long but was always moving back and forth between his missions, exhorting his co-workers to greater charity and zeal, encouraging the converts to higher spiritual lives.

Father Serra refused to allow Indians to be abused by the Spanish military. Once when a commandant practiced cruelty to Indians in his region, Father Serra walked 2,400 miles to Mexico City to get redress from the viceroy. No obstacle was too great if overcoming it would better the people among whom he had come to work. At last exhausted by his efforts, he died at the Carmel Mission, on August 28, 1784. With Father Serra's passing came the end of the Spanish penetration of the United States.

The missions of California are a lasting tribute to the effort of Father Serra.

Explorations For France

French explorer, Giovanni Verrazano

IT was an Italian, Christopher Columbus, who gave Spain a foothold in the New World. It was another Italian, John Cabot, who laid the claims of England. It was quite fitting, therefore, that still another Italian should be the man to make the first discoveries for France. His name was Giovanni Verrazano.

We know very little about the early life of Giovanni Verrazano, other than that he came from Florence. Somehow he entered the French maritime service, and became captain of a corsair that raided Spanish shipping. This is a polite way of saying that he was a pirate. In the year 1522, he captured two Spanish treasure ships, laden with gold and other wealth that Cortes had gained in his conquest of Mexico and was sending to Spain.

When Verrazano returned to France with that wealth, the French sovereign, King Francis I, was impressed by this evidence of what could be gained in the New World. He commissioned Verrazano to explore the possibilities for locating a French settlement in America, and also to search for the desired northwest passage to Asia.

Late in 1523, Verrazano, with three ships, sailed from France. Immediately he ran into bad weather. By the time he reached the shelter of the Madeira Islands, two of his ships were so badly damaged that they were useless. On January 17, 1524—in the remaining ship, the *Dauphine*—Verrazano began his journey of western discovery. He was plagued by bad weather until he reached the North American coast, in a region that is now the shore of the Carolinas.

Verrazano turned his course north. He landed at many points, made notes in his log of what he saw—beautiful forests, fine harbors, savages who wore skins—and systematically explored much of the eastern coast of the United States. He was the first white man to enter what is now New York Harbor. He continued his journey along the coasts of Massachusetts, Maine, Nova Scotia, and Newfoundland. Then he returned to France and reported his findings to his royal employer.

France was at that time engaged in a war with Italy, and King Francis could not immediately follow up Verrazano's exploration. The Florentine captain did make another journey to the New World: it was in 1527, to Brazil. Tragedy and not success ended that voyage. Verrazano was captured by Carib Indians, killed, and eaten. Today his memory is preserved in the name of a new bridge that spans the entrance of New York Harbor.

In 1534 the French ruler sent out another expedition. It was under the command of Jacques Cartier, who eventually made a number of voyages to America. Cartier discovered the Saint Lawrence River, and sailed down it in the thought that he had found the long-desired northwest passage. He was finally halted by great rapids. Using his native language, he named the place *"La Chine"* ("China"). He visited an Indian village on the shore of the Saint Lawrence River; it was at the foot of a very high hill, which he named *"Mont Real"* ("Mount Royal," now Montreal). Later the great Cartier claimed the whole area of his explorations for the King of France. After Cartier the explorer, French fishermen followed, and then French trappers. France's colonization of North America had begun.

PAINTING BY J.B. KELLY

An engraving showing the famous French navigator Champlain on Lake Huron. His explorations were in 1615.

The French Also Contributed

IF the Spanish contribution to the development of the United States has been downgraded in our history books, that of the French has received only slightly better treatment. Both the French and the English began settlements in America at approximately the same time. While the English hugged the Atlantic coast and went only as far west as the Allegheny Mountains, the French with intrepid daring criss-crossed the tremendous interior of our nation, reaching the Rocky Mountains, the Gulf of Mexico, and the Pacific northwest.

The French had two purposes in coming to America. They wanted to build an empire founded on the fur trade, and they wanted to convert the Indians to Christianity. As with the Spanish, wherever French explorers went, missioners were either ahead of them or with them. The founder of Canada, the great Samuel de Champlain, declared that it was better to convert a single Indian than to conquer an empire, and it was this missionary spirit that motivated many of the French in their actions.

The approach of the French to colonization was different from that of the Spanish. The Spanish also had a double motive in their conquests. They sought to spread Christianity and to gain personal wealth, and very often these two motives came into conflict. That is why at times, despite contrary orders by the Spanish crown and the intercession of the Church, abuses were practiced on the Indians. The wealth the Spaniards sought was gold and silver, and those metals had to be extracted from the ground. To accomplish this end, a labor force was needed, therefore, at times, some Spaniards practically enslaved Indians as laborers.

The French, on the other hand, sought to support their colony by means of the fur trade. There was no way to force Indians to trap fur-bearing animals and then trade. The French, therefore, sought to make friends with the Indians and win their good will. This was done very successfully with all but the warlike Iroquois. The French learned the Indian languages, established forts for protection against the Iroquois, built schools for the ed-

Jacques Cartier, he explored the St. Lawrence River.

Samuel de Champlain, the French founder of Quebec

ucation of Indian children, and intermarried. These mixed people were called *"metis,"* and they were a bond between French and Indians. By the time the United States was founded, the *metis* could be found as far west as the Red River Valley.

The first French missioners arrived in Quebec in 1615, at the request of Champlain, who had raised the money for their support. They were members of the Recollect Order, a branch of the Franciscans. They began work among the Huron Indians. The Recollects soon realized the enormity of the task and knew that their own order did not have sufficient priests available to accomplish it. They asked the French Jesuits to help them. In 1625, the first band of Jesuits arrived and took up work in Huronia. Success came to the missioners, and Huronia became a model of Christianity. Then tragedy took place.

The Iroquois, who had remained unfriendly to the French because of the latter's alliance with their enemies, the Hurons, wanted to get the kind of guns and knives and other goods that the Hurons received for their fur trade. So the Iroquois began trading with the Dutch and English. But the area of New York State that the Iroquois occupied was not rich in furs, and therefore they decided to destroy Huronia and take over that region. One

by one, the Huron villages were captured and burned; the inhabitants, including missioners, were killed or enslaved. As a result, the flourishing Huron mission perished.

The Jesuits took the surviving Huron Indians to Quebec and set up a new mission. The Black-robes, as the missioners were called, also decided that they would try to convert the Iroquois who then controlled the whole Great Lake region. The Iroquois, interested more in goods than principles, began trading with the French, and as a result allowed Jesuits to come among them. But the Iroquois only tolerated the missioners and would not listen to their teaching.

The Jesuits were finally forced to withdraw. Relations between the French and Iroquois grew worse. The Mohawks, one of the five "nations" that made up the Iroquois confederacy, began attacks against the French; and they were supported by the English. The King of France decided that his colony could not survive without help. A strong force was directed against the Iroquois. The French invaded central New York, burned the Indian villages, and forced the Mohawks to beg for peace. One of the terms for peace was that the Mohawks should receive missioners and allow them to perform missionary labors.

Isaac Jogues was born in France. This saint of the Church died at Mohawk hands in New York.

Founded in 1680, Fort Creveceour was soon destroyed.

The Blackrobes returned, and for twenty years worked without interference. They had modest success. In 1687, when a new war between the French and Iroquois threatened, the Jesuits took their Mohawk converts and went to Montreal. There today many descendants of the Christian Mohawks still live. With this second failure, the Jesuits decided that they would turn west and evangelize other tribes. And so they set out over the trails and streams pioneered by the French *voyageurs*, and began to penetrate the heartland of America.

Champlain: Father of New France

Raising of a cross marks the founding of Montreal.

IN any roll call of the great figures of the Americas, the name of Samuel de Champlain would be close to the top. A man of wisdom and courage, he it was who planted the French flag in the New World, and he it was who earned the title of "Father of New France." Like Columbus, Champlain was a man of great religious feeling and of loyalty to the Catholic Church; he, also, was hopeful of finding a water passage westward to the Pacific Ocean. He was an excellent governor and administrator, and his sensible policies towards the Indians were of great benefit to France.

Champlain's first venture to the New World was aboard a Spanish ship. He visited the West Indies, Mexico and Central America. His foresight is revealed in his suggesting a ship canal across the Isthmus of Panama — the first man to do so. He recorded his observations of this journey in a journal that won for him the attention of the French authorities.

Champlain returned to the New World, this time to explore Canada. He went up the St. Law-rence River until halted by Lachine Rapids, and he learned a great deal from the Indians about the network of rivers and lakes beyond. He returned again to Canada in the expedition of Sieur de Monts, which tried to settle a colony in Acadia but failed. In 1608, Champlain was back in Canada once more, this time in charge of an expedition.

Three purposes motivated Samuel de Champlain. First, he hoped he could find a water route across the American continent; what he had previously heard from the Indians led him to believe that it might be possible. Second, he realized that the St. Lawrence River was the key to the fur trade, and the nation that controlled the St. Lawrence would control that trade; so he intended to make a strong French settlement on the St. Lawrence. Third, he sought the conversion of the Indians to the Catholic Faith.

Champlain selected a spot along the St. Lawrence where the river passed through some high hills. The Indians called it *Kebec* ("The Narrows") and there Champlain founded the city of Quebec— a very humble city of three wooden buildings for living quarters, a storehouse and fort. Several small cannons commandeered the river. Champlain and his twenty-eight men settled there to pass the first winter in Canada.

It was a terrible winter. Hunger, starvation

A map of the Great Lakes as explored by Champlain

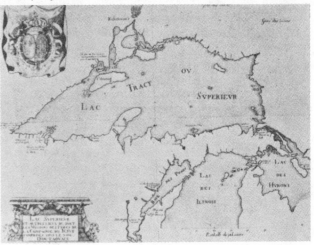

and cold were constant enemies. Scurvy broke out. When spring came, only Champlain and seven companions were alive out of the original twenty-eight. But the time had not been completely lost. Champlain had allied himself with the Huron tribe, and had promised to help these Indians in their fight with their enemies, the Iroquois. Supplies and more men arrived from France. Champlain seized the opportunity to explore the region and to assist his Indian allies.

A war party of Hurons and Algonquins was organized; and because it would go into the region Champlain wished to explore, he took two soldiers and joined it. The party traveled by canoe, traversing several rivers and finally entering a beautiful lake. Champlain was the first white man to see that lake, and it bears his name today—Lake Champlain. The plan was to travel the length of the lake, enter another lake (now Lake George), and finally reach the Hudson River, where Mohawk villages were to be found. There the attack would be made.

However, halfway down Lake Champlain, the invaders came upon a war party of Iroquois, out to launch an attack on the Hurons. Since it was nearly dusk, the battle was not joined until the next day. When morning came, the three Frenchmen encased in steel armor moved out with their Indian allies. The two sides moved forward; then suddenly the Huron ranks parted, and out stepped the steel-clad Champlain. The apparition must have startled the Iroquois, who had probably never seen a white man.

"I looked at them, and they looked at me," Champlain recalled later. "When I saw them getting ready to shoot their arrows at us, I leveled my arquebus, and aimed straight at one of the three chiefs. The shot brought down two and wounded another. The Iroquois were greatly astonished and frightened to see two of their men killed so quickly in spite of their arrow-proof armor."

The Iroquois broke in panic and fled. The Huron-Algonquin party captured their enemy's camp, canoes and food. It was an important day in history because it marked the break between the French and the Iroquois. From that time on, the five nations were the enemies of the French. Champlain has been accused of poor judgment in provoking this resentment, but actually it was a very well-considered judgment on his part. He believed rightly that the St. Lawrence River was the way to the fur trade. The Hurons and Algonquins controlled the St. Lawrence area; and if he were to succeed as a trader, he must have their friendship. It was impossible to be friends of the Hurons and the Iroquois at the same time, so he made a choice—the best choice that he could.

In 1611, Champlain established a trading station farther down the river, and named it Montreal (Mount Royal). Like Quebec, it was to grow into a great Canadian city. He explored westward, around Lakes Huron and Ontario. But gradually his duties as governor of New France kept him so busy that he had to forego further exploration. Instead, he sent young men into the wilderness to pioneer the way west.

When Champlain died at Quebec, on Christmas Day, 1635, he left behind him an army of missioners and *voyageurs* who were to bring great wealth, both spiritual and material, to France. Champlain had lived as a brave soldier and Catholic gentleman. His death was mourned by all in the colony, for he was not only "Father of New France" but he was also a father to every settler, soldier, trader and missioner.

A typical Mohawk. He belonged to the Iroquois tribe.

The Blackrobes

ONE of the most inspiring chapters in the history of Catholic missions is the story of the Jesuit missioners who worked in Canada and the northern United States. Theirs is a story of educated and cultured men who willingly entered the Indian wilderness to live under the most primitive and dangerous conditions, ever ready to sacrifice their lives for the advancement of Christianity. It is a story of heroism and love that demonstrates the best in the missionary tradition of the Church.

Eight of those Jesuits, all martyrs, have been canonized. Three of those missionary saints belong to the United States: Saint Rene Goupil, a lay Brother who was tomahawked by the Iroquois in 1642 at Auriesville, N.Y.; and Saints Isaac Jogues and John de Lalande, who also won their crowns of martyrdom at Auriesville four years later. The remaining Jesuit martyrs died during Iroquois attacks on Huronia, an area north of the Great Lakes that is today part of Canada.

The Jesuit missioners wrote copious diaries, reporting the places they went and the things they saw. Those diaries are today a treasure house for historians and anthropologists, who find in them the history and customs of lost tribes. The diaries are also as exciting reading as one can find. For example, Father Christopher Regnaut's account of the martyrdom of Saint John de Brebeuf has, in its simplicity, an authenticity of horror that leaves nothing to the imagination.

The Blackrobes preached and taught among the Indians. Eight of these Jesuits were martyred by the Iroquois.
NEW YORK STATE DEPARTMENT OF COMMERCE

Father Regnaut described how 1,200 Iroquois sprang from ambush on the village of Saint Ignace. In the surprise attack, Fathers de Brebeuf and Gabriel L'Alemant were captured. The Indians stripped their prisoners naked and tied them to posts. They tore the nails from their fingers, and beat them with clubs all over their bodies. Boiling water was poured upon Father de Brebeuf in imitation of baptism; then a string of red-hot hatchets was hung about his neck. Then the Indians put a belt of pitch on him and lighted it, roasting his body. Next they cut out his tongue and began to peel the flesh from his bones.

"Those butchers seeing that the good Father began to grow weak," continued Father Regnaut, "made him sit down on the ground; and one of them, taking a knife, cut off the skin covering his skull. Another one, seeing that the good Father would soon die, made an opening in the upper part of his chest, and tore out his heart, which he roasted and ate. Others came to drink his blood, still warm, which they drank with both hands."

No writer of fiction would be taken seriously if he invented such a series of torments, yet these are what one Jesuit missioner underwent without a single complaint! Indeed, until Father de Brebeuf's tongue was cut out, he "did not cease continually to speak of God, and to encourage all the new Christians who were captives like himself to suffer well, that they might die well, in order to go in a company with him to Paradise."

The story of Saint Isaac Jogues, who is a saint of the United States, is another good example of the bravery and unselfishness of the missioners of that time. Father Jogues was returning to Huronia from Quebec with supplies. With him were two young lay missioners, Rene Goupil and Louis Coutoure. Suddenly, the party was attacked by Mohawk Indians. Father Jogues managed to escape into the brush; but when he saw some of his converted Indian guides taken captive, he determined to go with them, so he gave himself up. Coutoure also had escaped, but he decided to go back and be with Father Jogues. Goupil had been captured.

For thirteen dreadful days, the Mohawks made their way back with their captives to their village on the Mohawk River, forty miles west of the Hudson River. During that time the captives were made to run the gantlet and were tortured, but the main torture was reserved until the Indians reached home. There Jogues and Goupil were savagely tested. Father Jogues was beaten with sticks; his hair

and nails were torn out; his fingers were chewed by Indian women, and his left thumb cut off. Both men survived the terrible ordeal and were forced to serve as slaves. Goupil died a few weeks later; he was murdered for making the Sign of the Cross over a child.

For the next ten months, Father Jogues occupied the lowest position in the Indian village. He was obliged to haul water, gather wood, and perform any other drudgery his Indian masters as-

A monument to the work and dedication of the Jesuit

A drawing of Sainte Marie I. The Jesuits were forced to put the mission to the torch when the Iroquois attacked. A. Dwelling; B. Chapel; C. Carpenter shop; D. Smithy; E. Cookhouse; F., G. Dwellings; H. Barracks; J. Barn; K. Indian Church; L. Huron Long house; M. Hospital; N. Algonquin dwelling; P. Huron Long house. 1, 2, 3. Locks; 4. Loading basin; 5. Landing basin; 6. East-west water channel; 7. North-south water channel; 8, 9. Aqueducts; 10. Main gate; 11. escape tunnel; 12. Bitchworks; 13. Christian cemetery; 14. Well. Sainte Marie I was eventually destroyed in 1649.

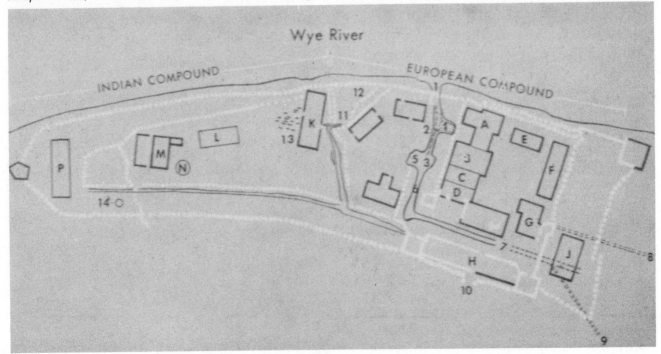

signed. Nevertheless he dared to tend the Huron captives and secretly baptized seventy Indians. Finally, a chance came to escape when the Indians took him to Fort Orange, the Dutch outpost that is now the city of Albany and capital of New York State.

After many close calls and dangers, Father Jogues succeded in getting away. The Protestant Dutch hid him aboard a boat that took him down the river to New Amsterdam. There he was received kindly. Given new clothing to replace his skins, and welcomed into the home of the governor. A Protestant minister, seeing how horribly Father Jogues' hands had been mutilated, fell on his knees and asked the priest's blessing. Later that same man introduced the priest to the pupils of his school, declaring: "Today you have the privilege of beholding a saint."

Father Jogues returned to France and to great honor. The Queen Mother received him by kissing his mangled hands. The Holy Father conferred on him the rare privilege of offering Mass although his fingers were largely useless. "It would be unjust," Pope Urban VII observed, "if a martyr of Christ were not to drink the blood of Christ."

A year later, recovered from his ordeal, Father Jogues was back in Montreal. He begged to be sent on a mission among the Mohawks; he stated that he knew the language and customs, and was suited for the task. His superior hesitated and then gave consent. Father Jogues knew he was making his last sacrifice. He told a friend before he left Quebec, "I shall not return."

His end came in 1646 as he entered a cabin of the Bear Clan in Ossernenon, the Indian village where he had lived as a captive; he was tomahawked from behind. Thus the blood of one more missionary pioneer enriched the soil of the United States. The blood of martyrs is the seed of Christians, says an old Catholic motto. It was on such sacrifices that the Church and the United States have been built.

Martyrdom of Brebeuf and L'Alemant by the Mohawks

Saints Among Savages

Although the Mohawk Indians killed Father Jogues, not all Mohawk Indians were enemies of Christianity. Many were converted by the examples of their captives, and others by the teachings of the heroic Jesuits. In the list of martyrs that the United States hierarchy has proposed for canonization, there are the names of three Indians of the Northeast.

Stephen Tegananokoa was a Huron who was captured by the Cayuga tribe; he was taken to Onondaga and there was tortured and killed. As he was being executed, he told his murderers, "I willingly give my life for a God who shed all His blood for me!"

Two Mohawk women were put to death near Auriesville, New York, because they refused to give up Christianity. One of them, Margaret Garan-

Brebeuf and L'Alemant as they are about to be murdered by the Mohawks. Many more were destined to follow.

gouas, was the daughter of an Iroquois chief. She suffered terrible torture before being burned to death. Her last words were the holy names of Jesus, Mary, Joseph.

Another Mohawk was the saintly Indian maiden, Kateri Tekakwitha. The movement for her canonization has already been begun. Kateri was born in Ossernenon, the village where Saint Isaac Jogues was tortured, held slave, and finally killed. Ossernenon is now Auriesville, and it is the shrine of the North American Martyrs. Kateri's father was a Mohawk chief of the leading Turtle clan, and her mother was a captive Algonquin.

The Mohawks were one of the five "nations" that made up the Iroquois confederacy and inhabited central New York. The Indians of the Five Nations were called "Iroquois" by the French because they ended every conversation with the words "hiro koue"—which mean, "I have spoken with joy" or "I have spoken with sorrow," according to the tone of the speaker's voice. Iroquois Indians were warlike people; and of the Five Nations, the Mohawks were the boldest and fiercest.

Four years after Kateri was born, a terrible smallpox epidemic swept Ossernenon. Kateri's father, mother, and brother died of the disease; Kateri recovered, but she was left with a pockmarked face and weak eyes. The orphaned girl was adopted by an uncle who had succeeded to her father's position of chief. As Kateri grew into womanhood, some Blackrobes came to her village. They taught the Christian religion. The chief, her uncle, hated the Blackrobes and their teaching. But he dared not oppose them because, a few years earlier, French soldiers had forced the Iroquois to seek peace, and one of the requirements was the presence of Blackrobes in those villages where there were Christian captives.

Kateri was much moved by the story of God's love for men. She wanted to become a Catholic but dared not approach the missioner, for fear of her uncle. She had already opposed his wish to marry her to a Mohawk brave, and her refusal was bringing her much suffering. Finally she summoned up courage, told her uncle that she intended to become a Christian, and went to the priest for instructions. On Easter Sunday in 1676, when she was almost twenty years old, the convert was baptized with the name "Kateri" — Iroquois for "Catherine."

At her home, persecution then increased. Kateri was treated as a slave. Because she would not work in the fields on Sundays, she was given no food on those days. The hatred of her uncle was so great that Kateri's life was in danger. The Blackrobe, Father de Lamberville, suggested that she go to the Christian Mohawk village near Montreal. There she would be safe and free to practice her religion. One night while her village slept, Kateri stole away from the Mohawk long house and joined a Christian chief on his way to Montreal.

Safe at last in the Christian village, Kateri gave herself entirely to God. She performed many penances and spent long hours in prayer, asking God for the conversion of the Mohawks. Her health, never strong after her childhood attack of smallpox, became worse. Kateri was happy with the suffering God gave her, because she could offer it to Him for her people. At last she grew gravely ill, and she died after receiving Holy Communion on April 17, 1680.

There were many other Indians who lived lives of heroic sanctity, and there were many Indians who died because of their newfound Faith. Those Indians were evidence of the civilizing influence of the missioners who labored throughout New France. In the march westward across the United States, many men of Anglo-Saxon heritage saw the answer to the Indian problem in the extermination of Indians. But that was not the view of the missioners, whether of Spanish or of French nationality. The missioners saw in every Indian a creature of God, who had been equally redeemed, with them, by the blood of Christ. And when the Indians were given an opportunity, many of them proved that they had the capacity for sanctity and sacrifice.

Kateri was baptized against her Mohawk uncle's will.

Marquette was the explorer of the Mississippi.

Marquette:
The Mississippi is Explored

ALTHOUGH Father Jacques Marquette and Louis Joliet are often referred to as the discoverers of the Mississippi River, other men were there before them. Cabeza de Vaca and Hernando de Soto had both been on the mighty river. But Louis Joliet and Father Marquette were the explorers of the Mississippi. They proved that the many rivers draining the heart of the United States join, at various places, the Mississippi, and that it flows, through a delta, into the Gulf of Mexico.

Louis Joliet was an old friend of Father Marquette. He had been born in Canada and was educated by the Jesuits. He was an intelligent man, and courageous. He was a merchant who traded with the Indians. Some of his trading trips took him to the west, and we know that at least once he visited Father Marquette at the latter's mission station in Sault Sainte Marie.

Father Marquette had been born in France in 1637 of a well-to-do family. When he was seventeen, he became a Jesuit novice, and after ordination he was assigned to the Canadian missions. His first year was spent at Three Rivers, learning the Indian language and customs. In April, 1668, he was assigned to work among the Ottawa Indians and was sent to Sault Sainte Marie. The Ottawas included such tribes as Chippewas, Creeks, Hurons, Winnebagos, Miamis, Illinois, and Sioux.

Father Marquette founded the Mission of Saint Ignace for the Huron Indians. That mission was established at the head of a Michigan peninsula jutting into the Straits of Mackinac, the body of water that joins Lakes Michigan and Huron. Today one end of a mighty bridge is anchored at Saint Ignace, near where Father Marquette built a chapel. The missioner gained experience and knowledge. He became skilled at map-making, and his journal was full of geographical notes.

On the Feast of the Immaculate Conception (December 8) 1672, Father Marquette was surprised to see a canoe paddle into the mission landing and debark his old friend, Louis Joliet, who had come all the way from Quebec. Joliet waved a paper at the priest. It was a commission for both friends to begin a voyage of exploration along the "Great Water" of which the Indians often spoke.

The two explorers were to determine if the mighty river flowed to the Pacific Ocean; also they were to claim, for the kingdom of France, the land through which the river flowed.

The two friends spent the winter making plans for their voyage. They interviewed Indians, gathered some supplies, and enlisted five *voyageurs* to accompany them. On May 17, 1673, Father Marquette turned over his mission to another priest, and the explorers set out in two birch-bark canoes. They paddled along the shore of Lake Michigan, entered Green Bay, and stopped at the DePere mission on the Fox River, in Wisconsin. They went up the Fox and onto Lake Winnebago. Beyond was unknown land.

Friendly Miami Indians guided the French party through the upper Fox River. When they reached a portage, the canoes were carried overland to the Wisconsin River, and the Indian guides departed. For seven days the explorers paddled down the rapidly flowing Wisconsin River. Then, one month to the day after they started the expedition, their canoes shot out of the Wisconsin into a stream a mile wide. They had reached the "Great Water"!

Down the mighty river they paddled, passing many joining streams — the Wapsipinicon, Rock, Iowa, Skunk, Des Moines. Somewhere near the point where Iowa, Missouri, and Illinois come together, they halted at an Indian village. The Illinois chief was a friend of the French, and they were made welcome and given the gift of a calu-

Louis Joliet, the explorer   *Marquette, preacher*

ment, a peace pipe, which was a guarantee of safe conduct among the allies of the Illinois Indians.

On the exploring party went, past the Illinois, Missouri, Ohio, and Arkansas rivers. Several times when they were threatened by hostile Indians, the calumet saved them; it was a passport to every village. Father Marquette preached in each village, using local interpreters who understood the Illinois language. The river grew wider, and the days hotter. Swarms of mosquitoes attacked the explorers by day and night. They passed the spot where De Soto was buried and where he had had his camp.

When they reached an Arkansas Indian village, they stopped to take stock. They were then

The Indians of the western plain lived a simple, harsh existence.

Marquette and Joliet as they sail down the Mississippi River. They passed the grave of Hernando de Soto.

in a region where the Indians had Spanish guns. The Frenchmen believed that they must be close to Spanish settlements; and if so, they were in danger. They knew that they were on the lower end of the Mississippi River, and that it emptied into the Gulf of Mexico. There was nothing to be gained by going on, and there was the possibility of capture by the Spanish. In that eventuality the result of their explorations would be lost. They decided to return to Michigan.

Father Marquette chose a different route for going back, and they ascended the Illinois River. Friendly Indians, won by the charm of the missioner, guided the explorers up the Des Plaines River and to Lake Michigan, near the present Chicago. Keeping close to shore, they finally reached Green Bay. They had paddled some 2,500 miles; pioneered two routes to the Mississippi River; and proved that a waterway existed from the heart of America to the Gulf of Mexico.

Father Marquette had contracted a disease on the journey, and for months he was very sick. In October, 1674, he felt strong enough to travel south to the Illinois Indians, to whom he had given a promise that he would return and tell them about God. By the time he reached the Chicago River, it was frozen over. He wintered there among the Indians, preaching and instructing them.

When spring came, Father Marquette was desperately ill. He knew that death was near, and he wanted to die at a mission that had a priest at hand. He left the Illinois region and started north. On May 18, 1675, near the site of the city of Ludington, Michigan, he died in the wilderness. The Indians buried the missioner's body on the banks of the river that now bears his name. In the following year his body was transferred to the mission at Saint Ignace, and there his remains still rest.

The State of Wisconsin placed the statue of Father Marquette in National Statuary Hall in 1895. His real monument should be, however, in the hearts of all Americans. The great missionary pioneer exemplified the noblest in unselfishness, sacrifice, devotion to duty, and faith in God.

Like most Jesuit missioners in America, Marquette kept copious records and journals. In one he confided: "No one must hope to escape crosses in our missions, and the best way to live happily is not to fear them but in the enjoyment of little crosses to hope for others still greater." It was his cross that after only nine years of mission work and at the early age of thirty-eight to die a solitary death in the forests of upper Michigan. But this was the material of which our American pioneers were made.

The discovery of the Mississippi River by de Soto. He and his men were under constant fear of Indian raids.

LaSalle at the mouth of the Mississippi on April 9, 1682. He would not live to see his dream of New Orleans.

LaSalle: The Man Who Claimed an Empire

THE true mark of greatness is the ability to recognize opportunity. Many men have courage and daring; others have wisdom and the will to succeed. Not always do men have opportunity. Sometimes it passes unrecognized, and sometimes it is seized and conquered. One man who recognized opportunity was Cavelier de LaSalle.

When news of the discoveries made by Father Marquette and Louis Joliet reached New France, Rene Robert Cavelier de LaSalle immediately saw his own chance for success. At that time he was in charge of a settlement not far from Montreal. He had done some exploring; had lived in the Seneca country of western New York; and, although he was not rich, had become popular with the French governor of Canada, Count de Frontenac.

The Marquette-Joliet discoveries put an end to the idea that the Mississippi River might be a way to China. But a new idea came to LaSalle: the Mississippi was the key to inland America. The French already controlled the northern part of the Mississippi, with its access rivers. If the French could control the whole river, to its mouth, they would hem in the English on the eastern side of the Appalachian Mountains, and the vast interior with its prairies and fertile soil would be a French prize! Moreover, the Mississippi and its tributaries provided a vast network for bringing in settlers and supplies, and for taking out wealth.

LaSalle was not inexperienced in the region and may even have penetrated as deep as the Ohio country; we know he roamed Huntington County in Indiana. In 1673, he established Fort Frontenac on Lake Ontario. Five years later he was at Niagara Falls where the following year he built a fort and then a boat to take his men through the Great Lakes. He led his force to the site of the present Green Bay to trade. He traveled down into Lake Michigan, explored the St. Joseph River about the area of South Bend, descended the Kankakee to the Illinois. Now, the news of the Marquette discovery excited his imagination.

He talked over his ideas with his friend, Governor Frontenac, who sent him to France for advice. When he returned to Canada, he had a patent that gave him authority to "labor at the discovery of the western parts of New France," to build and man forts, and to go where he pleased between the eastern end of Lake Ontario and Mexico. LaSalle borrowed money, organized an expedition, and set out for the Mississippi River. After an almost incredible series of hardships that would have turned back a lesser man, he reached the Gulf of Mexico in April, 1682 — the first white man to travel the river to its mouth. There he ceremoniously planted a cross and claimed the whole Mississippi Valley for France: "the seas, harbors, ports, bays, adjacent straits, and all the nations, peoples, provinces, cities, towns, villages, mines, minerals, fisheries, streams, and rivers." In short, LaSalle claimed an empire that stretched from the Appalachians to the Rockies, from Canada to Mexico. In honor of his sovereign, King Louis XIV, he named the region "Louisiana."

The return voyage provided continuous hardships. Food supplies were exhausted, and LaSalle and his men had to eat alligators. There were attacks by Indians, and there was much sickness. At last the explorer reached Canada — to find himself pressed by creditors and no longer under the protection of the Count de Frontenac, because a new governor had been installed. LaSalle returned to France to report his enormous claim and to answer those attempting to discredit him. France and Spain were then at war and it seemed desirable for the French to have an outpost at the mouth of the Mississippi River. King Louis ordered LaSalle to establish a colony in Louisiana.

In July, 1684, LaSalle set sail for the Gulf of Mexico; his fleet consisted of four ships which carried four hundred colonists. From the start events went badly. The Spaniards captured one ship, and valuable supplies were lost. The three remaining ships entered the Gulf of Mexico but were unable to find the mouth of the Mississippi; the Spanish were not giving away their navigation secrets and LaSalle's navigators miscalculated. Early in 1685 the ships were in Matagorda Bay, between the present Galveston and Corpus Christi. Here, a second ship foundered during a storm. A third deserted with men and supplies. The remaining ship landed near the mouth of the Lavaca River and the survivors hastily erected Fort St. Louis but in a few months moved it to another site.

LaSalle took a party of soldiers and traveled west—the direction has never been explained. Was he lost? Was he trying to spy on the Spanish? In any event, he finally returned to Fort St. Louis where he learned that the last ship had been lost and that supplies were desperately low. Selecting seventeen men, La Salle declared that he would march north to Illinois, then Canada, and return with aid. It was a bold plan but the only one that offered hope to the stranded French.

LaSalle selected his companions and the party

La Salle's fleet docks at Matagorda Bay in early 1685.

95

Rene Robert Cavalier de LaSalle (1643 - 1685)

started out. This time he headed directly for the Mississippi River. It was a weary, hungry journey of already tired men. Some of the soldiers began plotting against their leader. One day, somewhere in east Texas, a group of the discontented waited in ambush, and as LaSalle walked along with a Recollect priest they opened fire. A bullet pierced the brain of the commander and he dropped dead. The murderers did not even bury him, only stripped the body and left it to the wolves. Thus perished the man who had done so much to open the American continent. He had launched the first ship on the Great Lakes; established the French in Illinois; made alliances with Indian tribes; and led the first party of white men to the Gulf of Mexico. His vision has been proved by time, for he was the first to realize the great commercial value of the Mississippi Valley.

The murderers compelled the innocent members of the expedition to go along with them. Among this group was Henry Joutel, one of LaSalle's closest friends. The march was renewed but it was not long before the mutineers fell to quarreling among themselves. Joutel persuaded the innocent survivors to attempt an escape; they agreed and it was successful. Joutel led his group to the Mississippi and at the mouth of the Arkansas River met a French rescue party, searching for LaSalle. They all returned to Canada where the tragedy was made known. Nothing was ever heard of the murderers again, except one—Jean l'Archeveque. He turned up in Santa Fe some years later, only to be killed by Pawnee Indians.

However, LaSalle's dream of a Louisiana colony did not die with him. Fifteen years later, a small French fleet put in at the mouth of the Mobile River. It was commanded by Pierre Lemoyne d'Iberville, who had with him his brothers, Sauvolle and Bienville. A settlement was made at Biloxi; then later new colonies were started at Cat Island, Dauphin Island and Mobile. When Pierre died, his brother, Bienville, took over the French command. In 1718, he founded the city of New Orleans, and at last La Salle's prophetic dream was accomplished. The city began to prosper. Soon Ursuline nuns arrived and opened a boarding school for girls.

In the years that followed, a series of wars broke out between France and England. The bitter rivalry did not end until the capture of Quebec and Montreal by the British. A peace treaty was signed in Paris in 1763, and by its terms, Canada was allotted to England and Louisiana to Spain. However, when Napoleon rose to power, he forced the Spanish to return Louisiana to France. This was upsetting to the young American Government: Americans did not wish Napoleon to control the Mississippi, which was playing a great role in American commerce.

President Jefferson sent James Monroe as a special minister to Paris, to see if he could buy New Orleans from the French. Napoleon considered the offer. He needed money to fight England—Louisiana was so far away that it was indefensible— and colonies were proving burdensome. Napoleon said that he was not interested in selling New Orleans alone, but he would sell all of the Louisiana Territory, including New Orleans, for fifteen million dollars.

Monroe agreed, and the purchase was made in 1803. It was one of the great real-estate bargains in history! Perhaps it was not so great as the purchase of Manhattan Island for twenty-four dollars' worth of trinkets; but it gave the United States 828,000 square miles of territory, at three cents an acre! The Louisiana Purchase doubled the territory of the United States, and it was the outstanding achievement of the Jefferson administration. With that purchase, the French exploration in the United States was ended.

A contemporary print of a Canadian voyageur

II. THE TIME FOR PIONEERS

Lord Baltimore Founds a Colony

ENGLAND had become a frightening place for Catholics. In his apostasy from the Catholic Church, King Henry VIII took the majority of his subjects with him. Under Henry and his successor-daughter, Queen Elizabeth, harsh laws were enacted against Englishmen who refused to desert the religion of their forefathers. Catholics were imprisoned and had their properties confiscated. Executions were not infrequent. Priests found it necessary to carry on their ministry in disguise and in secret. Many Catholics dreamed of a land where they might be free to worship God in the old way.

One of those who dreamed of a place of religious freedom was George Calvert, an Englishman of engaging personality and a high sense of honor. Calvert had been brought up a Protestant but had become a convert to Catholicism, an act that cost no small sacrifice. As a result of his conversion, Calvert had to resign as secretary of state and also to give up his seat in Parliament. However, Calvert did retain the friendship of King James I, who created him Baron Baltimore, a member of the Irish peerage.

Calvert conceived a plan for a colony in the New World, where men of various religious faiths could live together in good will. He approached his friend, King James, with the idea and received royal support. James died before the colony could be founded, but his son and successor, King Charles I, proved equally friendly and helpful. Calvert attempted a colony in Newfoundland in 1627; however, French attacks and harsh weather forced a withdrawal. Two years later he went to Virginia, but he was quickly informed that Catholics would not be welcome there. He then asked King Charles to grant him a patent to found a colony north of Virginia which he would name "Maryland." The royal reply was favorable.

Before the patent was issued, George Calvert died. He was succeeded by his oldest son, Cecil, who inherited the father's title, estates, and patent to Maryland. The second Lord Baltimore organized an expedition. He drew up a set of rules which stated that in the new colony all men would be equal before the law, that all would be free to practice their respective religions, and that no state religion would be established.

On November 22, 1633, aboard two ships, the *Ark* and the *Dove*, the colonists left Gravesend, England. The *Ark* halted off the Isle of Wight and there two Jesuit Fathers — Andrew White and John Altham — were taken aboard. They would never have been permitted to sail from England. The ships made a rendezvous at the island of Barbados, and then turned north. On March 25, 1634, the Feast of the Annunciation, the colonists landed on Saint Clement Island. Father White offered Mass in thanksgiving and erected a large wooden cross; and the Protestants, who were in the majority, held their own religious service.

The Maryland colony prospered. Fine estates were developed; manor houses were built; and farming, tobacco raising, and fishing put money into the pockets of the colonists. The Jesuit Fathers converted many Indians, including the chief of the Piscataway tribe. There were also some conversions among the Protestants. More colonists arrived: Protestants from England and Puritans from Virginia. In 1649, the Legislature passed Lord Baltimore's famous Toleration Act, which guaranteed all colonists religious freedom. It was an historic document.

"Ark and Dove", on November 22, 1633, these two ships sailed from Gravesend, England, to colonize Maryland.

Charles Calvert, the colonizer   *Cecil Calvert, first proprietor*   *George Calvert, colony governor*

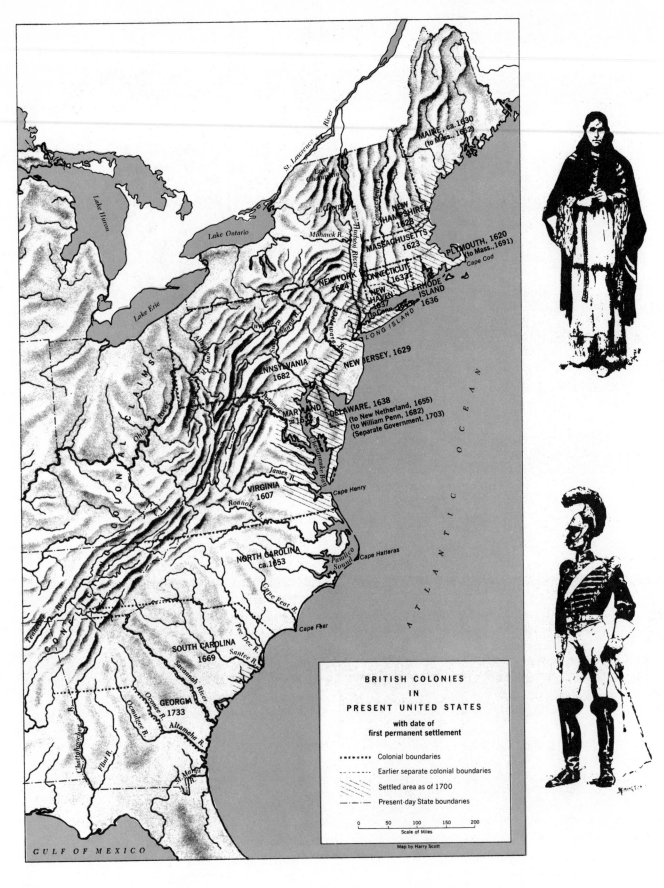

MAINE, ca.1630
(to Mass., 1652)

NEW HAMPSHIRE 1623

MASSACHUSETTS 1623

PLYMOUTH, 1620
(to Mass., 1691)

Cape Cod

CONNECTICUT 1633

NEW YORK 1624

NEW HAVEN 1637
(to Conn., 1662)

RHODE ISLAND 1636

LONG ISLAND

NEW JERSEY, 1629

PENNSYLVANIA 1682

DELAWARE, 1638
(to New Netherland, 1655)
(to William Penn, 1682)
(Separate Government, 1703)

MARYLAND 1634

VIRGINIA 1607

NORTH CAROLINA ca.1653

Cape Henry

Cape Hatteras

Pamlico Sound

SOUTH CAROLINA 1669

GEORGIA 1733

Cape Fear

Cape Fear R.

St. Lawrence River

Lake Champlain

Lake Huron

Lake Ontario

Lake Erie

Mohawk R.

Hudson River

Connecticut R.

Susquehanna R.

Delaware R.

Allegheny R.

Ohio River

Potomac R.

Chesapeake Bay

James R.

Roanoke R.

Pee Dee R.

Santee R.

Savannah River

Ocmulgee R.

Oconee R.

Altamaha R.

Chattahoochee R.

Flint R.

St. Marys R.

Tennessee River

CONTESTED COLONIAL CLAIMS

ATLANTIC OCEAN

GULF OF MEXICO

BRITISH COLONIES IN PRESENT UNITED STATES

with date of
first permanent settlement

‑‑‑‑‑‑ Colonial boundaries

– · – · – Earlier separate colonial boundaries

Settled area as of 1700

– · · – Present-day State boundaries

0   50   100   150   200
Scale of Miles

Map by Harry Scott

The settlers as they arrive at Maryland, this painting by Leutze portrays the colonists as they land in 1634.

The only source of trouble for the new colony came from Virginia. William Claiborne, the secretary of Virginia, had a deep hatred of Catholics and a personal dislike for the Calverts. Claiborne led many raids against the new colony; and in one of them, Father White was taken prisoner. Claiborne sent the Jesuit to England in chains, to be tried on a charge of treason. Somehow the priest managed to obtain his release. Claiborne also conspired with the Puritans who had moved to Maryland from Virginia, but whose hatred of Catholics blotted out their memory of the mistreatment they themselves had suffered in that other colony.

In 1652, the Puritans seized power in Maryland. They turned against the Catholics, plundering their estates and farms. Ten Catholics were condemned to death, and four were executed. Catholics were forbidden to hold office. Priests fled the colony in disguise. The Toleration Act was repealed. In 1657, Lord Baltimore regained control of the colony, forgave the rebels, and restored religious liberty. That liberty lasted until 1691, when the Baltimores were deprived of their holdings and Maryland became a royal colony. The Church of England became the official Church, and Catholics were taxed for its support. Catholic services were forbidden, and even the right to vote was denied to Catholics.

Catholics in Maryland made up less than ten percent of the population, yet among their numbers were some of the richest families in the colony: the Carrolls, the Darnalls, the Brookes. Their manor houses became centers where priests said Mass, taught catechism to children, and administered the sacraments. Their wealth enabled them to send their children to Europe for Catholic educations and in that way the children of wealthy Catholics of Maryland received better educations then the children who were taught at home. Many were to become great leaders.

It is of interest that the first experiment of religious freedom in America should have been attempted by Catholics. Sanford H. Cobb, an American historian, has written, "In face of the remarkable fact that, during the half century in which the Romanists governed Maryland, they were not guilty of a single act of religious oppression, the legislation against them was unwarranted and base."

A Catholic First Family

N O Catholic family played a greater role in the foundation of the American nation than did the Carrolls of Maryland. The head of that patriotic American family was Charles Carroll, a scholarly and brilliant man. An Irish Catholic, Carroll had been educated in the exiled English college at Douai, France. Later he made a brilliant record for himself in the English government. He was secretary to a cabinet minister when the third Lord Baltimore asked him if he would go to Maryland and accept the post of attorney general of the colony. Carroll accepted, partly because of the challenge the new post offered and partly to be free to worship God as a Catholic.

Charles Carroll fell in love with Maryland and its religious freedom. He changed the family motto from "Strong in Faith and War" to "Liberty in All Things." Lord Baltimore presented him with large grants of land; and in the years that followed, he held important political positions. Carroll prospered in the New World and raised a large family. Three of his grandsons were to play important roles in the development of our country: Charles, Daniel, John. Two of these were brothers; the first-named was their second cousin.

Charles Carroll vigorously supported the Revolution.

Charles Carroll of Carrollton

Charles Carroll of Carrollton, namesake of his grandfather, was born at Annapolis, September 19, 1737. As a boy, he was educated by the Jesuits at Bohemia Manor. When he was eleven years old, he and his cousin John crossed the Atlantic to enroll at the College of Saint Omer in France. In the years that followed, he studied at Rheims, Paris, Bruges, and London. At the age of twenty-eight, he returned to Maryland, an educated man, skilled in law and the classics and possessing a thorough knowledge of his religion.

Charles was given an estate at Carrollton, Maryland. He married and settled down at his new home. In the American colonies, at that time, there was a great deal of agitation against England, and Charles Carroll soon found himself caught up in it. He took the side of the colonies and wrote articles for the *Maryland Gazette*, which won him a large

following. His intellectual brilliance and his power as a debater overrode the fact that he was a Catholic, and although Catholics were deprived of the vote, Carroll was elected to the State Legislature, ending the discrimination against Catholics. From then on, he was to hold many public offices.

Carroll, in 1775, was elected to the Continental Congress, having already pledged himself to armed resistance against England. On July 4, 1776, he cast the vote that separated Maryland from England. On August 2, 1776, he strode up to a table in Philadelphia and signed his name to the Declaration of Independence. No signer risked more than Charles Carroll of Carrollton, for he was the wealthiest man of all who signed the historic document.

As Carroll penned his name to the Declaration, one member of the Congress is said to have remarked, "There are so many Carrolls in Maryland, Charles can feel safe from reprisal!"

Charles Carroll quickly added "of Carrollton" after his name, and declared, "Now King George will know with which Carroll he is dealing!"

Charles Carroll served his country and state in many posts. He was a member of the Board of War, a Congressman, president of the Maryland Senate, a member of the committee that drew up the Maryland Constitution, and a United States Senator. He advocated placing the national capital on the Potomac. As the years passed, he became the last surviving signer of the Declaration of Independence, and America's esteem for him grew proportionately.

Shortly before his death, Charles Carroll said: "I have come almost to the threshold of ninety-six years; I have always enjoyed the best of health. I have been blessed with great riches, prosperity, public esteem, and more of the good things than the world usually concedes; but in looking back, the one thing that gives me the greatest satisfaction is that I practiced the duties of my religion."

On November 4, 1832, Charles Carroll died peacefully. The entire nation mourned his passing. Charles Carroll was a great American, a noble patriot, a man of honor. The outstanding Catholic layman of his time, he never compromised his religious beliefs but proved to his country that Catholics can be good citizens.

Daniel Carroll

Another Carroll who rendered outstanding service to the newly founded nation was Daniel Carroll, brother of Archbishop Carroll and cousin of Charles Carroll. Daniel Carroll was born in Maryland in 1733. He was educated in Europe and returned home in time to take part in the struggle for independence. He served in the Colonial Congress and in the House of Representatives. He was named by Maryland to represent that State in the Constitutional Convention.

Daniel Carroll played an important role in drawing up our Constitution. He was a leader in the fight against having the President elected by Congress. The theological training he received in Europe, his studies of Saint Thomas Aquinas and Saint Robert Bellarmine, and his native intelligence, stood him in good stead. His amendment to the Constitution (Article X), which protected States' rights, was accepted as he presented it. Daniel Carroll called the finished Constitution "the best form of Government that has ever been offered to the world."

Daniel Carroll authored the State's Rights amendment.

When the Constitution was completed, Daniel Carroll returned to Baltimore and led the campaign for its ratification. Over great opposition, he succeeded in getting Maryland to adopt the Constitution. He was one of three men chosen to pick a site for the national capital. The site that was selected included one of his own farms, which he promptly transferred to the new Government. Daniel Carroll personally chose the site on which the White House was to be built, and on April 15, 1791, he was one of the two men who laid the cornerstone of the District of Columbia.

The esteem with which Daniel Carroll was regarded is indicated by one incident. When

George Washington hesitated about accepting a second term as President of the United States, Alexander Hamilton, among other leading citizens, stated that the only logical successor to the Father of His Country was Daniel Carroll. That patriotic American died in Washington, in 1829, at the age of ninety-six. Today the Capitol of the United States stands on a hill that once belonged to him. A finer monument no man could ask.

The Capitol building stands on land that was owned by Daniel Carroll. Alexander Hamilton considered him to be the only possible successor to the first president of the United States, George Washington. As the author of the State's Rights amendment, he also led the campaign for popular election of the President.

Archbishop John Carroll

The third of the illustrious Carrolls was John Carroll, younger brother of Daniel. John was born in Maryland on January 8, 1735. In 1747, he joined his cousin Charles at Bohemia Manor, a school conducted by Jesuits to prepare American Catholics for colleges in Europe. After a year at Bohemia Manor, John and Charles went to Flanders and the Jesuit College of St. Omer.

At St. Omer John decided to devote his life to the service of God as a priest. He applied for admission to the Society of Jesus and was accepted in the novitiate at St. Omer. In 1761, he was ordained and was assigned to teach philosophy and theology at St. Omer and later at Liege. Father Carroll was traveling in Europe when word reached him that Pope Clement XIV had dissolved the Society of Jesus. The year was 1773, and it marked a turning point in the life of the young American.

The reasons for the suppression of the Jesuits are varied and complex and will not be dealt with here. The suppression meant that Father Carroll was a free agent without a superior. He then de-

In CONGRESS. July 4, 1776.

The unanimous Declaration of the thirteen united States of America.

When in the Course of human events, it becomes necessary for one people to dissolve the political bands which have connected them with another, and to assume among the powers of the earth, the separate and equal station to which the Laws of Nature and of Nature's God entitle them, a decent respect to the opinions of mankind requires that they should declare the causes which impel them to the separation.

We hold these truths to be self-evident, that all men are created equal, that they are endowed by their Creator with certain unalienable Rights, that among these are Life, Liberty and the pursuit of Happiness.—That to secure these rights, Governments are instituted among Men, deriving their just powers from the consent of the governed,—That whenever any Form of Government becomes destructive of these ends, it is the Right of the People to alter or to abolish it, and to institute new Government, laying its foundation on such principles and organizing its powers in such form, as to them shall seem most likely to effect their Safety and Happiness.

We, therefore, the Representatives of the united States of America, in General Congress, Assembled, appealing to the Supreme Judge of the world for the rectitude of our intentions, do, in the Name, and by Authority of the good People of these Colonies, solemnly publish and declare, That these United Colonies are, and of Right ought to be Free and Independent States; that they are Absolved from all Allegiance to the British Crown, and that all political connection between them and the State of Great Britain, is and ought to be totally dissolved; and that as Free and Independent States, they have full Power to levy War, conclude Peace, contract Alliances, establish Commerce, and to do all other Acts and Things which Independent States may of right do.—And for the support of this Declaration, with a firm reliance on the protection of divine Providence, we mutually pledge to each other our Lives, our Fortunes and our sacred Honor.

John Hancock

cided to return to America. Near the middle of the year 1774, he arrived in Maryland and took up residence on his mother's estate. There he built a small chapel for Sunday Mass; but it served only as his center, because he spent a great deal of time on horseback, visiting distant Catholics to counsel them, to administer the sacraments, and to attend to sick calls. Meanwhile the winds of revolution were blowing about him.

In 1776, Congress decided to send a commission to Canada, to seek the aid of the Canadians against England. Benjamin Franklin and two Catholics from Maryland — Daniel Chase and Charles Carroll — were appointed to the commission. Because the group had to deal with Bishop Briand, of Montreal, it was suggested that a Catholic priest would make a valued intermediary. Father John Carroll was chosen as the man to go with them.

The Canadian mission was a failure. Bishop Briand refused to use his position to help the Americans. He pointed out that most American colonies were influenced by anti-Catholic sentiment, and that even in Maryland there were laws against Catholics. But in Canada, the bishop stated, Catholics were protected by the Quebec Act, which admitted them to public office and guaranteed them freedom of religion; Catholics in Canada had all the rights of any English subject. The Quebec Act had been passed only after a great deal of diplomacy by Bishop Briand, and he did not wish to lose what he had gained after years of hard work. Moreover, most Canadian people did not wish to break with England.

The mission was not a complete failure, however. Although Canada did not enter the war on the side of the colonies, it did remain neutral. Moreover, many Catholic Canadians did fight for American independence, forming a special regiment called "Congress' Own." A number of Canadian priests sided with the Americans. Father de la Valiniere, who argued for the American cause, was therefore deported to France; Father Lothiniere became chaplain to the rebel Canadians; and Fathers Gibault and Flouquet were among others who openly agreed with the Americans.

Daniel Chase and Charles Carroll remained in Montreal on other American business, while Benjamin Franklin and Father Carroll returned home together. Franklin was ill, and Father Carroll took great care of him. The two men became close friends; and later, when Franklin was Ambassador to France, he recommended to the Holy See that Father Carroll be appointed first Bishop of the United States.

During the war, Father Carroll continued to carry on his priestly work in Maryland and Virginia. He was ardent in the cause of independence, and his letters to former Jesuits in England defended that cause. He led his people in prayer for success of the American venture and for the return of peace. After the war ended, the American clergy felt that it was inappropriate for the United States to remain under the ecclesiastical jurisdiction of the Vicar Apostolic of London. A petition was sent to the Holy See, asking that Catholic Americans be given a superior of their own.

Benjamin Franklin recorded, in his Paris diary, this event: "1784. July 1. The Pope's Nuncio called and acquainted me that the Pope had, on my recommendation, appointed Mr. John Carroll Superior of the Catholic clergy in America, with many of the powers of a Bishop, and that, probably, he would be made a Bishop *in partibus* before the end of the year."

The document appointing Father John Carroll Prefect Apostolic of the United States did not arrive in America until November of 1784. As Prefect Apostolic, he had the power to administer Confirmation and had authority over all priests in the United States. In 1789, the then Monsignor Carroll was named Bishop of the United States, with his see at Baltimore. In the following year, he was consecrated in England.

When Bishop Carroll returned to the United States, he made a survey of his Church. The first national census (1790) showed that the United States had a white population of 3,200,000 people, of whom about 30,000 were Catholics. There were a few more than thirty priests in the country, caring for a widely distributed Catholic population. Maryland had 16,000 Catholics—more than half the total. There were 7,000 Catholics in Pennsylvania; 3,000 around Detroit and Vincennes; 2,500 in Illinois. In all of the rest of the United States, there were only 1,000 Catholics.

Bishop — later Archbishop — Carroll was to direct the American Church for twenty-five years. He convened the first synod of Baltimore, and the rules and regulations adopted by the body are wise even to this day. He founded Georgetown University. When the Jesuit order was restored in 1801, he asked his old Society to take over Georgetown. He persuaded the Sulpicians to come to Baltimore and open a seminary. Augustinians, Dominicans, Carmelites, Visitation nuns, and Sisters of Charity began work at his invitation.

Immigration to the United States swelled the number of Catholics. In 1807, there were 14,000 Catholics in New York City where, seventeen years earlier, there had been less than a hundred. Many French priests driven from France by the French Revolution came to assist Bishop Carroll in his work. In 1808, the Holy See raised Baltimore to an archdiocese and created four new dioceses: Boston, New York, Bardstown, Philadelphia. When Archbishop Carroll died in 1815, at the age of eighty-one, the Church, numbering 200,000 souls, was firmly established. Archbishop Carroll was truly the spiritual father and founder of the Catholic Church in the United States.

Bohemia Manor

BEFORE passing on to more history of our country, a word should be said about Bohemia Manor, because from this center missioners evangelized much of the eastern seaboard. At one time the "parish" included Delaware, Maryland, Virginia and southeastern Pennsylvania.

Bohemia Manor was the center for the Jesuit Fathers and was founded in 1704 by Father Thomas Mansell. It was designed as a place that would support the missionary activities of the Jesuits, and hence was self-sufficient. The church and rectory were surrounded by a 1,200 acre plantation. There was a water-powered grist mill that ground corn,

Saint Francis Xavier Shrine in Warwick, Maryland, the shrine of "Old Bohemia" was founded by Father Mansell.

Bohemia Manor was founded by Father Thomas Mansell in 1704. The Manor was the center of the Jesuit fathers.

wheat and other grains grown on the mission's farm. The establishment also had a saw mill, a brick factory, a smithy, barns and warehouses.

In 1742, Father Thomas Poulton began an academy to train students from wealthy families in the area so that these boys would be equipped for study in Europe. It was to this academy that Charles and John Carroll came before going abroad.

The official name of the mission was St. Francis Xavier, after that great Jesuit pioneer in the Far East. It was the center of Catholic activity for the most populous Catholic area of the American colonies. Ten priests, mostly Jesuits, are buried in the cemetery on the east side of the church. These priests came from England, Ireland, Germany and France — the pioneer missioners of the east coast; the first was buried there in 1748 and the last almost a hundred years later. Around them lie the remains of the early Catholic colonists.

Today this shrine of pioneer Catholicism has been restored by the Old Bohemia Historical Society, and Mass is still offered at intervals in the church, although it no longer serves as a parish. The rectory has been made into a museum where many artifacts of colonial days are on display. Among the exhibits are religious objects used by the priests when they traveled throughout their large area to offer Mass for isolated Catholics. There is a missal dating back to 1645 and a chalice used at Mass from the same period.

Catholics in the Revolution

AT the time of the American Revolution, Catholics numbered only about one per cent of the colonies' population, but the important contribution Catholics made to the war effort was far out of proportion to their numbers. In addition, when the count includes Europeans such as Lafayette and Pulaski, who served the American colonies as volunteers, the contribution of Catholics rises even higher. Some Catholics held high positions; for example, Commodore John Barry, Father of the American Navy. Others played minor roles.

Patrick Colvin, a resident of Trenton, was one of the latter. Colvin was a member of Saint Mary's Parish in Philadelphia, and every Sunday he traveled the thirty-two miles from Trenton to Philadelphia to attend Mass. Colvin's moment of glory came on Christmas Eve in 1776. At that time it seemed as if the cause of the American Revolution was hopelessly lost, but General Washington had one more card to play. With a handful of poorly clothed, shivering men, Washington undertook the daring plan of crossing the ice-clogged Delaware River and attacking the English camp at Trenton on Christmas morning. Two ferrymen worked all night, taking their boatloads of Americans across the Delaware. One ferryman was a Presbyterian, named McConkey, the other was Patrick Colvin. Every schoolboy knows how Washington's surprise attack was successful — and the success was due in no small part to Patrick Colvin's ferrying.

Saint Mary's Parish in Philadelphia was the center of Catholic life in that city. Many parishioners played important roles in the Revolution. From that parish came the leading Catholic soldier, Brigadier General Stephen Moylan. A native of Ireland, where his brother was Bishop of Cork, Moylan arrived in Philadelphia in 1768. At the outbreak of war, he went to Boston and joined the Continental Army. Washington recognized the Irishman's business skill, named him aide-de-camp, and appointed him quartermaster general of the Army. Moylan organized his own cavalry outfit, Moylan's Dragoons, which fought bravely at Brandywine and Germantown. After the war, Moylan organized the Friendly Sons of Saint Patrick and

Comte de Grasse blockaded the British at Yorktown.

became first president of that organization. He died in 1811 and is buried in Saint Mary's Cemetery.

Thomas Fitzsimmons, a wealthy Philadelphia Catholic, used his own personal fortune to finance the war. He had arrived in Philadelphia when a youth of seventeen; had gone into merchant shipping, and had made a grand success. He was heart and soul behind the break with England. When war came, he was commissioned a captain in the state militia and took part in the battle of Princeton. In 1782, he was elected to the Continental Congress. In 1787, Fitzsimmons took part in the Constitutional Convention and was one of the two Catholics who signed the historic document. Later he served three terms in Congress.

Frederick Remington portrays life of the American in a simple and rustic style.

Another prominent Catholic was George Meade, Fitzsimmons' partner and a grandfather of the later Civil War general, George Meade. Meade was very active in the patriotic movement, used his own money to help finance the fight, and served in the Third Battalion of Associators. He, too, is buried in Saint Mary's Cemetery. Other prominent Philadelphia Catholics were Matthew Carey, America's greatest editor of the period, and Thomas Lloyd, "father of American stenography." Lloyd was present in Old Federal Hall on Wall Street, New York, when Washington delivered his Inau-

gural Address. Lloyd took it down in shorthand and then gave it to the world.

Thirty-eight per cent of Washington's troops had Irish names. How many of them were Catholics and how many Protestants, we have no way of knowing. But certainly there were many like Sergeant Andrew Wallace, a known Catholic, who served his adopted country heroically. Sergeant Wallace first fought in the French and Indian War. In the Revolution he participated in the battles of Brandywine, Germantown, and Monmouth. He survived the Paoli Massacre, where his brother was killed; he was captured by the British, but released in time to join Anthony Wayne in the storming of Stony Point. Later he fought at Camden, Cowpens, Eustace Springs, and Yorktown. He remained in the Army until 1811, when he was mustered out at the age of eighty.

Many stories can be told about such men as Colonel Morgan Connor, Major Michael Ryan, Major John Doyle, Colonel John Moore, Colonel John Fitzgerald. But the summary of one other Irish Catholic will be sufficient to indicate the breed of men who fought in the war for independence. Although Timothy Murphy came from New York State, he enlisted in the Pennsylvania Riflemen, probably to be with other Irishmen. He fought at Boston, Stillwater, and Saratoga, where he is reputed to have shot the British General Fraser and swung the tide of battle. Later he went on expeditions to punish the Indian tribes for the Wyoming and Cherry Valley massacres. He had many narrow escapes from Indians, and his reputation as a marksman and Indian fighter became legendary in his own time. He died quietly in New York's Schoharie County, in 1818.

The Irish, however, did not have a monopoly on patriotism. They merely had the largest numbers of participants in the fateful endeavors. Other nationalities, also, contributed to the struggle for freedom. No one could give more than young Richard Tagliaferro, who at the age of twenty fell mortally wounded in Virginia's battle of Guilford courthouse. There was another man known only as "Francesco, the Italian," who at the cost of his own life protected General Washington from British bayonets at the Battle of Monmouth. Two other Italian Catholics played important roles in the struggle for freedom.

The first, Philip Mazzei, went to Virginia to begin the specialty of his native Tuscany—viniculture. He settled near Monticello and became a friend of Thomas Jefferson. When war came, Mazzei enlisted in the Williamsburg regiment. Later he was sent, as an agent of Virginia, to Europe to solicit military funds. After the war, some of his friends wanted to get him a consular post; but because he was a foreign-born Catholic, he was turned down.

The other Italian who contributed greatly to the success of the colonies was Francesco Vigo; born in Sardinia, he became a fur trader working out of Saint Louis. Vigo joined the frontierman-soldier, George Rogers Clark, in a bold scheme to wrest Detroit and the Indian territories from the British. Disguised as a Cuban merchant, Vigo penetrated the British stronghold at Fort Sackville (Vincennes, Ind.) and gathered information that made possible the capture of that fort (1779). He also loaned Clark almost seven thousand dollars to buy arms and gunpowder for the campaign. Finally Vigo and the French missionary, Abbe Pierre Gibault, persuaded the French Catholics of the area to support the cause of revolution. It was

The engineer, Thaddeus Kosciusko   *Pulaski, Polish Catholic Soldier*   *Rochambeau, aide of Washington*

The first draft of the Declaration of Independence is presented to the Continental Congress in July, 1776.

A Frenchman came to the aid of Americans, Lafayette

Abbe Gibault who administered the oath of allegiance to the United States. The success of their work was recognized in the Treaty of Paris, which established the legal right for the United States Government to obtain all the territory between the Allegheny Mountains and the Mississippi River. Vigo also used his money and influence to get priests for Indiana Territory.

It was a Polish Catholic, Thaddeus Kosciusko, who is sometimes called the "Father of Army Engineers." Kosciusko, descendant of a noble Lithuanian family, came to the United States and offered his service in the cause of democracy. General Washington appointed him an engineering officer. The brilliant Kosciusko erected the fortifications at West Point; he built the defensive works along the Delaware River; and his fortifications at Saratoga were responsible for the success of the battle there. Another Polish Catholic who fought for the Americans was Count Casimir Pulaski. He made a name for himself at the Battle of Brandywine, was appointed a brigadier general by Congress, organized an infantry-and-cavalry unit including his Polish followers; and then met death at the age of thirty-one, in the Battle of Savannah.

General George Washington, "Father of his Country" with Lafayette and an aide-de-camp at the end of the war.

His last words were: "Jesus, Mary, Joseph!"

Of all the foreign nationals who assisted the United States, the French take first place. In 1778, France signed a treaty of alliance with the United States, and French financial and military aid helped greatly in turning the tide of the war. The French contributed some 30,000 soldiers, 90 officers, and 109 chaplains to assist the American Army. The best-known Frenchman was the young Marquis de Lafayette, whose head swam with liberal idealism but who kept his own chaplain with him. He won the heart of America with his dashing ways. But the two Frenchmen who contributed most to American victory were Count de Rochambeau and Count de Grasse.

Count Jean de Rochambeau, Marshal of France, was sent to America by King Louis XVI, at the head of 6,000 soldiers. At an earlier time, De Rochambeau had studied for the priesthood but left the seminary when his brother's death made him head of his family and heir to the family estates. This French volunteer landed in Newport, Rhode Island, in 1780; and from then until the surrender at Yorktown, he was at the side of General Washington.

Count Francois de Grasse won his sea legs as a boy, when he fought for the defense of the Church against the Turks and Moors. He joined the French Navy and rose rapidly to the rank of admiral. De Grasse commanded a naval force of fifty-one ships during the last seven weeks of the American Revolution. He kept the British from sending reinforcements to the trapped Cornwallis. The English fleet had to retreat to New York, and the armies of Washington, Rochambeau, Lafayette, and Count de Saint-Simon forced the Yorktown surrender of General Cornwallis.

Some years later General Washington, in a letter to Monsignor John Carroll, stated that he recognized the important aid given by Catholics and "a nation professing the Roman Catholic Faith," to the establishment of our Government.

One final scene was to be played by Catholics. Following the Yorktown surrender, General Washington sent Colonel Tilghman, an Irish Catholic from Maryland, on an important mission to Philadelphia: he bore to the Congress a dispatch that announced the American victory. The French Ambassador, who had mortgaged his private fortune to help the struggle, immediately arranged a religious service to be held at Saint Mary's Church. The religious service, which consisted of a Mass of Thanksgiving and the singing of the hymn of

Benjamin Franklin, statesman, author and inventor

thanks, the *Te Deum*, was attended by the Continental Congress, the Supreme Executive Council, and the Philadelphia Assembly. Representatives of the whole nation joined the Catholics in thanking God for the wonderful victory.

The end came in Paris, in 1783, when the peace treaty with England was concluded. There, in the capital of "the eldest daughter of the Church," was signed the document that created the United States a free and independent nation. It was a document won by the blood and sacrifices of men of many religious faiths, but one for which the contribution of Catholics was proportionately great.

Father of The American Navy

G R E A T
ENCOURAGEMENT
F O R
SEAMEN.

ALL GENTLEMEN SEAMEN and able-bodied LANDSMEN who have a Mind to distinguish themselves in the GLORIOUS CAUSE of their Country, and make their Fortunes, an Opportunity now offers on board the Ship RANGER, of Twenty Guns, (for France) now laying in Portsmouth, in the State of New-Hampshire, commanded by JOHN PAUL JONES, Esq; let them repair to the Ship's Rendezvous in Portsmouth, or at the Sign of Commodore Manley, in Salem, where they will be kindly entertained, and receive the greatest Encouragement.—The Ship RANGER, in the Opinion of every Person who has seen her is looked upon to be one of the best Cruizers in America.—She will be always able to Fight her Guns under a most excellent Cover; and no Vessel yet built was ever calculated for sailing faster, and making good Weather.

Any GENTLEMEN VOLUNTEERS who have a Mind to take an agreable Voyage in this pleasant Season of the Year, may, by entering on board the above Ship RANGER, meet with every Civility they can possibly expect, and for a farther Encouragement depend on the first Opportunity being embraced to reward each one agreable to his Merit.

All reasonable Travelling Expences will be allowed, and the Advance-Money be paid on their Appearance on Board.

In CONGRESS, March 29, 1777.

RESOLVED,

THAT the Marine Committee be authorised to advance to every able Seaman, that enters into the Continental Service, any Sum not exceeding FORTY DOLLARS, and to every ordinary Seaman or Landsman, any Sum not exceeding TWENTY DOLLARS, to be deducted from their future Prize Money.

By Order of CONGRESS,
JOHN HANCOCK, President.

DANVERS: Printed by E. Russell, at the House late the Bell-Tavern.

Barry, founder of the American Navy

THE story is told that the English general, Sir William Howe, commander of the English forces in the colonies, once offered Captain John Barry $100,000 and command of any English frigate he might choose, if he would desert the American cause and join the British.

"Not all the money the British Government controls, nor the command of all the fleets it could bring upon the seas, would tempt me to desert my country!" Barry replied.

Captain John Barry, sometimes called "Commodore" although the title was not in use in his day, fought the first and last naval battles of the Revolution; was the first officer appointed by

Congress to command the first ship purchased (the *Lexington*); and because of all this, is referred to as the Father of the American Navy.

Barry was born in 1745, in Wexford, Ireland. He was about fifteen years old when he came to America and found a job in Philadelphia with a shipping firm. Ten years later he was captain of the *Black Prince*, one of the fastest packets of that period. By the time the Revolutionary War began, Barry was a prosperous man. But, according to his own words, he gave up "the finest ship, and entered the service" of his country.

The United States had no navy at the time, and Captain Barry was charged by Congress with equipping two merchant vessels and supervising the construction of a battleship. This latter, the *Lexington*, named after the first battle of the Revolution, was put in his command. Barry was ordered to clear American coastal waters of enemy ships. In his first engagement, he captured the *Edward*, an armed tender. In the succeeding years of the war, he captured the *Atlanta*, *Trepassy*, *Mars*, *Minerva*, and *Sybil*.

Captain Barry trained such naval heroes of the War of 1812 as Jacob Jones, Stewart, and Dale. He commanded such ships as the *Raleigh*, *Effingham*, *United States*, and *Alliance*. He was in command of the last-named ship when he captured the *Trepassy* and the *Atlanta*. In that battle Captain Barry received grapeshot through his shoulder. After considerable loss of blood, he was finally carried below. The *Alliance* had received heavy damage, and when Barry disappeared from deck, the crew lost heart.

One of his lieutenants reported the heavy damage and asked if the ship should be surrendered. "No!" exclaimed Barry. "If the ship can't be fought without me, then carry me back on deck!"

This answer traveled through the ship's company and put new spirit into the fighting men. The battle was resumed, and before long the British ships struck their flags.

Captain Barry's service to his country was rendered in other ways than on the sea. During the hard and cold winter of 1780, when hunger and mutiny jeopardized the Continental Army, Captain Barry spent his days on the streets of Philadelphia, recruiting soldiers for the Army and seeking pledges of financial support. He also served as aide-de-camp to General Cadwalader in the Battle of Trenton, commanding a company in charge of heavy cannon. In another foray he took two rowboats and twenty-eight men, and rowed down the Delaware River at night, to capture two English ships and a schooner — all heavily armed and full of supplies, much needed by the patriots.

Captain Barry continued to serve in the American Navy until his death in 1803. He lies buried in Saint Mary's Cemetery in Philadelphia.

An old song gives an indication of the esteem and affection that were rendered to Captain Barry by his fellow citizens:

There are gallant hearts whose glory
Columbia loves to name,
Whose deeds shall live in story
And everlasting fame.
But never yet one braver
Our starry banner bore,
Than saucy old Jack Barry,
The Irish Commodore.

Barry's statue stands in front of Independence Hall in Philadelphia

The Lithuanian Prince Who Became a Priest

Prince Demetrius Gallitzin conducted himself as one born to nobility. Tall, handsome, with black hair and dark, flashing eyes, a skilled swordsman and horseman, the prince was the target for ambitious mothers who wished to see their daughters well wed. Demetrius was born at The Hague in 1770, where his father was Russian Ambassador to Holland. His father came from a noble Lithuanian family; his mother was the daughter of a German field marshal who also belonged to the nobility.

The father of Demetrius prepared his son for a military career. The Senior Gallitzin was a man of his times, a scoffer at religion, an admirer of Voltaire and Diderot. He allowed no religious influence to touch his son; indeed, he had even de-

stroyed his wife's faith and led her away from religion. Young Gallitzin was brought up in a pagan atmosphere, his education heavily military.

When Demetrius was sixteen, his mother fell seriously ill. She had been born in a Catholic family and her soul was troubled by her years of unfaithfulness to God. Fearful of death, she called for a priest — much against her husband's wishes. She returned to the Catholic Faith, and upon recovery began to pray for her son. She particularly prayed to Saint Monica, whose own son, Saint Augustine, had led a life of luxury and dissipation for many years.

Demetrius later recalled his own conversion, when he wrote: "An intimacy which existed be-

117

tween our family and a certain celebrated French philosopher had produced a contempt for religion. Raised in prejudice against Revelation, I felt every disposition to ridicule those very principles and practices which I have since adopted. During these unfortunate years of my infidelity, particular care was taken not to let any clergyman come near me."

Referring then to his mother's conversion, Demetrius went on to tell how his own curiosity was aroused. He added: "I soon felt convinced of the necessity of investigating the different religious systems, in order to find the true one. . . . My choice fell upon the Catholic Church, and at the age of seventeen, I became a member of that Church."

The conversion of the young soldier did not turn him from his military pursuits. When he was twenty-two, he was aide-de-camp to the Austrian General Von Lillien in the campaign against the French. He seemed destined for a brilliant military career—until suddenly, for political reasons, all foreigners were dismissed from the Austrian Army.

Demetrius was aware of events in America. He knew that the infant army of the United States could use trained soldiers. In America were opportunity and a chance to apply his skills. Accordingly, under an assumed name, he took passage from Rotterdam, and the autumn of 1792 found him in the United States. He was immediately attracted to the young country, but one regrettable condition could not escape his notice: the United States was a vast spiritual wasteland, and there were very few priests. Without a glance backward, the young Russian offered his services to Bishop John Carroll to prepare for the priesthood.

Demetrius was accepted for the seminary in Baltimore; and after three years of study, he was ordained on March 18, 1795. He was the first American-trained priest. Previously Father Stephen Badin had been ordained in America by Bishop Carroll; but he had made his studies in Europe and had come to the United States only for ordination. Father Gallitzin was the first priest to have completed his studies in America.

After ordination, Father Gallitzin began work in Virginia and Maryland. He labored there for almost four years, before he was assigned to serve Catholics living along the frontier in western Pennsylvania. For forty-one years, Father Gallitzin labored in that area. He was ever active, traveling by horseback through the forest wilds, being caught in the rains, suffering in the heat, but al-ways ministering to his scattered flock of Christians.

Father Gallitzin used his own money to build a mission center at Loretto, Pennsylvania; shortly after his death, it had grown into ten churches and three monasteries. His work covered an area that now includes the dioceses of Pittsburgh, Harrisburg, Greensburg, and Erie. In between his travels from mission station to mission station, he wrote books defending the Catholic religion. He concealed the fact that he was a prince, introducing himself as "Father Smith." When he was naturalized as an American citizen, it was under the name of Augustine Smith. Only after his father died, did he assume his true identity.

Father Gallitzin was a great civilizing influence. He entered a wilderness and left a region of fertile farms. For his unceasing labors, western Pennsylvania will be forever in his debt.

SIGNATURE OF REV. D. A. GALLITZIN.

118

Their Works Praise Them

Sister Rose Duchesne was later declared "Blessed."

Two women played important roles in the early development of the United States. One did not begin the work she wished to do until she was seventy-two years of age; the other was the mother of five children. Both are undergoing the process of canonization.

A worldling looking at the life of Blessed Rose Philippine Duchesne would probably arrive at the conclusion that she was a failure. Born in France in 1769, she left a social whirl to become a Visitation nun. The French Revolution closed the convent, and Philippine returned home without accomplishing her desire. When France returned to peace, Philippine attempted to restore the Visitation convent, but her effort failed.

At the age of thirty-three, she met the future Saint Madeleine Sophie Barat and joined the Religious of the Sacred Heart. She confided to Mother Barat that it was her ambition to work among the Indians of North America, but years passed before she received permission even to go to America. Finally, at the age of forty-nine, Mother Duchesne, accompanied by four other religious, sailed from Bordeaux.

The group—the first Sacred Heart religious to be sent to the United States—spent eleven weeks at sea before New Orleans was reached. The trip up the Mississippi River to Saint Louis took forty-seven days. When Mother Duchesne finally reached her goal, it was to learn that she wasn't wanted! The bishop had misunderstood; there was no place for her to work among the Indians.

Mother Duchesne and her companions were sent to Saint Charles, in the same state. There they opened the first free school west of the Mississippi. A new foundation was begun at Florissant, in the Missouri Valley: a boarding school and novitiate. Later in St. Louis, she started an orphanage, an academy, and a free school. These works were done under almost-incredible hardships.

At last, when she was seventy-two years of age, Mother Duchesne received permission to begin mission work among the Indians of Kansas. It was impossible at that age for her to learn the Indian language, so she spoke the international language of kindness and love. Daily she spent four hours in the morning and four hours in the evening in the chapel, praying for the success of the work.

The Indians could not believe that anyone would spend so long in prayer, so they devised a test. One with typical Indian stealth would creep into chapel and place kernels of corn in patterns on the skirt of her habit. Coming back four hours later, the tester would check the corn. It was never found disturbed; and for that reason, the Indians

Sister Duchesne finally had her dream come true at the age of seventy when she began working with the Indians.

A simple hand bell and clock were once the possessions of of Blessed Rose.

named Mother Duchesne "Woman Who Always Prays."

The last years of her life were spent at Saint Charles, where she died at the age of eighty-three. In 1940, she was beatified by Pope Pius XII. This woman, whom contemporaries might have considered a failure, began in the United States a movement that has spread to South America, New Zealand, and Australia. The school she founded in Missouri has grown, and today colleges conducted by her successors extend from Lone Mountain, near San Francisco, to Purchase, on the outskirts of New York City.

Blessed Philippine Duchesne was a valiant woman. In the early days, when difficulties and poverty surrounded her at Florissant, her brother offered to pay her passage back to France.

"Use the money to pay the passage of two more nuns coming to America!" she replied. This was Blessed Rose Philippine Duchesne, frontier missioner.

The second woman whose contribution to the growth of Catholicism in the United States is inestimable, was Elizabeth Bayley Seton, mother of five, convert, foundress of the Sisters of Charity, and actually the creator of the parochial-school system in the United States.

Beautiful Elizabeth Bayley moved through New York City society with charm and grace. Daughter of well-to-do Doctor Richard Bayley, and a devout and practicing member of Trinity Episcopal Church, Elizabeth had all the attributes to make her sought after by the most-eligible bachelors of her day. William Seton, a handsome, young businessman, won her hand, and after a fashionable wedding at Trinity, the young couple moved into a house on the Battery.

For eight years Elizabeth Seton led a happy and social life. She had five children: two boys and three girls. Her charm won her a broad circle of friends, and her devotion to her husband was a model for every married woman. Then her husband suffered a business reverse; and almost at the same time, his health began to fail. Doctors prescribed a change in climate. The Setons decided to go to Italy, and their children—with the exception of the oldest, Anna—were placed with relatives.

But the journey was in vain. Not long after reaching Italy, William Seton died. Alone in a strange land, with four of her children an ocean away, the widow was taken into the home of the Filicchi family in Leghorn. There a revelation awaited her. The Filicchis were devout Catholics. There was daily Mass in the family chapel; morning and evening prayers and the Rosary were said in common. Elizabeth was drawn to the faith that surrounded her.

A year after her husband's death, Elizabeth Seton returned home with her daughter, to find a way to support her family. She knew that she should become a Catholic, but it would be a hard struggle. All her friends and relatives were Protestants; the New York Catholics were a tolerated minority. She waited almost a year, but finally in Lent of 1805, she made known her desire; and she was baptized at Saint Peter's, on Barclay Street, in time for Easter.

Elizabeth opened a school, but it failed for lack of pupils; her friends had forgotten her after she became a Catholic. She obtained a job teaching in a private school, but was unhappy because of the bigotry that surrounded her and her family. Providentially, a priest from Baltimore was visiting in New York at that time. He met the Widow Seton, heard her story, and invited her to Baltimore to open a Catholic school.

In 1808, Elizabeth journeyed to Baltimore with her daughters (her sons were in boarding school). A house on Paca Street had been rented for her, and it would serve as both school and home. There she was surrounded by Catholics, and she soon lost herself in her work. Other young women arrived to assist her. It was not long before she confided to Bishop Carroll her desire to begin a religious community that would be devoted to teaching.

Bishop Carroll was delighted. He suggested the rule of Saint Vincent de Paul, France's great apostle of charity. Mrs. Seton suggested that the garb of the Sisters be contemporary—the black dress and small bonnet of the Italian widow. Thus the Sisters of Charity came into being, and Elizabeth Bayley Seton became the first superior, Mother Seton. The headquarters for the community was set up at Emmitsburg, Maryland.

Mother Seton did not live a long life. She died on January 4, 1821, at the age of forty-seven, probably from tuberculosis. Behind her she left more than fifty Sisters of Charity, with foundations at Emmitsburg, Baltimore, Philadelphia, and New York. She had begun a vast movement that was to erect hospitals and schools across the United States, and eventually reach even beyond our own borders. Her spiritual daughters were to be numbered in many thousands. Mother Seton grew up in a time when the American nation was beginning, and it is impossible to consider the growth of the Church in the United States without realizing the contribution that Mother Seton made to it.

This "White House" at Emmitsburg served as the first Catholic parochial school founded in the United States.

Blessed Elizabeth Ann Seton

Francis Vigo settled in Vincennes.

Vincennes was the cornerstone of mid-western Catholicism.

Vincennes, Indiana

A wood carving of Bishop Simon Bruté, the founder of the historical parish of Vincennes in Indiana.

Memorial to the explorer, George Rogers Clarke.

Vincennes was the passageway to the western frontier.

Monsignor Conti is the founder of the historical Simon Bruté library which consists of over 11,000 volumes.

Two Southern·Justices

ON the last day of his life, William Joseph Gaston of North Carolina was hearing a case before that state's Supreme Court when he was taken ill and had to be helped back to his office where he passed into unconsciousness. When he was revived, he opened his eyes to find his chambers filled with solicitous friends. One of them, a Judge Ruffin, was suggesting that a hot mustard plaster be applied to the sick Gaston.

"It's astonishing, Ruffin, with how much courage you bear my troubles," remarked the revived jurist to the laughter of all present.

Then Justice Gaston, sitting up with some difficulty, told about a party he had been at during which a freethinker had sounded off about his disbeliefs. After pausing a moment, the sick judge continued:

"A belief in an overruling Divinity, who shapes our ends, whose eye is upon us, and who will reward us according to our deeds is necessary. We must believe there is a God, all wise and mighty."

Then with a sigh Judge Gaston lay back on his couch and within minutes was dead.

William J. Gaston, who has been called the greatest Catholic layman in Southern history, was born in New Bern, North Carolina, on September 19, 1778. His father, a physician, was an early supporter of the American Revolution, so much so that he was ambushed by Tories in 1781 and murdered. However, the family was well off financially and his mother, a devout English Catholic, enrolled him as the first student at the newly founded Georgetown College. Several years later, Bishop John Carroll suggested that young William be sent to Princeton where he was graduated at the head of his class. As a graduation gift for his mother he had his portrait painted by the famed James Peale.

Young Gaston decided that he did not wish to become a gentleman planter and he chose to become a lawyer. He entered the law firm of Francis X. Martin, a French Catholic, who later became the Chief Justice of Louisiana. At the age of twenty, Gaston was admitted to the North Carolina bar. He was first elected to the State Senate in 1800

William J. Gaston, from an engraving by A. B. Durant

and from that time on held one elective or appointive office or another. He was a member of the United States Congress during the War of 1812 and was in Washington when news reached him that the British had invaded North Carolina and marched directly on New Bern where the attack sent his wife into a violent convulsion and she died with a yet unborn child. He was shortly remarried in Washington by the president of Georgetown College, Father de Grassi. He later sent his children to Emmitsburg, Maryland—his girls attended a school founded by Mother Seton, while he entrusted his son to Father Simon Bruté at Mount Saint Mary's College.

Gaston and Bruté became fast friends as a result of the contact. Bruté was later to become the first bishop of Vincennes, Ind., and was a wise and scholarly man who held great appeal to the southerner. The Notre Dame University archives have some 150 Bruté letters written to Gaston, an indication of their friendship. Gaston was also friend and advisor to the gifted Bishop John England, of Charleston, S.C., one of the most prominent churchmen of his day. Bishop England was a frequent guest at the Gaston home, and the North Carolina jurist was able to gain entree for his friend to Congress and the White House. Gaston had a great interest in Bishop England's paper, *United States Catholic Miscellany*, contributing funds and articles. He helped his Church in many other ways.

By this time Gaston had a nationwide reputation. His plea for religious toleration delivered at his state's constitutional convention in 1835 was reprinted all over the country. Because of a speech, he was successful in changing the word "Protestant" to "Christian" as a qualification for holding office in North Carolina. He was not happy with the compromise that he had been able to effect because it eliminated Jews whose rights he had previously defended. He had the reputation for championing more minority causes than any other man of his day. Gaston's views on slavery were in advance of his times. He fearlessly defended the human dignity of slaves and ruled against slaveholders when that dignity was violated. A landmark decision was his ruling that freed Negroes were citizens of North Carolina.

This decision was used as support for a minority dissent in the ruling of another Catholic, Roger Brook Taney, in the famous Dred Scott case. Taney, a native of Maryland made law his career. A close friend of Andrew Jackson, Taney was appointed Attorney General of the United States (1831) after his friend became president. Other appointments as Secretary of the Treasury and Associate Justice of the Supreme Court were turned down by the Senate, largely because of Taney's Catholicism, which was under attack by the Know-Nothings.

Jackson later forced through Taney's nomination as Chief Justice of the Supreme Court to succeed Justice Marshall; the nomination was made in 1835 and he was confirmed on March 15, 1836. One of the objections made to Taney was that as an Associate Justice he spent some time in private prayer before entering the courtroom. Taney defended his religious beliefs, saying that all his reading and study "strengthened and confirmed my faith in the Catholic Church, who has never ceased to teach her children how they should live and how they should die."

The southern justice, Roger Taney

Taney, himself, was opposed to slavery and had freed his own slaves. But he was a strong supporter of the constitutional interpretation of states' rights. His Dred Scott ruling stated that Congress had no power to exclude slavery from the territories because that was a matter for the individual territories to decide. He also ruled that under the Constitution, Negroes had no claim to citizenship. He died in 1864, not soon enough to realize that a terrible civil war was to overrule him.

The political differences between Gaston and Taney should have been evidence that Catholics did not have a monolithic political position, but it would be another century until that fact became clear to all but the most bigoted. Gaston's respect for the law and his love for his country put him largely above criticism. Honors came frequently to him. For example, he was awarded honorary doctor of laws degrees from such American universities as Princeton, Harvard, Yale, Pennsylvania and Georgetown. He turned down appointments to the Cabinet and declined offers to run for the vice-presidency. He explained his decisions as a love for the law:

"To give a wholesome exposition of the laws, to settle the fluctuations and reconcile the seemingly conflicting analogies of judicial decisions; to administer justice in the last resort with a steady hand and an upright purpose, appears to me to be among the highest of civil functions. As long as God spares me health and understanding to perform these faithfully, how can I better serve my country?"

The Winning of The West

A sketch by Lailler of the French explorer, Cartier

THE United States was explored from the edges. Because the east coast was the closest to Europe, that received the first settlements. The expansion westward was slow, depending mainly on the pressure of population. The Appalachian Mountains formed a natural barrier, and the vast bulk of population lived on the east side of that range. There were Spanish settlements in Arizona, New Mexico, and Texas, pushed north from Mexico. California also was thinly settled. Although French

power had come to an end in 1763, with the Treaty of Paris, the French *coureurs de bois* (rangers of the forest) continued their penetration into unknown parts of America.

The dream of a northwest passage continued to occupy French minds. At first it was hoped that the Father of the Waters, as the Indians called the Mississippi River, would provide the opening. When Father Marquette finally proved that the great river flows into the Gulf of Mexico and not into the western sea, the French turned to the western part of the United States, hoping that some stream would be found that would carry ships to the Pacific Ocean and then to India and all the Orient.

This desired route was considered so important that the King of France, in 1720, sent Father Charlevoix, a celebrated historian and geographer, to explore westward. Father Charlevoix recommended two plans. The first called for following the Missouri River to its headwaters. Eighty-three years later, this plan was adopted by the Americans, Lewis and Clark, who followed the Missouri, crossed the Rockies, and then discovered the Columbia River—which led them to the Pacific Ocean.

The second plan was to establish a series of forts and trading posts westward, until the ocean should be reached. It was this plan that was adopted, and the man who attempted to follow it was Pierre de la Verendrye, a native Canadian. Verendrye had been a fur trader in his youth. When war broke out in Europe, between France and Spain, he hurried to France, asked to serve in that nation's forces, and was commissioned an officer. During the war, he nearly died from wounds; but he recovered, returned to New France, and went back to the forest as a fur trader.

One day an Indian told him of a river that flowed west, out of a lake, into water in which there was a tide. Immediately Verendrye thought of the western passage to the Pacific. He returned to Quebec and obtained permission to explore, but was told that he must do it at his own expense. Following Father Charlevoix's plan, he began to establish a series of forts westward until, by 1738, he had six stretching to Lake Manitoba.

Verendrye continued to probe and explore, both in person and through parties sent out by him. His sons, Pierre and Francois, led one such party. All through the summer, autumn, and early winter, they toiled, examining every lead given by Indians. On New Year's Day, 1743, they became the first white men to see the Rocky Mountains from the east. They had reached the Big Horn Range, near the present Yellowstone Park. The mountains were too much for them to cross, and they turned back.

In 1782, Alexander Mackenzie, an agent of the Hudson's Bay Company, set out from the Athabasca area and finally crossed the continent, ca-

Hunting, trapping and trading was the way of life for those westerners who chose against farming the land.

An ambush by hostile Indians on these fur traders was not an uncommon experience for these men in the west.

noeing down the Fraser River to the present Vancouver. Twelve years later an equivalent journey was made in the United States by Lewis and Clark. The discovery of America, begun three centuries earlier by Columbus, had been completed.

The fur trade played an important role in the development of the United States. Detroit, Saint Louis, and Chicago are three cities that owe their beginnings to French Catholics and the fur trade. The fur companies built forts and trading posts, and it was around them that the cities and towns of America grew. For example, Pierre La-

The proud and sometimes savage Indian of the west.

The La Verendrye
brothers at the Rockies

131

LANCASTER 7 MI.

CHININGUE 328 MI.

Sighting in the Rifles

Bridger, one of the mountainmen

RANCH HOUSE—BOW RIVER

Mountain men, though mostly "loners", helped many of the settlers by being guides, trappers or soldiers.

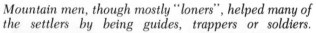

clede and Rene Chouteau built a fur-trading post in 1764 on the site that became Saint Louis. The Chouteaus were the first family of that city for many years.

The backbone of the fur trade was the French voyageur. Many a great fortune was amassed because of the labors of these men. John Jacob Astor, who became one of the wealthiest men in America, founded his fortune on the fur trade and the voyageurs. Those Frenchmen were a hardy and daring breed. They knew the interior of the United States better than any other white men. They had no equals when it came to understanding the Indian mentality and how to get along with the Indians; many of them married Indian women.

They dressed alike. A buckskin coat, sometimes trimmed in fur. Red or blue beret-like cap. A sash about the waist. A bright-colored beaded bag, sometimes thrown over a shoulder sometimes attached to the sash. For cold or rainy weather they wore a cape. A short clay pipe was always carried.

The voyageurs were short, stocky men, incredibly strong. They could paddle fifteen hours a day for weeks on end. A voyageur could portage up to 450 pounds on his back, travel through the forest with the silence and swiftness of an Indian. Voyageurs were happy fellows. They made up songs as they paddled canoes or sat around their campfires. They were full of practical jokes. Few voyageurs became rich. They were the middlemen between the Indians and the fur traders.

The Mountain Men

TO ENTERPRISING YOUNG MEN
The subscriber wishes to engage ONE HUN-
DRED MEN to ascend the river Missouri to
its source, there to be employed for one, two
or three years.
—William H. Ashley

THE above advertisement, which appeared in Saint Louis newspapers in 1822, marked a revolution in the fur trade. It also brought together one of the most daring and valiant groups of men this nation has ever seen: men such as Jim Bridger, Dick Wootten, Tom Fitzpatrick, Kit Carson, Jean Baptiste Gervais, William Sublette, and the incredible Jedediah Smith.

William Ashley and his partner, Major Andrew Henry, had a new idea. Instead of depending on Indians, who were fickle at best, to trap pelts and deliver them to the fur-trading centers, the partners decided to hire white men to go into the wilderness and trap systematically. The idea was immediately successful, even though its fulfillment entailed great hardships.

Not only were the "mountain men" (as they have since been called) obliged to undergo the rigors of weather and terrain, but they were constantly periled by marauding bands of Indians. In order to survive, the mountain men had to become as clever as the Indians. They lived off the land, mainly on buffalo meat, and yearly met at a predetermined rendezvous where they were to sell their furs. The mountains were their chosen homeland, and they had no desire to return to the amenities of civilization.

Yet, unknown to themselves, the mountain men were the vanguard of civilization. They explored and mapped much of the western region. They proved that barriers could be crossed. Jedediah Smith, for example, led a party across the searing Mojave Desert — to the disbelief of Mexican officials. William Sublette proved that wagons could cross the Rocky Mountains, and thus he opened the way for a stream of emigrants. The mountain men played an important role in the growth of the United States; and if many of their feats are now legendary, all Americans are still in their debt.

Along with the mountain men, went the private forts that were established far beyond the frontiers of our country. Those forts served as shelters against Indian uprisings, as places of rendezvous to which furs could be taken, and as trading posts for the Indians. Many of those forts gave rise to American cities.

Fort William was built by William Sublette, in Wyoming. It was a log stockade that contained living quarters, storehouses, and trading rooms. It developed into Laramie, Wyoming. Fort Pierre was built along the Missouri River in South Dakota, and was named after Pierre Chouteau, the Catholic fur trader of Saint Louis. It is now the State capital. One of the earliest forts was built by Manuel Lisa, a Spanish Catholic from New Orleans and a partner of Chouteau. Lisa built a fort on the Bighorn River; there he brought his wife, the first white woman to enter that country.

Manuel Lisa, who had been a sea captain, introduced the keelboat to the west. That boat did much to open up the country along the great rivers. Once Lisa gave a rival fur trader a nineteen-day head start from Saint Louis. By sailing his keelboat day and night, dragging it through turbulent waters, rowing when the wind failed, Lisa finally caught up to his rival after covering 1,200 miles in sixty-three days — a never-equalled record for keelboats.

The greatest fort between the Mississippi River and the Pacific Ocean was Bent's Fort, built on the Arkansas River in Colorado. It was an adobe structure with a front wall 137 feet long, fourteen feet high, and up to four feet in thickness. Its side walls were 178 feet long. Two eighteen-foot towers stood in opposite corners, equipped with small cannon. The fort had been built in 1833 by Charles and William Bent and their partner, Ceran St. Vrain, a French Catholic;

Wagon trains became an American legend but there was nothing glamorous about the long and difficult journeys

The Chiricahua Geronimo, legendary Indian outlaw

The victor over Custer was the Sioux, Sitting Bull.

that fort was the main American outpost astride the Spanish border. To its shelter went the famous mountain men: Kit Carson, Jim Bridger, Bill Williams, Dick Wootten, and many others. Americans, Canadians, Mexicans, and Indians met within its walls to sell or barter.

Behind the stout barricades was the main building, consisting of twenty-two bedrooms, a trading post, and many shops. The fort boasted an icehouse, and travelers leaving the wilderness could look forward to iced drinks and good food. The kitchen was presided over by a motherly Negro woman, affectionately known to all the mountain men as "Black Charlotte." Her stoves produced the only pies and biscuits to be found between Kansas and California. The fort boasted, also, the only billiard table west of Saint Louis. Bent's Fort was an island of civilization in an untamed and uncharted western wilderness.

With the arrival of American troops under General Kearney, and the predictable arrival of settlers who were sure to follow, Colonel William Bent realized that the west he loved was about to change. The Old West was dying, and the Wild West was being born. When the United States Government did not meet the price Colonel Bent placed on his fort, that doughty individualist

/S OF THE NATION
PAPER HISTORY OF THE UNITED STATES
DEMOCRACY FUNCTIONS
LOUISIANA PURCHASE
Copyright, 1943, by Sylvan Hoffman
OCTOBER 19, 1803   No. 10

LOUISIANA BOUGHT FOR 14½ MILLIONS

WASHINGTON, October 19, 1803—An extraordinary session of the Senate today officially accepted the purchase of the vast Louisiana Territory from France.

A three-point treaty which the Senate ratified by more than the necessary two-thirds majority sets forth the terms of the $14,500,000.00 real estate deal, whereby the United States assumes ownership of an uninhabited, unexplored, mostly unmapped land which doubles the size of the new nation.

So important to this country is Louisiana, however, that supporters of President Jefferson's accomplishment consider it the greatest single achievement in United States history.

Approximately 50,000 people are to become American citizens under terms of the treaty, which pledges this government to incorporate Louisiana into the Union.

No Boundaries

No boundaries are mentioned in the treaty and the only definite statement regarding territory is that the island of New Orleans, great Gulf Coast port, is included.

[An important section of the treaty also settles U. S. claims against France which nearly plunged the two countries into war several times during the past six or eight years.]

The United States is to retain about $3,250,000 of the purchase price to settle claims against France. Creditors who have claims growing out of French seizure of American ships and cargoes, losses caused by embargoes, or other "hostile acts" before September 30, 1800, are to be paid from this amount.

France Gets $11,000,000

The remaining $11,250,000 is to be paid to Napoleon's government in yearly installments beginning in 1818. This amount is to be put into interest-bearing stock and the 6 per cent interest is to be paid semi-annually beginning immediately.

Free entry into Louisiana ports is pledged for all French and Spanish ships for a period of twelve years. Prior to expiration of this treaty, all foreign agents other than Americans will be excluded.

French ratification of the treaty has already been announced by the ministers and the treaty details are expected to be ratified quickly on both sides.

BRINGING HOME THE BACON

PUBLIC NOTICE

We notify the public that tomorrow, the ninth of the present month, between the hours of 11 and 12, we will deliver Upper Louisiana to Captain Amos Stoddard, Agent and Commissioner of the French Republic, in accordance with our public announcement dated Nineteenth of February last. Saint Louis of the Illinois, March 8th, 1804.

Charles Dehault Delassus.

J. H. Hortis.

Published by the Public Notary.

Pierre Chouteau, a leader of early St. Louis

mined the massive structure with dynamite and, in one grand explosion, brought the end to the era of mountain men. There could be no more fitting salute!

The beaver trails were no more; man had taken his toll of the animals. The fur trade was coming to an end. The mountain men turned to other pursuits, some sedentary, others adventurous. Typical of those men was Uncle Dick Wootten—who, after he settled down, became a member of the Catholic parish in Trinidad, Colorado. Uncle Dick had been born in Virginia in 1816. The distant west held a lure for him, and he journeyed over the Santa Fe Trail and became a mountain man, trapping for Bent's Fort. He soon had more adventures than any dozen men might have in a lifetime. On one trapping trip of eighteen months, he had to carry an injured companion for two of those months. On another occasion, he rescued an Indian woman from dying in a snowdrift, and thus won the friendship of the Arapahoes. He had many encounters with Indians, won a fight against wolves, spent hours trapped in a tree by a grizzly bear.

After the destruction of Bent's Fort, Uncle Dick engaged in many businesses. He raised buf-

A map of the early town of St. Louis, through the work of men like Chouteau it became a leading trade center.

Liguest, the founder of St. Louis

William Bent, the trader and pioneer

Kit Carson, the legendary scout

falo to sell as meat. When he heard that sheep were selling at a high price in California, he drove nine thousand sheep to Sacramento. He ran freight over the Santa Fe Trail to Independence, Missouri. He formed a stagecoach line from New Mexico to Kansas. But his crowning achievement was building a twenty-seven-mile toll road over Raton Pass, on the border of Colorado and New Mexico. Before Uncle Dick built his road, there was only a steep and dangerous trail. On it wagon drivers had to use extra teams, and even then could only cover two miles a day. Uncle Dick's road ended all that trouble. The old man's foresight was justified also by the fact that later the Southern Pacific used the route he had pioneered.

Tom Fitzpatrick, a giant of an Irishman, who was partner of the Sublettes and Jean Baptiste Gervais, in the Rocky Mountain Fur Company, became a guide when the fur trade ended. He led the first California-bound wagon train through the Rockies. He led another emigrant wagon train to Oregon. The following year, with Kit Carson, he guided General John Fremont from Missouri to Oregon and then to California. In 1846, Fitzpatrick served as an Army scout for General Stephen Kearney in the march that won Santa Fe and New Mexico for the Union.

Finally, there was Kit Carson, a convert to Catholicism and one of the most romantic and legendary of the mountain men. Kit Carson always surprised people who met him for the first time. This was because of his small size. The things Carson did were big, and people expected to see a big man; instead they saw a short, bandy-legged, blue-eyed, sandy-haired individualist. The appearance was deceiving, for Kit was a veritable wildcat when he got into a fight. Kit was born on Christmas Day, 1809, in Kentucky and was christened "Christopher." He moved to Franklin, Missouri, where he was apprenticed to a saddler. The estimate of his worth there, and the kind of treatment he received, can be judged from this advertisement:

Notice Is Hereby Given To All Persons that Christopher Carson, a boy about 16 years old, small of age, but thick-set, light hair, ran away from the undersigned subscriber to whom he had been bound to learn the saddler's trade, on or about the first of September. He is supposed to have made his way to the upper part of the state. All persons are notified not to harbor, support, or assist said boy, under the penalty of the law. One cent reward will be given to any person who will bring back the said boy.

David Workman
Franklin, Oct. 6, 1826

139

What Kit had done was to join a wagon train heading west. He spent the winter in Taos, New Mexico, and then found employment as a horse herder on expeditions to Texas and Mexico. In 1830, Kit signed on with the Rocky Mountain Fur Company to trap in the northwest. His first trip kept him in the wilderness two years before he returned to Taos. On his next trip, he was with two partners, Joe Meek and Bill Mitchell, when they were attacked by a hundred Comanches. The mountain men cut the throats of their seven pack mules and arranged the carcasses in a circle. From behind that barricade, they held the Comanches off until dark. Then the Indians retreated, leaving behind forty-two dead. After their victory, Carson and his companions had to walk seventy-five miles to the nearest water.

Kit next signed on as a hunter for Bent's Fort, at thirty dollars a month. At the fort his Arapahoe wife died and left him with a daughter, Adelaide, whom he loved very dearly. Soon afterwards a niece of Ceran St. Vrain — Felicite St. Vrain — arrived to visit her uncle. She fell in love with Kit, but the wealthy and proud St. Vrains did not want her to marry a mountain man, and she was shipped off to a convent.

Kit was worried about his daughter in the wilderness, and he took her to Saint Louis and entered her in a boarding school. On that trip he met John Charles Fremont, who immediately took a liking to the small wiry young man. Fremont was an Army officer, mapping and exploring the western frontier. He offered Kit a job as guide and scout at a hundred dollars a month, which Kit promptly accepted. On his first assignment, he guided Fremont through the Rockies' South Pass. After Kit returned to Taos, he married a Mexican girl from a good family. It was because of that wife, Josefa, that he became a Catholic.

Almost immediately another call came from Fremont. Kit hurried off and, with his old friend, Tom Fitzpatrick, guided Fremont across the Great Salt Lake to Sutter's Fort in California. That was a particularly rugged journey, for the mountains were crossed in winter, and only the skill of the mountain men kept the party from disaster. Kit made many more expeditions with both Fremont and General Kearney, including two transcontinental trips to Washington. In between journeys he returned to his wife and family in Taos.

He had bought a farm and intended to settle down. But when the Civil War began, he joined the Union Army and was commissioned a brigadier general. He fought Apaches, Comanches, and Navajos. Nevertheless, he was a great friend and protector of the Indians. The Cheyennes named him "Little Chief."

In the late Sixties, Kit's wife died. Her death was a tragedy from which he never recovered. He died a few years later (1868, at the age of fifty-nine). He is buried in Taos. But the memory of his immeasurable contribution to the development of our country lives after him.

Kit Carson helped to obtain California and other Mexican territories for the United States. He opened trails over which the pioneer emigrants traveled. He made his fellow Americans aware of the tremendous possibilities and potential of the western region. In short, Kit Carson was a great American.

The gateway arch at the Old Cathedral of St. Louis

The Indians Suffer

ONE of the darkest pages in American history is the treatment of the Indian by the white man — an abuse that continues to our own day. Most Americans are aware of it generally but put it from their minds. The story of the People of Sorrows — the Cheyenne — has been told many times. There have been history books written about the exile of the Cheyenne to reservations selected by the white conqueror; fiction stories abound;

Henry Cross's "Red Cloud and Burning Heart."

the Sand Creek Massacre, the heroic but futile winter escape to their beloved Black Hills, and other incidents have been the stuff of which motion pictures have been made. But wherever the Cheyenne went Blackrobes were there to console them, to suffer with them, and to attempt to win them justice. First, there were Jesuits, then the Edmundites, and in more recent times the Capuchins.

Also told many times has been the story of the proud and gifted Navajos who originally roamed the southwest and to whom Spanish was a second language. They had been Christianized by the first Spanish missioners. They had a particular attachment to the land which they regarded as sacred and they resisted every attempt by the government to remove them to Oklahoma. Christ was first preached to this proud people by the Franciscans, and the sons of Saint Francis are still with them. Father Anselm Weber, O.F.M., who came from the Franciscans' Cincinnati Province, was the outstanding Navajo apostle of modern times. And while Father Anselm's work was a labor of the heart, Father Bernard Haile, O.F.M., performed an apostolate of the intellect to which the whole world is indebted; he was the first to make an alphabet for the Navajo, and his dictionary and anthropological works are the chief sources of knowledge about this complex people.

And what can be said about the Cheyenne and the Navajo can be multiplied many times with other tribes. If American civilization was the enemy to the Indians' nomadic ways, the Church was not. And when the encroachment of civilization forced back the red man, as often as not some unsung missioner accompanied him on his sad journey. Perhaps one lesser known incident will give an indication of the greater picture. It is one of the earliest recorded banishments of an Indian tribe.

The Potawatomi Indians were not a large number of people. They lived in present day Marshall County in Indiana, directly south of modern South Bend. In 1836 they were compelled to sign the Treaty of Yellow River which specified their removal to Kansas. Chief Menominee refused to recognize the treaty because he had been guaranteed lifetime occupancy of Potawatomi lands by an earlier treaty. The Indiana governor, David Wallace, ordered the Indiana militia to remove the Indians by force. The attack was made on a Sunday morning while the Indians, who had been converted to Catholicism, were at church. The militia surrounded the village and moved in after firing their muskets.

Serving the Indians at this time was a young priest, Father Benjamin Petit, who had been sent to the Potawatomi by Bishop Simon Bruté, from Vincennes. Father Petit was born in Rennes,

France (hometown of Bishop Bruté), in 1811. A pious and brilliant young man, he had studied law and was practicing that profession when Bishop Bruté came to Rennes to visit his birthplace and his relatives. The zealous bishop met young Petit, told him about his diocese, and captured the young lawyer's own zeal. Petit asked to join him in his work.

In 1836 Benjamin Petit arrived in the United States and made the difficult journey to Vincennes. He completed studies for the priesthood under Bishop Bruté, an old seminary professor, and was ordained October 14, 1827. In a letter to his mother he tells of his happiness: "I am now a

The last of the Sioux were killed in their tents after surrendering. This was the "Battle" of Wounded Knee.

143

priest, and the hand which is writing to you has this day borne Jesus Christ. . . . How my lips trembled this morning at my first Mass when, at the Momento, I recommended you all to God. . . . You recollect that I often said I was born happy. I can say the same still. I had always desired a mission among the savages; there is but one such in Indiana, and it is I whom the Pottawattomies call their father black robe."

Father Petit was with his Potawatomi when the militia came and it is his journal from which their "Trail of Death" can be reconstructed. After the militia entered the village, Chief Menominee came from the Mass and refused to bargain. When ordered to round up his people and leave, he drew his knife and stood his ground. A lasso whistled through the air, fell about him and was jerked; the chief was yanked to the ground. In a moment soldiers were upon him, tied him hand and foot, and threw him in the back of a wagon. The Indians were lined up and under American guns were forced to march from the village. Other soldiers set fire to the cornfields and the wigwams. Father Petit saw smoke curling from the roof of his chapel. He knew that it signaled the end of the village and no return for his people.

From a camp near Danville, Ill., Father Petit wrote a letter to Bishop Rosati, of St. Louis, through whose diocese the exiles would be passing. He said in part: "Last year Monseigneur Bruté sent me to the Pottawattomie Indians to replace M. De Seilles whose death left them orphans; that mission, in full vigor and growth, was about to be destroyed in Indiana by the policy of the government which seeks to unite all the Indians on the other side of the Mississippi. As a great many of these (are) very fervent and pious Christians . . . Monseigneur Bruté permitted me to accompany them to their new settlement so that I may reestablish their church and their mission; he has given me temporarily the faculties and jurisdiction which are necessary; today, I am asking Your Lordship to confirm these faculties. . . .

"I am not coming to establish a mission in the midst of the good Indians for myself, although I am attached to them with all the affection of my priestly heart (they are my first mission); I am coming solely to hold this mission together (so that these precious souls may not be lost). . . . Your Lordship knows so much better than I can tell you how important it is for subsequent development of the Indian missions not to let them disperse and perish by the abandonment of that Christianity fully developed which Providence sends today into the midst of the nearby Indians.

"Our trip is a harsh experience; we have much sickness; two of the Indians were buried today. Monseigneur, please pray to God to sustain us and to bless the Christian resignation of these good Indians deprived by force of their fatherland and of all their notions of blessing, the Faith excepted. . . . The emigration will cross the Mississippi at Quincy and our destination is the Osage River."

From Illinois Father Petit reported that "almost all the babies, exhausted by the heat, are dead or dying." Again he describes how the Indians dropped by the dozens on the wayside to die. He writes of one halt to consider whether or not to kill a dying one hundred-year-old squaw; it was finally decided to "let her die a natural death." After several months of this agony, the Indians arrived in Kansas Territory. Out of 859 Indians who started the trek, over 150 died en route. In summing up the incident, Edward A. Leary, writing in The Indianapolis Star, said: "It was not a proud record, less proud when one considers that the white man had made promises he had not kept, and to a good and Christian Friend. Chief Menominee's people had been one of the few tribes who had not sided with the British in the War of 1812."

Young Father Petit himself took sick on the journey. He made his way back to St. Louis for help but died there February 10, 1839. His remains were later brought to Notre Dame by Father Sorin, the university's founder. Father Petit had been a priest and missioner for sixteen months.

The Alamo: The Mission That Is a Monument

IN the pages of American history, few names evoke a greater pride in patriotism than that of The Alamo, for in this historic structure the dedication of pioneers was made visible to the entire world. Here died such popular American heroes as David Crockett, Jim Bowie, James Bonham, and Colonel W. B. Travis. But a share in the glory of The Alamo belongs to Catholic heroes, too: Charles Despallier, a Cajun from Louisiana; the Irishmen, Andrew Duvalt and John Gavin; and the brave band of Mexicans under Captain Juan Seguin, who chose to fight with the Americans for Texas independence.

The Alamo compound was originally the Franciscan mission of San Antonio de Valero, established in 1718. The early buildings were of wood and crudely constructed. Franciscans and their Indian converts cleared the land and started to build. In 1744 the cornerstone of the church was set in place. By 1761, the mission was completed, consisting of church, monastery, workshops, store rooms, and houses for Indians. Any visitor to The Alamo today finds it hard to visualize the mission in its original state, for the modern city of San Antonio has grown up about it. However, San Jose Mission, a few miles away, can be visited. That mission, still in use, is impressive in size. It was built about the same time as The Alamo. Its tremendous granary gives an idea of the large number of people the mission once supported within its thick walls.

In 1793, the San Antonio Mission was secu-

The Mission San Antonio de Valero, known as the Alamo, as it stands today in the center of San Antonio, Texas.

larized, the same fate as befell San Jose Mission, as recorded earlier. While San Jose tried to continue offering spiritual ministration, it was decided to close San Antonio because there were too few Indians left in the vicinity, and hence no workers to till the fields and tend the herds. The mission was turned over to civil authorities; land and tools were divided among the remaining Indians; and some of the livestock was sent to other missions. The missioners returned to headquarters in Mexico for reassignment.

Ten years after the mission was closed, a company of Mexican soldiers was sent to San Antiono to take up garrison duty at the mission. Those soldiers were from the pueblo of Santiago del Alamo, and the mission-outpost became known

simply as "Alamo." Few repairs were made to the compound until 1835, when the Mexican General Cos strengthened it as a fort against rebel Texans. Later that same year, the Texan Army stormed San Antonio, drove General Cos back to Mexico, and left a small garrison to occupy the area. Those Texans were strengthened by Captain Seguin and his company of young Mexicans, also Crockett and his seventeen followers from Tennessee, and a unit organized by Colonel Travis.

On February 23, 1836, advance troops of Mexican General Antonio de Santa Ana's army reached the outskirts of San Antonio. Colonel Travis, senior officer for the Texans, moved the garrison into the old mission building. Earthen embankments were built, and cannon mounted on

The historic defense of the Alamo, Travis and the volunteers fought to the last man in the legendary battle.
SAN ANTONIO CHAMBER OF COMMERCE

the walls. Travis expected that reinforcements would come to his assistance. Although General Santa Ana flew a blood-red banner of "No Quarter" from the tower of the cathedral, the spirit of the Texans was high. Crockett, particularly, kept up the jovial mood with his tall stories and his fiddle.

But as the days dragged past, the weary defenders began to realize that no help would come. Rain and mud prevented the movement of supply wagons. Colonel Travis called his men together and told them that he intended to fight to the last. He added that any man who wished to try to escape could do so, and that as commander he would be comforted by those who chose to stay and die with him. Only one man went over the wall and deserted his comrades; the rest surged about their heroic leader.

Shortly after midnight on March 7, the final attack began. Companies of Mexicans with scaling ladders swarmed over the walls. Santa Ana circled his cavalry around The Alamo to prevent any Texan from escaping. But none tried. The 180 defenders fought where they stood. When their ammunition ran out, they used their guns as clubs, and each defender was surrounded by Mexican dead. When dawn came the battle was over and not a defender remained alive. Santa Ana came into the fortification with the Alcalde (mayor) Ruiz to identify the corpses of the leaders. The body of Col. Travis was sprawled across a cannon; Crockett was slumped in the doorway of the church; Bonham was found dead by his cannon; Bowie, who had come down with typhoid-pneumonia, had been murdered on his cot. The haughty Santa Ana, in one last petty act, ordered the bodies of the defenders to be burned. Thus their ashes were mingled with the ruins and soil of The Alamo.

Today The Alamo is owned by the people of the State of Texas and is cared for by a group of patriotic women. Each year thousands of Americans from every part of our country visit this historic shrine. The Alamo is a sacred spot where Catholics and Protestants and men of no religious belief stood together against tyranny and where death made brothers of them all.

Many Mexican volunteers fought and died with the Texans at the heroic battle of the Alamo.

The Priest Who Went To Congress

When Joseph Pleiss, Bishop of Quebec, visited Detroit in 1816, he was completely enchanted by a tall, gaunt, balding priest who, the bishop confided in his journal, "has the talent of doing, almost simultaneously, ten entirely different things." Father John Tracy Ellis, the distinguished historian, says of this priest that "his life was identified with practically every important event in Michigan." Malcolm Bingay, the Detroit editor, referred to the priest as "the soul of the city."

The man on whom so many encomiums have been lavished was Father Gabriel Richard, a Sulpician priest who had been driven from France by the French Revolution. After working for a time in Illinois, Father Richard answered the call of the French population about Detroit, and arrived there in June, 1798. He was soon the center of life in that growing city, adapting himself completely to American ways.

Father Richard became so American that, when the British occupied Detroit during the War of 1812, he refused to take the oath of allegiance to the British crown, which all Detroiters were required to swear.

"I have taken an oath to support the Constitution of the United States," the French exile told the British authorities. "I cannot take another."

He denounced the British from his pulpit and begged all Detroiters to stand firm against the enemy. That the British feared him is shown by the fact that he was arrested, deported to Windsor, Canada, and put under house arrest.

As the only Catholic priest in the Detroit area, Father Richard had enough spiritual work to keep an ordinary man busy day and night. Yet without neglecting the spiritual care of whites and Indians, he somehow managed to find time to engage in a host of extracurricular activities. He founded the University of Michigan and persuaded his friend, Doctor John Montieth, a Presbyterian minister, to become the first president, while he himself served as secretary. Being a wise man, Father Richard knew that the university would best succeed with a cultured American as its head. Doctor Montieth, a graduate of Princeton and a schol-

arly man, fitted the need perfectly. The two men divided the thirteen classes between them.

Before Doctor Montieth arrived in Detroit, in 1816, there was no Protestant minister. Father Richard gathered the Protestants every Sunday afternoon and preached to them. The story is told that when Doctor Montieth arrived at Detroit, Father Richard was on the shore of the Detroit River to meet him. The priest embraced the minister and turned over one of his school buildings to him. The two men became close friends and co-operators.

Father Richard had been a professor in France, and he brought a passion for education with him to the New World. He used to gather all the news he could, write it up, and then send his sacristan about town, as a sort of town crier, to inform the people. In 1809, he imported the first printing press to come west of the Alleghenies; and he founded Michigan's first paper, the *Michigan Essay and Impartial Observer*. His press turned out schoolbooks and catechisms. He began elementary schools, a manual-training school for farmers, and a normal school for training teachers. Well might he be called the father of Michigan education. He also organized the first circulating library, town-hall meetings, and lectures.

Father Richard had a deep and abiding civic sense. In 1805, a terrible fire practically wiped out Detroit. The people thought of giving up and leaving the area. Father Richard designed a seal for the city, putting on it the words that are still the Detroit motto: "*Speramus Meliora; Resurget Cineribus*" ("We hope for better; it shall arise from the ashes"). Because the people of Detroit were destitute and starving as a result of the fire, Father Richard organized the French rivermen into a relief battalion, and they were soon bringing canoes loaded with food from surrounding farms. He rationed the supplies according to each family's need. The Indians, who loved Father Richard, also helped, bringing supplies from their own camps.

When Michigan was organized as a territory, Father Richard was appointed to represent the area in Congress. Thus he became the first priest ever to sit in our national legislature. His main accomplishment in Congress was to get that body to approve building a road between Detroit and Chicago. The road was named "Michigan," and as Michigan Boulevard in Chicago it still exists.

Early in September, 1832, the steamer *Henry Clay* docked at Detroit. On board were 370 soldiers, on their way to fight in the Black Hawk War. On board also was an unseen enemy—Asiatic cholera. The disease swept the city, and in a few days hundreds of the inhabitants were dying. Panic gripped the people, and many of them fled. Father Richard once more rose to the occasion. He worked almost without sleep, taking care of the sick, administering the Last Rites, holding funeral services.

On the morning of September 13, Father Richard was kneeling on a Detroit street, comforting a dying man. Suddenly he collapsed across the man he was aiding. He died in a few hours. The people of Detroit have named a park after him and put in it an heroic statute of this extraordinary priest. His greater monument, however, is the city he helped build and save, and also the great state that has grown up around it.

Bishop Baraga was the first of the American bishops to issue his pastoral letters in English and Indian. He wrote and studied in depth on the Indian dialect.

FATHER GABRIEL RICHARD
1767 - 1832
PIONEER PRIEST-PATRIOT-FOUNDER
OF CHURCHES AND SCHOOLS-CO-
FOUNDER OF THE UNIVERSITY OF
MICHIGAN-MEMBER OF CONGRESS-
PRINTER-MARTYR OF CHARITY-PRO-
PHET AND APOSTLE OF CHRISTIAN
CIVILIZATION-HE SERVED GOD
AND COUNTRY ON THE
MICHIGAN FRONTIER

150

The Best Friend the Indians Ever Had

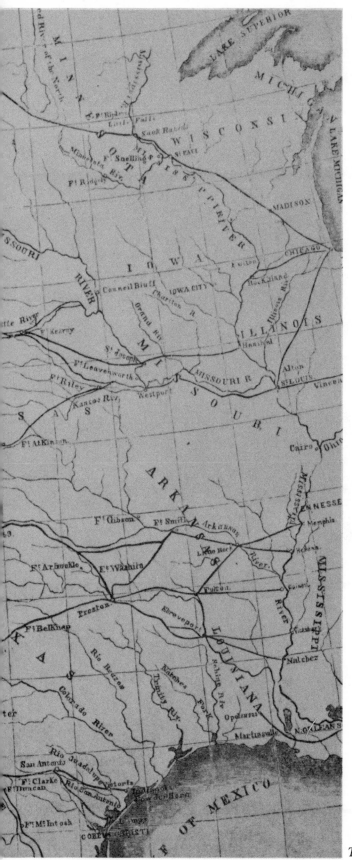

IN 1884, Senator George Vest arose on the floor of Congress to speak on the Indian problem. "Nowhere in the United States have such satisfactory results been obtained as in the Jesuit missions," the senator declared. "I defy any one to find me a single tribe of Indians on the plains — blanket Indians — that approximate in civilization to the Flatheads, who have been under the control of the Jesuits for fifty years. I say that out of eleven tribes that I saw — and I say this as a Protestant — where they had Protestant missionaries, they had not made a single solitary advance towards civilization — not one; yet among the Flatheads, where there were two Jesuit missions, you find farms, you find civilization, you find Christianity, you find the relation of husband and wife and of father and child scrupulously observed."

The man who made such a tribute possible, more than any other, was Father Peter De Smet, the greatest missioner to the Indians the United States has known. Father De Smet not only was respected by the Indians but also was loved by them. He could go into any Indian camp and receive a warm welcome reserved only for a trusted friend. His efforts on behalf of the Indians were untiring, and he himself figured that he had traveled 260,929 miles by foot, horseback and boat in their cause.

Father De Smet was born in Belgium, in 1801. As a boy his imagination was caught by Napoleon's Grand Army. He was inclined to a military career, but later decided to enter the preparatory seminary at Mechlin. It was there that Father Charles Nerinckx, the famous missioner to Kentucky, came seeking recruits for the American missions. Father Nerinckx spoke to the seminarians, and two applied to go to America with him. One of them was Peter De Smet.

The Western plains of the United States in the 1880's

151

Father Peter De Smet

Peter left Belgium without saying good-by to his parents, because as he afterwards said: "To have asked consent of our parents, would have been to court a certain and absolute refusal!" Father Nerinckx escorted his recruits to Baltimore, left them there, and went on to Kentucky. The recruits entered the Jesuit novitiate in Maryland. Shortly afterwards, a request to begin a Jesuit foundation in Missouri was made, and the Jesuit superiors decided to open a novitiate and seminary for the express purpose of training missioners for the Indians. De Smet, of course, volunteered. It was in Missouri that he was finally ordained, on September 23, 1827.

There is one interesting sidelight on the development of the West. When De Smet arrived in Saint Louis, the town had 4,000 people and one church. He noted this fact in a letter to a friend in Belgium, written in 1872. Then he added, "Today its population numbers 450,000, and next Sunday the bishop will bless the thirty-sixth church."

Father De Smet did not begin his Indian work at once. He was assigned to other tasks, including one trip to Europe to raise funds. But late in the

"Buffalo" Bill Cody

Captain Throckmorton's historic steamer which carried Father De Smet along the Missouri River many times.

summer of 1839, a delegation of Flathead Indians arrived in Saint Louis, on their fourth attempt to secure a Catholic priest to live among them and teach them. Father De Smet was struck by their zeal and faith, and he begged his superior for permission to go to the Flatheads. The permission was granted; and in March of 1840, Father De Smet left on his first trip to the Rocky Mountains.

From that day on, the Jesuit was to work solely for the Indians and their welfare. He became the foremost American authority on American Indians, and his letters and diaries and maps are of tremendous value to historians. He knew the rivers and trails of the West as no other white man knew them. He was a friend of the famous men of his time—Doctor John McLoughlin, Jim Bridger, Tom Fitzpatrick, and Major Culbertson, to mention but a few. He was the first priest most of the Indian tribes ever saw, and his baptisms were counted in thousands. He administered the earliest-known baptisms among the Crows, Cheyennes, Arapahoes, and Assiniboins. He was welcomed at Indian councils and used the opportunities to make conversions. At the 1851 council, held near Fort Laramie, Wyoming, he baptized 1,586 Indians.

Father De Smet's work brought him national attention. In 1852, Senator Benton declared that Father De Smet could do "more for the Indians' welfare and keeping them in peace and friendship with the United States than an army with banners." The Secretary of War asked the Jesuit to accompany General Harney on the Utah expedition, and later to assist the general to put down Indian revolts in the Northwest. In that latter region, the friendly relations that were established between Indians and whites were entirely due to Father De Smet. But his crowning achievement as an official peacemaker was won among the warlike Sioux.

Alone, in 1868, he penetrated the Sioux stronghold on the Powder River. Open warfare existed between the Sioux and the United States; and the Sioux, under Chief Sitting Bull, were adamant in their desire to continue the war. They refused to disarm, or even to talk with the American peace commissioners. Father De Smet was asked to intervene. He was then sixty-eight years old and in poor health, but that intrepid missioner forgot his own personal discomforts and set out on the long journey from Saint Louis.

For thirty-three days, Father De Smet traveled up the Missouri River. Then he crossed the Bad Lands and moved into the valley of the Yellowstone — a journey of sixteen more days. Finally he reached the camp of the hostiles, where he was met by scouts from the camp.

"Blackrobe," the scout leader told him, "entrance to our camp is given to you alone. No other white man could come out of it with his scalp!"

Father De Smet was taken to Sitting Bull, who had prepared for the Jesuit a large lodge in the middle of the camp. Exhausted by his journey, Father De Smet asked if he might take a nap. Without any worry or fear, he lay down and slept soundly, despite the fact that he was in the midst of thousands of Indians who had sworn to kill all white men. When he awoke, Sitting Bull was standing before him.

"Blackrobe," declared the famed chief, "I am hardly able to stand because of the weight of the white men's blood I have shed! The whites provoked the war—their injustices, their indignities to our families. I have done all the hurt to the whites that I could! Today you are among us; and in your presence, my hands fall to the ground as if dead. I will listen to your good words; and as bad as I have been to the whites, just so good am I ready to become towards them!"

Father De Smet asked Chief Sitting Bull to call a council at which the Jesuit might speak to the Indians. The chief agreed, and a four-hour meeting followed. It ended with the Indians promising to enter peace negotiations. They agreed to send a delegation back with Father De Smet, to meet with the peace commissioners. When Father De Smet returned to his lodge after the council, he found it crowded with Indian mothers who wanted him to bless their children. His mission had been a complete success.

Father De Smet died in Saint Louis, on May 23, 1873. The Missouri Republican reported: "In him the world loses one of the most intrepid pioneers of Christian civilization." Father De Smet had not tried to be a history maker; he wished to be solely a missioner who loved the Indians. As one of his biographers has written: "Although he was powerless to prevent the extermination of the Western tribes in the United States, he procured for the Indians in the bosom of the Catholic Church the assurance of a better life and a kingdom that could not be taken from them through the injustice of men."

OVERLAND TO THE PACIFIC.

The San Antonio and San Diego Mail-Line.

THIS Line, which has been in successful operation since July, 1857, is ticketing PASSENGERS through to San Diego and San Francisco, and also to all intermediate stations. Passengers and Express matter forwarded in NEW COACHES, drawn by six mules, over the entire length of our Line, excepting the Colorado Desert of one hundred miles, which we cross on mule-back. Passengers GUARANTEED in their tickets to ride in Coaches, excepting the one hundred miles above stated.

Passengers ticketed through, from NEW-ORLEANS, to the following points, via SAN ANTONIO:

To Fort Clark,.........Fare, $52.	To Fort Bliss,.........Fare, $100.	
" Hudson,........ " 60.	" La Mesilla,........ " 105.	
" Port Lancaster, " 70.	" Fort Fillmore,..... " 105.	
" Davis,........... " 90.	" Tucson,........... " 135.	
" Quitman,........ " 100.	" Fort Yuma,........ " 162.	
" Birchville,...... " 100.	" San Diego,....... " 190.	
" San Elizario.... " 100.	" Los Angelos, ... " 190.	
" El Paso,......... " 100.	" San Francisco,..... " 200.	

The Coaches of our Line leave semi-monthly from each end, on the 9th and 24th of each month, at 6 o'clock A.M.

An armed escort travels through the Indian country with each mail train, for the protection of the mails and passengers.

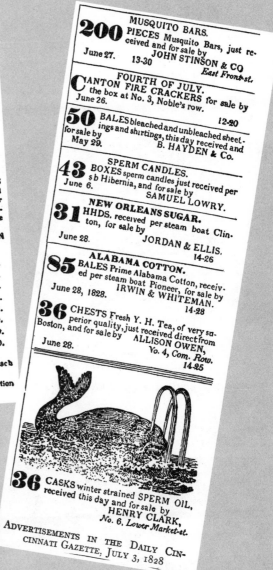

ADVERTISEMENTS.
A Servant Boys Time for 4 Years to be difpofed of. He is about 16 Years of Age, and can keep Accompts, Enquire at the Blue Ball in Union Street, and know further.

RUN away the 27th of *Auguſt* laſt, from *James Anderſon* Miniſter of the Goſpel in *Dongal*, in the County of *Lancaſter* in *Penſilvania*, a Servant Man named *Hugh Wier*, aged about 30 Years of a middle Stature and freſh Complexion, ſandy Beard, and ſhort dark brown Hair, he went off very bear in Cloathing, and is ſuppoſed to have got himſelf dreſs'd in *Indian Habit*, (He having been uſed among *Indians*, when he run away from other Maſters before) He is by Trade a Flax-dreſſer, Spinſter and Woolcomber, and it is ſuppoſed he can Weave; He alſo does moſt ſort of Women Work, ſuch as waſhing of Cloaths or Diſhes, milking of Cows, and other Kitchen Work, and uſually changes his Name, Whoever takes up ſaid Servant and ſecures him either in this or any of the neighbouring Provinces and let his Maſter know of it, by Poſt or otherways, ſo as his ſaid Maſter may have him again, ſhall have *Three Pounds* as a Reward, and all reaſonable Charges paid by me,   *James Anderſon*

RUN away from his *Maſter* Philip Caverly, of Colcheſter, in Connecticut, in New-England, on *the 24th of* *April* laſt, a *Negro Man* named Japhet, aged about 21 Years, of a tall Stature, ſpeaks good Engliſh, and pretends to be free; has the Toes of one Foot froze off, and part of the other; had on when he went away, a great Coat of a brown Colour, a cloſe bodied Coat of the ſame Colour, Tow-cloth Breeches, and grey Stockings. Whoever takes up ſaid Runaway, and conveys him to his Maſter ſhall have Twenty Pounds Reward, Old Tenor, and all reaſonable Charges, paid by
Philip Caverly.

ADVERTISEMENT IN THE WEEKLY NEW YORK POST-BOY, DECEMBER 22, 1746

Westerners spent most of their lives on horseback.

An old Western mission still greets worshipers today.

The contributions of Catholics to the expansion of American civilization in its march westward have never been fully described. Much has been written about individual Catholics, but the total picture is difficult to assay. This is because in many instances the pioneers were also missioners, whose primary role was the development of the Church; yet in filling that role, they also established respect for law and order, and other foundations of civilization. Those pioneers were men like Bishop Benedict Flaget, the apostle of Kentucky; Blessed John Neumann, the Redemptorist missioner, who later became Bishop of Philadelphia and developed that diocese tremendously; Father Edward Sorin, an apostolic missioner in Indiana and Michigan, and founder of Notre Dame University; Bishop Francis Blanchet, the developer of the Church in the Northwest; and Archbishop John Lamy, who has been nominated for National Statuary Hall by the State of New Mexico, and who was the inspiration of Willa Cather's famous book, *Death Comes to the Archbishop.*

There is, also, a long list of Catholic converts, who in their lifetimes made important contributions to American development. Those converts included Colonel William F. Cody (Buffalo Bill), who served as Pony Express rider, Army scout, and provider of food for the construction crew of a continental railroad, and who became legendary to Americans while still alive; Stephen A. Douglas, an American statesman who represented Illinois in both branches of Congress, who authored the Kansas-Nebraska Bill, and who is best remembered for his debates with Abraham Lincoln; Thomas Ewing, senator from Ohio, who later became Secretary of the Treasury and Secretary of the Interior. Some of those converts will be treated in another section of this book.

Two who were born of Catholic families and who made inestimable contributions were James Shields and John McLoughlin. Both men have been selected by their States for inclusion in our Capitol's National Statuary Hall. James Shields was born in Tyrone, Ireland, in 1806. He came to the United States as a young man and settled in Illinois. He fought in the Black Hawk War; he was a general in the Mexican War. He led the famous charge of the New York Irish and South Carolina volunteers in the Battle of Churubusco, a painting of which now hangs in our National Capitol. He was also a general in the Civil War.

In the political field, Shields has a record difficult for any man to match. He was at various

Thomas Ewing

Stephen Douglas

Blessed John Neumann of Philadelphia

The cathedral of the Cincinnati, Ohio, diocese

Chicago, Ill., in 1820

times senator from Illinois, Minnesota, and Missouri. He was also governor of the Oregon Territory. He finally died in Iowa, in 1879. Although he was connected with many States, it was Illinois that placed him in Statuary Hall.

John McLoughlin is recognized as the founder of Oregon, because he was instrumental in getting United States settlers for the Oregon Territory and then in making it part of the Union. McLoughlin was truly an heroic figure of the American frontier. Born in Canada in 1784, he came from a devout Catholic family, and he had a sister who became Mother Superior of the Canadian Ursulines. Most Catholic writers who report on McLoughlin state that, although he was baptized a Catholic, he was brought up a Protestant and did not return to the Church until late in life. This story is a complete falsehood.

The false story has its only foundation in a paragraph of Archbishop Blanchet's *Historical Sketches*, in which the archbishop told of McLoughlin's conversion, his profession of Faith in 1842, and the blessing of his marriage. But on page 139 of the same book, Archbishop Blanchet retracts his earlier statements, saying that, since the first pages had gone to press, he had received positive information that McLoughlin was a Catholic all his life. Moreover, there is supplementary evidence from a number of Protestant missionaries, who were in Oregon long before Archbishop Blanchet and who, in existing letters, stated that John McLoughlin was a Catholic. The real fact of the matter was that McLoughlin was in the wilderness for forty years, before the Church caught up with him and enabled him to receive the sacraments again.

Archbishop Lamy, Santa Fe Archbishop (1875-1885)   *John McLoughlin, the founder of the Oregon territory*

John McLoughlin was educated to be a doctor, but he spent little time in the practice of medicine. He joined the Northwest Company, a fur-trading outfit largely controlled by John Jacob Astor, and a competitor of Hudson's Bay Company. He first worked at Fort William, an outpost on Lake Superior. There was bitter rivalry between the Northwest and Hudson's Bay Companies. When their trappers met in the wilderness, a fight was certain to break out. Oftentimes trappers from one or other company failed to return to their home base; but although while foul play was suspected, it could never be proved. McLoughlin was sent to London to work out a solution, and the two companies were merged into an enlarged Hudson's Bay Company.

When McLoughlin returned to Canada, he was assigned to Oregon, where he built a trading post on the Columbia River. It was called Fort Vancouver, and it became the capital of a tremendous "kingdom" that included Washington, Oregon, California, Idaho, Nevada, Utah, Colorado, Wyoming, part of Montana, and a stretch through Canada to the Yukon. In that vast region, John McLoughlin was the sole authority, and he developed the trading post into the most valuable of the Hudson Bay holdings. His yearly gathering of furs was worth up to one million dollars — an enormous sum in those days.

McLoughlin's foresight was evident in the farm he developed near the fort. He stocked it with cattle, horses, sheep, goats, and hogs. He set out apple, pear and quince orchards. The farm produced annually the following bushels; wheat, 8,000; barley, 5,500; oats, 6,000; peas, 9,000; potatoes, 14,000. He also established two sawmills

159

and two flour mills. He shipped flour to Alaska, and boards to the Hawaiian Islands, opening up new trade for his company. McLoughlin also brought many French-Canadian settlers into the region.

Fort Vancouver became an important outpost, the only civilization in miles and miles of wilderness. To the fort went many great men of that day: Kit Carson, John Fremont, Father De Smet, Father Blanchet. The fort was also a beacon for American emigrants who fought their way over the Oregon Trail to find new life on a new frontier. The first wave of the prospective settlers arrived in 1841; they were 125 strong. In 1843, a big party of 875 men, women, and children made the journey from Independence, Missouri. The wagon master of that expedition was Peter Burnett, who later became first governor of California, and who wrote a book called *The Path that Led a Protestant Lawyer to the Catholic Religion.* After six months of agony, that party reached Fort Vancouver. The members were in a starving and pitiful condition, and McLoughlin welcomed and fed them. He also gave them seed and implements for farming, and even money — much of which was never repaid. In 1844, a party of 1,400 settlers arrived; and in 1845, a party of 3,000. Each of those parties received similar help from McLoughlin.

McLoughlin's aid to the settlers caused trouble for him with his company. The territory was in dispute between the United States and Canada, and for a time it seemed certain that war would break out over the boundary. McLoughlin was denounced as being sympathetic to the invading Americans; and he was forbidden to give any assistance to future immigrants, no matter how desperate their plight. His conscience would not permit him to ignore suffering, and he resigned from the Hudson's Bay Company.

Anticipating the annexation of Oregon by the United States, McLoughlin staked out a claim of land, which was to develop into Oregon City. But the Methodist Mission Society contested the same land. The group denounced McLoughlin as a British subject, and sent a delegation to Washington to further its charge. McLoughlin wrote a spirited defense, stating that he had been condemned by the British because he had saved American men and women from starvation and helped them to settle on farms; now he was being condemned by Americans on the accusation that he tried to prevent their settlement of Oregon.

"I did all I could to promote its settlement!" McLoughlin declared. "I could not have done more for the settlers if they had been my brothers and sisters, knowing as I did that any disturbance between us might lead to war between Great Britain and the United States. This is a treatment that I do not deserve and do not expect!"

But opposition won the day. The missionaries, mostly with New England connections, managed to have considerable pressure put on various congressmen. The final ruling was against McLoughlin. The Donation Law was passed, depriving him of his claim. Nevertheless, he took the oath of allegiance and became a citizen of the United States.

McLoughlin began to fail in health. He died at Oregon City, September 3, 1857. Five years after his death, he was vindicated. The Donation Law was repealed, and his heirs gained his property. Thirty years after his death, his portrait was hung over the speaker's desk in the Oregon senate, with the inscription under it, "Founder of Oregon." In 1953, the State of Oregon placed his statue in National Statuary Hall. Time has placed the great American, John McLoughlin, in true perspective.

Bustling communities grew from the various trade outposts. These grew up rapidly throughout the west.

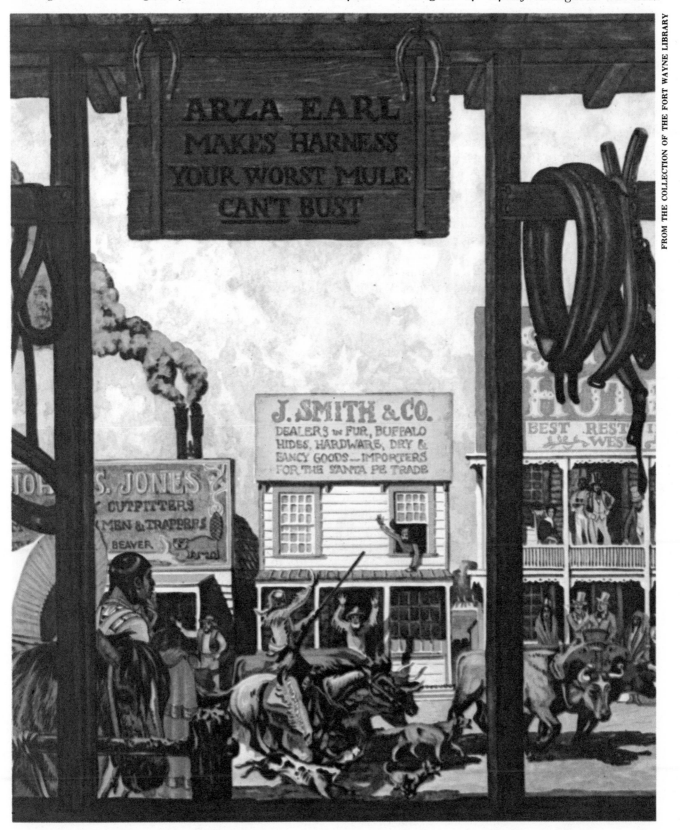

Women Also Were Pioneers

IN the history of the American West, little attention is given to the role played by pioneer women, yet those wives and mothers were the stabilizing influence on the adventurous spirit of the men. It was the woman who made the pioneer home, who insisted on education for her children, and who argued for law and order. Those pioneer women were an heroic breed, equally ready to get behind a plow or a gun. Often they were the only defenders of their homes against Indian attacks. Wagon-train journeys may make interesting television fare, but an actual journey was tortuous for the brave people who made it. Baked by the prairie sun, coated with layers of dust raised by hooves and wheels, frozen by unrelieved cold, wearied by back-breaking work of helping to get the wagons over rough terrain, the pioneer women had to be as mighty as the plains, mountains, and rivers they crossed. Only the hardy survived; for the others, there were lonely graves at the sides of the trail.

In the vanguard of the pioneers were the Catholic religious Sisters. They, too, possessed indomitable spirits. They went West, not for riches, not for escape, not for a chance to start over again, but to save souls — Indian and white souls. And for this, they were ready to face any danger. Not unusual is the story of one wagon train that rolled out of Leavenworth, Kansas, one fine June day in 1867. That train of a hundred wagons was organized by the saintly Bishop Lamy, of Sante Fe, New Mexico. He was taking supplies and recruits to his diocese, and among his passengers were five Sisters.

The wagon train moved along steadily. By July it was deep inside the prairie, in the heart of Kiowa country. Suddenly the bishop gave an order for the wagons to circle. This was hardly done when a large party of Kiowas attacked. The battle went on until sunset. Then the Indians withdrew; but at dawn their war whoops were heard again, and once more the battle was joined. Suddenly, among the defenders, word spread that cholera had broken out in camp. One of the Sisters

collapsed, and died almost immediately from the disease. Then a young man was stricken. While arrows showered about her, one of the Sisters crawled under wagons to reach and comfort the dying man. For the rest of the day, the fight continued, with the Indians making repeated attacks and the Sisters nursing the sick. Every one of the defenders suffered terribly from thirst.

Bishop Lamy knew that the caravan could not hold out another day, so a desperate ruse was decided upon. Several of the teamsters risked their lives to transport some provisions and a keg of whiskey out onto the prairie. They got back safely, before the Indians found the supplies and broke open the barrel of whiskey. Then an order was given, as the sun went down, to light campfires as if the evening meal were to be prepared. By that time the Indians were dropping off to sleep from the whiskey. Under cover of darkness, the teams were hitched; and with the fires burning as if all were normal, the caravan stole away. Two months and one day after the train had rolled out of Leavenworth, the safety of Santa Fe was reached.

Another of those pioneering women was Sister Blandina Segale, a most extraordinary and enterprising Sister of Charity, who labored for many years in Colorado and New Mexico. She was born in Italy, in 1850; came to the United States with her parents when she was still a child; and joined the Cincinnati Sisters of Charity when she was a young girl. In 1872, Sister Blandina was assigned to Trinidad, Colorado. (She thought she was going to an island of the same name in the Caribbean. It was the only Trinidad she could find in her atlas.) At that time Trinidad was one of the wickedest cities in the West, a rendezvous for outlaws and other bad men. The Sister's contribution was to start the first public school there, then a private academy and a hospital. Later she moved on to Albuquerque and Santa Fe.

Sister Blandina's experiences during her twenty-one years in the West were fantastic. She was protected by Billy the Kid after she treated

Billy the Kid was known by Sr. Blandina.

buried the dead. Later in Albuquerque, she outmaneuvered the town's politicians to advance her school and hospital.

Sister Blandina's secret was her solid belief in the goodness of God. It was her faith that made no labor too difficult and no sacrifice impossible. Pioneering was merely part of the day's work; hardships were the expected routine. Sister Blandina typifies all the Catholic Sisters who advanced to the American frontier. Not all had her spectacular energy, but all had her faith and courage. Those Sisters, many of whose names have been lost to history, played an important and deliberate role in the building of a new country, and to them America must always be indebted.

one of his band who had been shot, and whom no one else would help. When Billy entered Trinidad to kill the town's doctors because they had refused to aid his companion, Sister Blandina faced the outlaw and talked him out of the murders. On another occasion, when a man was to be lynched after a shooting, Sister Blandina took the threatened shooter to the bedside of his dying victim, persuaded the shooter to seek forgiveness for the shooting, and then talked the wounded victim into granting forgiveness. There was no lynching. Once when some Apaches, angered at the unprovoked and cruel murder of one of their people by the whites, were about to go on the warpath, Sister Blandina, alone and with crucifix held aloft, went out and talked the Indians out of their proposed war.

Sister Blandina did not know the meaning of the word "failure." Once she decided on a project, it was as good as done, even if she had to do it herself. In Trinidad she shamed townspeople to come to her aid in building a decent schoolhouse to replace the dilapidated adobe structure that was there when she arrived. Lacking funds, and at first not receiving offers of help, she took a crowbar and began tearing down the old building. Trinidad's women could not bear to see her doing that work, and so they found assistants for her. In Santa Fe she begged money from miners and railroad workers to build a three-story hospital; and when some poor soul died, she herself built a coffin and

The Sisters tend to the sick and wounded in battle.

The Cycles of Bigotry

It is an over-simplification to state that the American colonies were founded by people who came to the New World seeking religious freedom. It is true that the early settlers in the Northeast did seek freedom to worship in their own way—but it was a freedom that they were not prepared to give to others who might differ in belief. Religious prejudice existed between sects, and it was responsible for driving Roger Williams from Massachusetts to Rhode Island, the Puritans from Virginia to Maryland, but it was particularly virulent in the case of Catholics.

The prejudice against Catholics was conceived mainly in the anti-Papal passion of Queen Elizabeth. Prejudice became a fixed state of mind, a fanatical compulsion, against which logic and reason had no effect. The Christian doctrine of love was implicitly amended to exclude Catholics. Separation of Church and State was interpreted to mean that Catholics should have no influence on civil government. The colonists, the vast majority of whom were Protestant, made provision for the union of Church and State in all colonies except Pennsylvania and Rhode Island. Maryland was founded as a place of religious freedom; but when Protestants gained control, Catholics faced discrimination.

The coming of the Revolution did little to alter anti-Catholic sentiment. George Washington

"Off to America", a common scene from Irish history

had to rebuke the Boston patriots for their anti-Catholicism. It is an arguable opinion that, except for the Americans' anti-Catholicism, Canada would have joined the colonies in breaking away from England. In 1788, Massachusetts put through a Puritan-inspired law that excluded Catholics from public office. In the following year, the Massachusetts Constitution was adopted, and it provided for public support of Protestant teachers of "piety, religion, and morality."

This union of Church and State was not confined to Massachusetts. In 1784, the New Hampshire Constitution was approved, and it included a religious test that barred Catholics from public office, and the provision for public support of Protestant teachers of religion. The State Constitution of North Carolina, adopted in 1776 and in force until 1835, denied office to all but Protestants. New York, New Jersey, Delaware, Pennsylvania, and Georgia limited their officials to others than "Papists." When President Andrew Jackson appointed a Catholic, the competent Roger Brooke Taney, first as attorney general and then as chief justice of the Supreme Court, he provoked political storms. When President Franklin Pierce appointed a Catholic, William Campbell, to his Cabinet as postmaster general, another brouhaha resulted— the accusation was even hurled that the act was a plot for the Pope to get access to the mails and read United States Government correspondence.

Over the years, various organizations were started and developed, each aimed at keeping political rights from Catholics. In 1830, the American Protestant Association was founded in New York by a Dutch Reformed minister. Its announced aims were to maintain the principles of the Reformation and to "expose Popery." This was followed by a group known as the Native-Americans, begun in 1837. The Native-Americans strove to promote legislation against Catholics and immigrants, particularly the Irish. The idea was to have only native-born American Protestants eligible to hold office.

Hatred and distrust of Catholics was, and in many ways still is, a common phenomenon in parts of America.

The burning cross and hooded figure are still in strong evidence today as they preach hatred and intolerance.

HANDS FROM "ACROSS THE SEA"

In 1852, the Know Nothing Party was founded, and it spread like wildfire throughout the country. "Americans must rule America!" was the rallying cry. Under the Know Nothings, religious bigotry reached a high point not previously attained. The party elected officials to office, and for a time held considerable power; it was anti-Catholic, anti-immigrant, terroristic and brutal. The Know Nothings provoked riots in many sections of the country, each riot aimed at injuring Catholic immigrants.

On Election Day, 1855, in Louisville, Kentucky, the Know Nothings attacked the homes of Catholics, setting them afire; the occupants were shot as they rushed out. It is not known how many Catholics were murdered, but the newspapers estimated the number as between twenty-five and one hundred. Xaverian Brothers, who conducted a school in Louisville, were warned that the Know Nothings were marching on it with the intention of setting it afire. For two days the Brothers had to hide in the countryside. The Louisville *Journal* had the effrontery to blame foreign residents who had—supposedly—been incited by their priests.

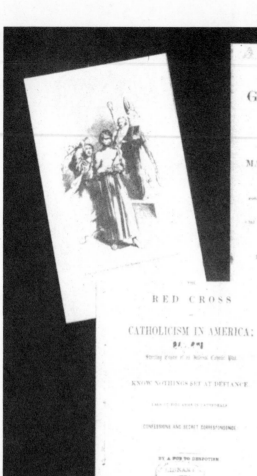

THE
GREAT RED DRAGON;
OR THE
MASTER-KEY TO POPERY.
BY
ANTHONY GAVIN,
FORMERLY ONE OF THE ROMAN CATHOLIC PRIESTS OF SARAGOSSA, SPAIN.

BOSTON:
PUBLISHED BY SAMUEL DONE,

THE
RED CROSS
OR
CATHOLICISM IN AMERICA:

KNOW NOTHINGS SET AT DEFIANCE.

CONFESSIONS AND SECRET CORRESPONDENCE.

BY A FOE TO DESPOTISM.

PUBLISHED BY THOMPSON AND COMPANY

HANNAH CORCORAN:
AN AUTHENTIC NARRATIVE
OF
HER CONVERSION FROM ROMANISM,
HER ABDUCTION FROM CHARLESTOWN,
AND
THE TREATMENT SHE RECEIVES DURING HER ABSENCE.

BY
THOMAS FORD CALDICOTT, D.D.,
PASTOR OF THE FIRST BAPTIST CHURCH, CHARLESTOWN, MASS.

BOSTON:
GOULD AND LINCOLN,
54 WASHINGTON STREET.

Bring me before a Court
Maria Monk

THE
HISTORY OF ROMANISM:
FROM THE EARLIEST CORRUPTIONS OF CHRISTIANITY
TO THE PRESENT TIME.

BY REV. JOHN DOWLING, A.M.
PASTOR OF THE BEREAN CHURCH, NEW YORK.

THIRTEENTH EDITION.

NEW YORK:
EDWARD WALKER, 114 FULTON STREET.
1846.

FURTHER DISCLOSURES
BY
MARIA MONK,
CONCERNING THE
HOTEL DIEU NUNNERY OF MONTREAL;
ALSO, HER
VISIT TO NUNS' ISLAND,
AND DISCLOSURES CONCERNING THAT SECRET RETREAT.

PRECEDED BY A REPLY TO THE
PRIESTS' BOOK,
BY REV. J. J. SLOCUM.

NEW YORK:
PUBLISHED FOR MARIA MONK.
1877.

The Know Nothings set torches to a Carmelite convent in Baltimore and an Ursuline academy near Boston. Churches in New York and Philadelphia were burned. In Boston, New York, Paterson, Philadelphia, and Louisville, the Irish residential areas were attacked. In Maine, Father John Bapst, a Jesuit, was caught by Know Nothings and was tarred and feathered, simply because he was a priest.

One of the most spiteful and petty acts committed by the Know Nothings was carried out in our nation's capital. The Washington Monument was being completed, and some foreign governments sent granite or marble blocks to be used in the construction. The gifts were made in honor of the Father of our country and to show friendship to our country. Pope Pius IX, as sovereign of the Papal States, sent a block to be set in the monument—and his gift caused a furor. Critics proposed that a block with an anti-Papal inscription be set next to it. The quarrel was settled when a mob of Know Nothings seized the block one night and threw it in the Potomac River. That block was never recovered.

The Know Nothings gained control of many State legislatures and therein they passed nuisance laws against Catholics. Particularly offensive were the "nunnery inspection" laws, which allowed civic officials to invade the privacy of convents at awkward hours. Those laws were later found unconstitutional. The Know Nothings even put up candidates for the office of President. The greatest tragedy was the violence the Know Nothings provoked. Catholics were kept from voting by beatings and killings. Catholic school children were barred from public schools or forced to read the Protestant Bible.

Despite their evil accomplishments, the Know Nothings represented no one but themselves—a bigoted and lawless minority. Abraham Lincoln was only one of many Americans who repudiated them. He once wrote against the Know Nothings in words that almost might be applicable today. He said: "I am not a Know Nothing; that is certain. How could I be? How can anyone who abhors the oppression of Negroes be in favor of degrading classes of white people? Our progress in degeneracy appears to me to be pretty rapid. As a nation we began by declaring that 'all men are created equal.' Now we practically read it 'all men are created equal, except Negroes.' When the Know Nothings get control, it will read, 'all men are created equal, except Negroes and foreigners and

A satirical study of the Irish propensity for drink

Catholics.' When it comes to this, I shall prefer emigrating to some country where they make no pretense of loving liberty—to Russia for instance, where despotism can be taken pure and without the base alloy of hypocrisy."

The undoing of the Know Nothing movement resulted from mob violence, plus the incompetence of persons the members of the movement elected to office. Gradually sensible Protestants worked against the Know Nothing party, and it disappeared beneath the weighty problems facing America in pre-Civil War days. While there was a basic mistrust and suspicion of Catholics, the root of the problem was fundamentally economic. There was a fear that Catholic immigrants would depress wages and take "Protestants'" jobs. There was also the threat of political control by the growing number of urban Catholics. The situation was repeated in our own times by the Negro emigration to the North.

The next anti-Catholic movement, springing from the same causes, appeared in 1887; it was stimulated by the American Protective Association —popularly known as the A.P.A. The Association began in a small town in Iowa, and it soon spread throughout the country, although its greatest strength remained in the Midwest. At its height it claimed millions of members, but the exact figure was kept secret. The A.P.A. sought to repeal naturalization laws, to forbid teaching any foreign languages in public schools, and to tax Church property. Its forays into politics became its undoing, because politicians used the organization for their own ends.

Some years later—on Thanksgiving night, 1915—thirty-four men gathered on a mountain top near Atlanta, Georgia. There, under a blazing cross, they pledged loyalty to the Invisible Empire, the revived Knights of the Ku Klux Klan. That movement, which used murder, whippings, and tar-and-feathers as weapons, was anti-Catholic, anti-Negro, anti-Semitic, anti-alien. Father James Gillis, the celebrated Paulist orator and writer, called the Klan "the most curious combination of comedy and tragedy, of buffoonery and villainy," ever to appear on the American scene. The Klan went into semi-retirement during World War I, but after the war returned stronger than ever. By 1922, the estimate was 3,500 American males were joining the organization every day. Its annual revenue was estimated at eight million dollars, and total membership was placed at 1,200,000. The Klan found its main strength in small towns and rural areas, but members lived in every State, including the Canal Zone and Alaska. By 1925, the Klan claimed five million members; burning crosses and hooded figures were part of the American scene.

The Klan became so ruthless that many Americans were forced into counteraction. The Governor of Louisiana sought Federal assistance to put the Klan down. The Governor of Georgia accused the Klan of 135 lynchings in his state over a two-year period. Many ministers denounced the Klan from their pulpits. In a Pennsylvania court trial, evidence was given by ex-Klansmen of Klan-inspired riots, floggings, kidnappings and murders in that State.

The Ku Klux Klan had considerable strength inside the Democratic Party; and in 1924, it was influential in blocking Governor Alfred E. Smith, a New York Catholic, from the nomination for President. The Klan managed to split the party and create all sorts of factions within it. A platform resolution condemning the Klan was so watered down that it was meaningless. The Klan attempted to keep Governor Smith from the 1928 nomination, and the kick-off of its campaign was a three-hour speech in the Capitol by Senator Tom Heflin of Alabama. Copies of the speech, an anti-Catholic and anti-Knights of Columbus diatribe, were distributed widely. The tactic failed, however, and Smith won the nomination.

The bigotry that was released by the 1928 Presidential campaign rocked the United States. Scurrilous literature, wild accusations, anti-Catholic sermons, were the order of the day. One of the most effective weapons used against Smith was a fraudulent document that purported to be the secret Knights of Columbus oath. The "oath" first appeared during a Congressional campaign in 1912, and an investigation by the House Elections Committee proved it a fraud. The Klan and other bigoted groups circulated almost countless copies of the "oath." The Knights of Columbus prosecuted when sufficient evidence could be obtained, and they gained many convictions.

Governor Smith attempted to conduct a high-level campaign, dealing with principles and issues. He attempted to dispose of the religious question by showing that there is no conflict between Americanism and Catholicism. But logic has no effect on prejudice, and intellect does not overcome emotions. The distortions and lies were too powerful. They helped to send the Happy Warrior down to defeat.

In more recent times, the A.P.A. and the Native-Americans have been succeeded by the awkwardly named "Protestants and Other Americans United." This organization, better known as POAU, has produced reams of anti-Catholic literature. It backed the California ballot amendment that would have taxed parochial schools; and it repeats anti-Catholic charges that have long since been refuted. Large sums of money are still being spent in anti-Catholic diatribes, and a considerable number of people make successful livings by baiting Catholics and other groups.

The Presidential campaign of 1960 gave ample evidence that bigotry is far from dead. The same type of literature that appeared in 1928 was present again; the bogus Knights of Columbus oath reappeared; and sermons once more rang out to tell why a Catholic could not be President. But if bigotry is not dead, neither is it as vigorous as it once was. In a masterful presentation, John F. Kennedy met the religious issue head on. The majority of Americans voted for him because they considered him the best man. The Constitutional provision that "no religious test shall ever be required as a qualification to any office or public trust of the United States" was finally applied, if not by all Americans at least by a majority, to the highest office in our land.

Catholics in the Civil War

The first naval officer killed in action in the Civil War was Capt. James H. Ward, a convert to the Catholic faith. He took the place of a wounded gunner and was mortally wounded himself. A crewman re-enacts the scene of 1861.

THE decision of President Abraham Lincoln that no State, once it had accepted the Constitution, could withdraw from the Union, tore the American nation in two and precipitated one of the bloodiest and most tragic wars ever fought. In the division of the nation, Catholics also were divided. Although Catholic theology teaches respect for civil authority and obedience to civil power, the question that faced bishops, priests, and people was: "Where does that power reside?" The Catholics of the North remained loyal to the Federal Union, while those of the South transferred their loyalty to the new Confederate Government.

Once the matter of loyalty was determined, the Catholic clergy gave steadfast support to their chosen cause. The bishops, particularly, played important roles. Archbishop Hughes, of New York, traveled to Europe to gain sympathy for the North. The performance of his mission was particularly effective in France, where officials favored the South. Diplomatically, Archbishop Hughes was able to neutralize those officials and prevent recognition of the Confederacy. Bishop Domenec, of Pittsburgh, was able to accomplish the same type of mission in Spain, where he persuaded the Spanish Queen to adopt a neutral position. Bishop Fitzpatrick of Boston used his influence in Belgium.

Southern bishops were active in behalf of their cause. Bishop Patrick N. Lynch was a fiery critic of the North. The Charleston (S.C.) prelate in a letter to Archbishop Hughes charged that the

Patrick Lynch—Bishop of Charleston, South Carolina

J. J. Hughes, Archbishop of New York and diplomat.

Yankees in "taking up antislavery, making it a religious dogma, and carrying it into politics, they have broken up the Union." He was sent to Europe by Confederate President Jefferson Davis but the South was already collapsing and the war ended before he could accomplish anything. After the war, Bishop Lynch was refused permission to return to his diocese; however, through the influence of Baltimore's Archbishop John Spalding, President Andrew Johnson granted Bishop Lynch a pardon and he was allowed to resume his duties in Charleston.

Archbishop John Purcell of Cincinnati exercised considerable leadership during the war. He held that all the principles of the Catholic Church

"gravitate around the idea of union. What is the principle of secession but the carrying out of the principle of private judgment?" His paper, the *Telegraph*, gave strong support to the Union cause, so much so that an Indiana pastor, Father Pontavice, wrote condemning the "Abolitionist articles in the stupid *Telegraph*." In another letter to a former bishop, he attacked: "Thanks to the exhortations of the Archbishops of New York and Cincinnati, the bishops of Chicago and Dubuque, all Irish, there are already about 160,000 Irish killed in this war. When the Catholics are so exhausted that they are no longer able to defend themselves or their churches, then shall come the infernal joy." He concludes by saying that Archbishop Purcell has made himself a recruiting officer "for Lincoln and Co." It seems as if there was a civil war going on inside the Church as well in the states.

The Draft Act of the Federal Government did not exempt priests from military service but there is no recorded instance of a priest from either North or South having been compelled to fight. Congress did assign chaplains to the troops, but the choice was left to the individual unit. In the North, chaplains were given a rank equivalent to a cavalry captain and a salary of $100 a month, plus benefits. In the South, there was no rank. Both sides agreed

The long and bloody American Civil War was the "great test" of democracy as brother fought against brother.

The soldiers of the 69th N.Y.S.M. hear Sunday Mass during a lull in the fighting in the early months of the war.

to free captured chaplains, a consensus which was sometimes tardily but regularly kept. There were forty assigned Catholic chaplains with the armies of the North, and twenty-eight with the South. In addition to these, there were many priests who administered to the needy on local battlefields, others who gave irregular and unassigned service, plus hospital and prison chaplains.

The best-known chaplain was Father Abram J. Ryan, a man whose poetry had won him a modicum of fame and many followers; he served with the Confederacy. Another prominent Confederate chaplain was Father Francis Leray, who became Archbishop of New Orleans. Two important Union chaplains were the future Archbishop John Ireland and the future Bishop Lawrence McMahon.

Some of the stories told about chaplains make interesting tales. There was a Father Ouellet who during the battle of Malvern Hill went about the field of combat with a lantern, peering down at each wounded man and asking, "Are you a Catholic? Do you wish absolution?" At Antietam, called "The Bloodiest Single Day of the War," Notre Dame's Father Corby mounted a horse and dashed along the front lines shouting at the soldiers to be sorry for their sins because he was going to give a general absolution. Another Notre Dame priest, Father Gillen, was almost imprisoned by General Grant. Father Gillen, unassigned and without orders, followed the troops in a buggy in which he slept and from which he said Mass. One day General Grant came upon him inside the lines as he went about his unofficial duties. He

Thomas Meagher, lawyer and governor of Montana.

William S. Rosecrans, Civil War general and diplomat

ordered the priest arrested and freed him only when he accepted a commission.

A Northern chaplain, a Benedictine named Bliemel, was shot at the battle of Jonesborough while bending over a dying soldier whose confession he was hearing. He died from his wound. He is the only Northern chaplain known to have died as the result of battle.

The priests who served in the war gave themselves wholeheartedly to their cause. A good example was Father James Sheeran, a Confederate chaplain, who was acquainted with such popular heroes as Generals Lee, Jackson, Longstreet, Ewell, Stuart, Mahone, and Pelham. Father Sheeran was born in Ireland, and was a Redemptorist priest stationed in New Orleans when the war began. A man of quick and vigorous action, he was convinced in favor of the Confederate cause. He called Northern troops "Lincoln's bandits," and he wrote that the war was started by New England fanatics to undermine the South. "The consequence," he de-

clared, "is a war unjust, cruel, barbarous, and inhuman."

Father Sheeran was dedicated to his soldiers and would do anything for them. He was ready to take on Confederate officers if he thought they were not acting in the best interest of his "boys." He accused officers of setting bad example for the troops, and once demanded and obtained the resignation of an officer who, he thought, had acted in a cowardly manner in battle. More than once he rebuked doctors because he did not think they were treating wounded soldiers correctly. If he didn't get what he wanted, he was ready to appeal to the highest military authority.

If Father Sheeran was not fighting with the officers for a better deal for his soldiers, he was fighting with the soldiers because they did not lead better lives. He was uncompromising against gambling, profanity and drinking. He gave sermons up to three hours in length on these vices! Whenever he found the soldiers gambling, he broke

175

up the game and confiscated the money for his favorite charity, an orphanage. Several times he threatened to resign and go back to Louisiana if the soldiers did not stop swearing.

Although Father Sheeran hated the Union cause, he did not hate Union soldiers but was always ready to give them spiritual assistance. It was not unusual for him to take care of a wounded Northerner and then, when the spiritual ministrations were finished, to lecture the man on the Irish chaplain's idea of the rights of the South. After one battle, Father Sheeran crossed into the Union lines to care for Yankee wounded. He was promptly arrested and hailed before General Philip Sheridan —who also was a Catholic. General Sheridan offered to release the captive, on the condition that he would not give "aid or comfort" to the enemy.

Father Sheeran exploded with wrath. He said he would give aid and comfort where they were needed; and besides, he himself was the enemy. Father Sheeran was then sent off to the Union prison at Fort McHenry, near Baltimore. There he attempted to reform a gang of deserters, robbers, and cowards. After several weeks, Secretary of War Stanton ordered Father Sheeran's release.

One Confederate priest played an amazing ruse on the Union Army. He was Father Bixio, pastor in Staunton, Virginia. When the Union forces occupied his area, he offered his services as chaplain with the Union troops. As soon as he was accepted, he used his authority to get wagonloads of supplies from the Union commissary, and then promptly took them through the lines and distributed them to the Southern people who were suffering under General Sheridan's scorched-earth policy.

In our nation's capital, there is a monument called "Nuns of the Battlefield." The statue was erected as public tribute to the more than six hundred Catholic Sisters who volunteered as nurses to care for the sick and wounded immediately behind the battle lines. Those Sisters gave devoted service under the most difficult conditions. Their hospitals were converted barns and warehouses; medicine and doctors were scarce; sanitation was almost impossible. Among the religious communities that participated in this heroic work were the following: Sisters of Charity, Sisters of Mercy, Ursulines, Sisters of Saint Dominic, Sisters of the Poor of Saint Francis, Sisters of Saint Joseph, Sisters of Providence, Sisters of the Holy Cross, Sisters of Our Lady of Mount Carmel.

The name of one group of Sisters is missing from the above list and that is because they deserve a paragraph of their own. This is the Daughters of Charity of St. Vincent de Paul. From this community, 231 volunteered as nurses; 26 were represented on the battlefield of Gettysburg, alone. Another 87 served in the ambulance corps that followed the troops into battle. At Lincoln Hospital in Washington 29 served and at Saterlee Hospital in Philadelphia there were 89 of these dedicated women. Although Sisters from other communities were represented among the wounded, it was the Daughters of Charity who won for all Sisters the popular title "Angels of Mercy."

Except for the work of the Sisters, there was no organized nursing during the Civil War — no Nurses Corps had yet been established, and the Red Cross was not as yet organized. But the Sisters did more than to nurse the wounded. Because of the shortage of priests in the country as a whole, chaplains were scarce. The Sisters, therefore, had to take on many of the duties of chaplains. As Theodore Maynard aptly observed, "Often, after having made all efforts to save life, they had to show men how to die."

Sisters brought back to the Church Catholics who had been away for years; they also prepared many Protestants to meet God. Through the Sisters' efforts, many converts were made both during and after the war. The Sisters did much to break down bigotry and antagonism towards the Church.

The compulsory draft law was not welcomed by many immigrants, the majority of whom were Catholics. Large numbers of immigrants had not been in this country long enough to feel close ties, and they had little understanding of Northern aims. However, the main opposition to the Draft Act was its basic injustice in administration. Any man with social or political power could get an exemption for almost any reason; and if that failed, the act enabled him, if he had three hundred dollars, to buy a substitute. There were firms that existed solely to provide substitutes; and it was not uncommon for a man to accept a bounty as a substitute, and then desert and join again for another bounty. The immigrants, who did not have social or political influence and who were poor, felt discriminated against, particularly when many native-born Americans were able to escape military service. The result was the Draft Riots of 1863.

Archbishop John Hughes, who years earlier had focused the attention of the nation on the civil rights of Catholics and other minorities, was a key figure in bringing the Draft Riots to an end. He had made his position clear in speeches and

At the battle of Perryville during the war, a Union officer rallies his men to meet the Confederate attack.

sermons that he favored conscription but one in which "every man, rich and poor, will have to take his share." When the riots did break out because his caution was not followed, he invited some of the leaders to his residence, where as an aged man he was in failing health. He spoke to the rioters, promising that he would fight in their behalf for an equitable draft. He emphasized that the war was being fought not to end slavery as was popularly depicted but to uphold the Constitution and maintain the Union. The next day he wrote to Secretary of State Seward reiterating his views and adding that he believed some of the hostility also arose from the fear of workmen that emancipated Negroes would flood the North and depress the labor market and take white jobs. His firm stand brought reason back into the dispute and

ended the violence. He died a few months later.

Catholics held more than their share of generalships in both armies. There were fifty Catholic generals in the Union Army, and twenty with the Confederacy. General William Starke Rosecrans had become a Catholic while teaching at West Point; his example converted his brother, Sylvester, who later became first Bishop of Columbus. Rosecrans left the Army in 1853 and built a new career as businessman, architect, teacher and engineer. When the war began, he returned to the Army as aide-de-camp to General McClellan, rising to Major General of Volunteers. After the war, he served as Ambassador to Mexico, congressman from California and Registrar of the Treasury. He once turned down the nomination for governor of his home state of Ohio. What is not very well

Pierre Gustave de Beauregard

Ambrose Everett Burnside

Stephen Russell Mallory

Philip Henry Sheridan

Sheridan rallies the soldiers at the famous Civil War battle of Cedar Creek. The response was a wild cheer of recognition.

known is that he probably could have been the first Catholic president of the United States had not that office been stolen from him.

It happened this way. The New York editor, Horace Greeley, had become a bitter foe of Lincoln and planned to dump him at the 1864 Republican Convention. He approached General Rosecrans with the proposal to make him the presidential candidate in place of Lincoln. Rosecrans refused to have any part in the scheme. Lincoln was appreciative when he heard of the General's refusal. Forewarned, Lincoln developed counter moves to Greeley and in the Baltimore Convention won the nomination to run for a second term. He chose

General Rosecrans as his running mate, knowing he could count on his loyalty and realizing that the General would strengthen the ticket because of the respect in which he was held.

Lincoln wired Rosecrans the offer of second place on his ticket. Rosecrans wired back immediately his acceptance. Rosecrans' favorable reply was intercepted by Secretary of War Edward M. Stanton, whose department had charge of the military telegraph and who had ordered that all telegrams from generals should be brought to his attention. Stanton was a vain man whose actions often bordered upon megalomania and who regularly usurped presidential powers. Stanton did

179

Longstreet left West Point to serve the Confederacy.

Edward Cresap Ord, Union general of the Civil War.

not like Rosecrans and he delayed the telegram. When Lincoln received no reply from his choice and the convention had to conclude, Andrew Johnson was selected for the vice-presidency. Later when Lincoln learned of the deceit, it was too late to do anything. Lincoln was assassinated a few months later and Johnson became president, a post that would have been Rosecrans' except for Stanton's duplicity.

Another prominent Catholic was General Patrick Guiney, father of the poetess, Louise Imogen Guiney. He commanded the Thirteenth Massachusetts and received a bullet in a lung—which was to be the cause of his death. Other general-rank Catholics in the Union Army included such names as: Hunt, Ord, Corcoran, Sturgis, Hardie, Stone, McMahon and Newton.

One of the more important officers in the war was the fiery Catholic, General Philip Sheridan, the popular cavalry leader, of whom Grant said had "no superior as a general, either living or dead, and perhaps not an equal."

Sheridan had been born in Ohio, had attended West Point, and rose rapidly in rank. Affectionately known to his soldiers as "Little Phil," he had gallantry, daring and the peppery ingenuity so often associated with the Irish. More than once his inspiration on the battlefield turned defeat into victory. Grant considered him as a "right arm" and he emerged from the war as one of the North's most popular figures.

Sheridan held many posts, all of which he filled brilliantly. As commander of the Potomac Cavalry, he went to the aid of Grant at Old Cold Harbor, driving the Confederates from strong positions. Despite incessant counterattacks, he held the position all through the night, until relieved the next morning by reinforcements. As commander of the Army of the Shenandoah, he drove the Confederate force from that rich valley.

One of the most dramatic events in the Civil War was General Sheridan's brilliant victory at Cedar Creek. His troops were encamped at Cedar Creek, twenty miles south of Winchester. Confederate General Jubal Early was in the vicinity, but Sheridan had given him two good drubbings, and he was not expected to attack. Sheridan went to Washington on business. Returning to the front, he had reached Winchester early in the morning, when he received word that Early had attacked with strong forces and that the Union soldiers were fleeing in disorder.

The weary Sheridan remounted his horse. In a

The war was costly to both sides but not just in matters of economics as many were not to return.

Major General Philip H. Sheridan

wild ride, he headed for the battle twenty miles away. He met fleeing fragments of his troops and turned them back to the front. Towards three o'clock in the afternoon, he launched a counter-attack that overwhelmed Early and destroyed his future effectiveness. Not only did Sheridan recapture his own cannons, which had been taken by the rebels, but he seized twenty-three more. By his daring, he had turned threatened defeat into victory.

Sheridan's cavalry was the decisive factor at Missionary Ridge. In the Battle of Five Forks, Sheridan was directed by Grant to attack General Lee's five brigades, which were holding an important railroad junction. Sheridan attacked and drove the enemy back, taking six thousand prisoners in the action. It was the end for Lee; two days later he began a retreat. Sheridan attacked the flanks of the retreating Confederate Army again and again. The wounds were mortal. Eight days after the attack on the railway junction, General Lee surrendered to General Grant at Appomattox Court House, and the Civil War came to an end.

General James Shields, a Catholic whose exploits in the West have been previously described, was a brigadier general for the Union forces. He made a good record in the Shenandoah Valley fighting, and then took command of a division that opened the fighting in the Battle of Winchester. Although wounded himself, he directed the fight against Stonewall Jackson, the almost-invincible Southern general. Wounds received in that battle caused Shield's retirement a year later.

One of the most colorful of the Union's Catholic generals was the silver-tongued Thomas Meagher. General Meagher was born in Ireland, of Catholic parents. He was educated in a Jesuit school in Kildare. He became active in the cause of Irish independence; was caught by the British and sentenced to death for treason; then had the sentence commuted to exile in Australia. He managed to get away from Australia to the United States, where he became a lawyer. When the Civil War began, Meagher threw himself wholeheartedly into the Union cause. In a speech made in 1861, at the Boston Music Hall, he exhorted his Irish compatriots to serve the Union. The speech not only was responsible for the formation of two Irish volunteer Massachusetts regiments, but also it put into American tradition one of the most beautiful tributes to the flag ever written.

"A national flag is one of the most sacred things a people can possess," declared Meagher.

"It is the symbol of national authority. This morning as I looked out on Bunker Hill, what did I see? I saw English troops evacuating New York. I saw George Washington seated as the first President of the United States. I saw the majestic forehead and lean figure of Andrew Jackson. I saw the Bay of Smyrna, Austrian prey, redeemed by the Stars and Stripes. I saw the towers of Mexico and those majestic roads glistening in a greater glory than that which Cortez conferred on Spain. These and a host of other events passed like a vision above those stars, while I remained in its shadow. Oh, that never, never again may that flag meet with another disaster. Henceforth, the troops carrying it in action should have this motto to guide them: 'Death if you will, victory if God grants it, but no defeat and no retreat!' "

Meagher joined the famous Irish Brigade of New York's Sixty-Ninth Regiment. He fought at Bull Run and at Antietam. In the autumn of 1862, he was with the Army of the Potomac, 122,000 strong, before Fredericksburg. There Meagher's commander was General Burnside, a man who did not feel himself capable of command. Rebel sharpshooters were stationed in the houses of the town; and on the hill behind Fredericksburg, Lee's forces were strongly entrenched. Burnside ordered Meagher's forces to make a suicidal, frontal attack. There was nothing to do but attempt to take the heights — and half of the Irish Brigade were wiped out. Burnside was relieved of his command as the result of the failure of the battle of Fredericksburg.

General Meagher remained with the Irish Brigade through the battles of Antietam and Chancellorsville, but by that time the Irish Brigade was almost nonexistent because of casualties. Later he joined General Sherman in Georgia, where he fought until the war ended. After the war he was appointed secretary of Montana Territory, and for a year acted as governor. In 1867, he drowned while on an inspection trip on the Missouri River.

Catholics also held prominent positions in the Marine Corps and the Navy. Commander James Ward, a marine, was one of the founders of the United States Naval Academy. When the war broke out, he was charged with organizing naval activities on the Potomac River. While leading the attack on Confederate batteries at Matthias Point, he was fatally wounded—the first naval officer to give his life in the war. Benjamin Sands served as an admiral, and his son, James, was an officer in the Atlantic Blockade.

CHARLESTON
MERCURY

EXTRA:

Passed unanimously at 1.15 o'clock, P. M., December 20th, 1860.

AN ORDINANCE

To dissolve the Union between the State of South Carolina and other States united with her under the compact entitled " The Constitution of the United States of America."

We, the People of the State of South Carolina, in Convention assembled, do declare and ordain, and it is hereby declared and ordained,

That the Ordinance adopted by us in Convention, on the twenty-third day of May, in the year of our Lord one thousand seven hundred and eighty-eight, whereby the Constitution of the United States of America was ratified, and also, all Acts and parts of Acts of the General Assembly of this State, ratifying amendments of the said Constitution, are hereby repealed; and that the union now subsisting between South Carolina and other States, under the name of " The United States of America," is hereby dissolved.

THE
UNION
IS
DISSOLVED!

SPRAGUE
LIGHT CAVALRY!

NOW IS THE TIME TO JOIN THE BEST CORPS IN THE FIELD!

This New and Splendid Regiment is being organized at PLATTSBURGH, N. Y., under the immediate supervision of

Adj't Gen. Sprague,

OF THIS STATE, WHOSE NAME THE REGIMENT BEARS.

Highest Bounties paid Promptly.

The Colonel has carefully inspected the Barracks, and pronounces them the finest and most comfortable in the State. Neat Rooms, well warmed, properly lighted, and good clean beds, furnished to all Recruits immediately on their arrival.

Men allowed to furnish their own Horses

IF IN GOOD CONDITION AND FITTED FOR SERVICE.

RECRUITS UNIFORMED IMMEDIATELY ON ARRIVAL AT CAMP.

owned and popular CAPTAIN LOT CHAMBERLAIN, the leading mover of this organization has the subsisting the same. The simple fact of his having subsisted Three Regiments prior to this, is sufficient assurance that the men will be well fed cared for.

SPENCER H. OLMSTED, Col. Commanding.

Clarry & Reilley, Printers & Engravers, 12 & 14 Spruce-st. N.Y.

A Union advertisement for cavalry recruits during the Civil War as "men may supply their own horses"

2000 ARMY HORSES
WANTED!

I want to purchase immediately at the Government Stables at this station,

TWO THOUSAND ARMY HORSES!

For which I will pay the prices named below, IN CASH. Horses must pass inspection under the following regulations, to wit:

FOR HORSES

Sound in all particulars, well broken, in full flesh and good condition, from fifteen (15) to sixteen (16) hands high, from five (5) to nine (9) years old, and well adapted in every way to Cavalry purposes—price

160 DOLLARS!

FOR HORSES

Of DARK Color, sound in all particulars, strong, quick and active, well broken, square trotters in harness, in good flesh and condition, from six (6) to ten (10) years old, not less than fifteen and one half [15 1-2] hands high, weighing not less than ten hundred and fifty [1050] pounds each, and adapted to Artillery service,

170 DOLLARS!

N. B. VAN SLYKE,

Fr. Corby was at the front at the battle of Antietam

A haunting reminder of the youth who died in the war

Fr. Gillen was almost imprisoned by General Grant.

(Top) After a battle, the troops are blessed and thank God for their lives. The wounded are brought closer.

Alexander Gardner's photograph of Confederate dead by a fence bordering on a cornfield. The war came home.

(above) The very young must also serve in war.

(upper left) A Southern classified for "subs."

"_. . . His heart was as great as the world, but there was no room in it to hold the memory of a wrong._" Emerson

A description of the "voluntary" methods of recruiting in the South, implying that they "shanghied" drunks.

New York Draft Riots

MULLIGAN'S BRIGADE!

LAST CHANCE TO AVOID THE DRAFT!

$402 BOUNTY!

TO VETERANS!

$302 to all other VOLUNTEERS!

All Able-bodied Men, between the ages of 18 and 45 Years, who have heretofore served not less than nine months, who shall re-enlist for Regiments in the field, will be deemed Veterans, and will receive one month's pay in advance, and a bounty and premium of $402. To all other recruits, one month's pay in advance, and a bounty and premium of $302 will be paid.

All who wish to join Mulligan's Irish Brigade, now in the field, and to receive the munificent bounties offered by the Government, can have the opportunity by calling at the headquarters of

CAPT. J. J. FITZGERALD

Of the Irish Brigade, 23d Regiment Illinois Volunteers. Recruiting Officer. Chicago. Illinois.

Each Recruit, Veteran or otherwise, will receive

Seventy-five Dollars Before Leaving General Rendezvous,

and the remainder of the bounty in regular instalments till all is paid. The pay, bounty and premium for three years will average $24 per month, for Veterans; and $21,30 per month for all others.

If the Government shall not require these troops for the full period of Three Years, and they shall be mustered honorably out of the service before the expiration of their term of enlistment, they shall receive. UPON BEING MUSTERED O the whole amount of BOUNTY remaining unpaid, the same as if the full term been served.

J. J. FITZGERALD.

Chicago, December, 1863.

Recruiting Officer. corner North Clark & Kenzie Stre

The son later became an admiral and head of the Naval Academy. Other Catholic naval heroes included Admiral Ammen and Commanders Febiger and Beaumont.

The Confederacy had many Catholic connections. Its President, Jefferson Davis, had been educated by Dominicans in Kentucky. After the war, when Mrs. Davis was destitute in Georgia, the Catholic Church aided her. Of that experience, she wrote: "No institution of my own Church offered to teach my poor children. One day three Sisters of Charity came to see me and brought me five gold dollars, all the money they had. They almost forced me to take the money, but I did not. They then offered to take my children to their school in the neighborhood of Savannah, where the air was cool and they could be comfortably cared for during the summer months."

Among the Confederate generals were William L. Cabell of Virginia, who helped design the Confederate battle flag and after the war was elected mayor of Dallas, Texas, for four terms; William Joseph Hardee of Georgia, a West Pointer who became a planter and is buried in Selma, Alabama; Lawrence O'Bryan Branch, a former Congressman from North Carolina, who was killed by a sharpshooter; Paul Jones Semmes of Georgia, veteran of Seven Pines, Sharpsburg, Fredericksburg and Chancellorsville, who died at the Battle of Gettysburg; William Henry Carroll, forced to resign because of ineptness, he went to Canada and later died in Montreal; and Generals Beauregard and Longstreet. These latter two deserve special mention.

General Pierre Beauregard was born in New Orleans, was graduated from West Point, and fought in the Mexican War—from which he emerged a major. He resigned his commission with the Army as the war approached and threw his lot with the Confederacy. He precipitated the Civil War by directing the initial attack on Fort Sumter, and he was the victorious leader of the first Battle of Bull Run. He was the commander at Shiloh, and then for two years successfully defended Charleston against the Union siege. In late 1864, he was assigned as commander of the West, with instructions to halt Sherman's march to the sea. Sherman was too strong, and the Confederates were forced to surrender. After the war, Beauregard was adjutant general of Louisiana. Later he was offered the command of the Roumanian Army and that of the Egyptian Army, but he declined both offers. He died in New Orleans in 1893.

Doctor Samuel Mudd

General James Longstreet was one of the ablest and most successful of all Confederate generals, and he held the respect of both the Union and the Confederate military leaders. General Longstreet was born in South Carolina, was graduated from West Point, was wounded in the Mexican War at Chapultepec, and then served on the Texas frontier. When the Civil War broke out, Longstreet resigned his commission and joined the Confederacy as a brigadier general. He commanded a brigade at the first Battle of Bull Run, and for his gallantry was promoted to the rank of major general.

Longstreet commanded the Confederate right wing at Antietam, and was made a lieutenant general after the Battle of Fredericksburg. He was placed in charge of one of the three corps that made up the Army of Northern Virginia. In the Battle of the Wilderness, he was severely wounded, but he returned as soon as possible to his command. He was a close friend of General Lee and, next to Stonewall Jackson, was probably Lee's most trusted adviser. After the war, Longstreet held a number of governmental posts, including that of Minis-

"Under My Wings everything prospers." The United States continued its rapid growth in the 1800's.

ter to Turkey. He died in Georgia in 1904, the last member of the Confederate high command.

A Confederate naval hero was Captain Raphael Semmes, member of an old Catholic family of Maryland. Originally Captain Semmes served the United States Navy as midshipman and lieutenant. Later he joined the Confederacy and was assigned to the command of the *Sumter,* first vessel of the Confederate Navy. Next he was put in charge of a fast ship being built in England. He named that ship *Alabama,* fitted it out with guns, and went to sea against Union shipping. He captured sixty-four Union ships and burned all but seven of them. The *Alabama* was finally sunk by the *U.S.S. Kearsarge,* off the coast of France.

Some other Catholics might be mentioned. The war song of the South, *Dixie,* was written by Dan Emmett. Other popular Confederate songs — *Bonnie Blue Flag* by Harry McCarthy, and *Mary-*land, *My Maryland* by James Randall — were written by Catholics. A Catholic politician, Stephen R. Mallory, of Florida, represented his State in the national Senate; later he was secretary of the Navy in the Confederate Cabinet.

From the strife of the Civil War, the Nation emerged torn asunder, the Reconstruction accomplished nothing to ameliorate the resentment of the South. House had been divided against house. Even religion did not escape, and Protestant churches divided according to geography, divisions that remain to this day. But the unity of the Catholic Church was demonstrated when, in 1866, the Second Plenary Council of Baltimore was held, and priests and bishops from North and South sat down together. However, that lesson and its wider implications went unheeded, as fanatics of the North bent their entire effort to humiliating the conquered South.

The Contribution of Religious Orders

THE labors and sacrifices of many individuals are recorded between these covers. But some words should be spared for the religious communities from which so many of them came because it was these communities—societies, orders, or what you will—that formed them.

In doing research for this subject an article was uncovered that was written by Father Thomas McAvoy, C.S.C., the distinguished archivist of the University of Notre Dame and author of a number of historical works. The article appeared in *Ave Maria* (March 17, 1962) at a time when that veteran magazine was at the apex of interest, information and usefulness. Because of its scholarship and conciseness, it would be foolish to attempt to cover the same ground anew. Therefore, with the gracious permission of Father John Reedy, C.S.C., director of Ave Maria Press, Father McAvoy's contribution (slightly condensed) is added to these pages:

To understand the role of the religious orders of priests, Brothers and Sisters in the present prosperity of the Catholic Church in the United States requires the examination of nearly every page in the history of the Church in this country. Perhaps the most romantic episodes are the accounts of the evangelization of the primitive Indians who lived within the borders of the present United States during the 16th and 17th centuries.

There are many reasons for the presence of religious priests in these early frontiers. Before the regular organization of the Church with her parish churches and schools and dioceses and bishops can be set up among such primitive peoples, they must be converted and civilized. In some countries, Catholic governments paid the cost of these missionary endeavors. But usually only a group of religious living under the vows of poverty, chastity and obedience, who share their property in common, can afford to support the frontier missionary.

Thus, when the Spanish first visited the shores of Florida they brought with them heroic Franciscans, Dominicans and Jesuits, many of whom suffered martyrdom in an effort to establish missions and to convert the natives. And if one turns to the early French missions of the Great Lakes and the Mississippi River one finds again the heroic exploits of the Jesuits and Recollects, among others. They, too, were dealing with primitive savages who could scarcely understand the Christian gospel and who sometimes killed the missionary instead of listening to him.

The Jesuit reports are filled with accounts of long canoe trips through lakes and rivers into the woodlands, the sharing of savage food and shelter, and long journeys on foot combined with the difficulties in instructing the simple minds. There are many writings that give witness to the martyrs among the Jesuits of the New York missions.

The suppression of the Jesuits in the French missions in 1663, carried out with a bureaucratic stupidity, erased much of the grand work of these missionaries. There were not enough other missionaries to replace them, but the tradition of their labors and fragments of Christian teachings lingered on in the savage memory until decades later when other missionaries came to open permanent missions in what is now Minnesota, Wisconsin and Michigan.

When Lord Baltimore's company arrived in Chesapeake Bay to establish the colony of Maryland in 1634, again the Jesuits were there in the persons of Fathers Andrew White and John Altham and Brother Thomas Gervase. They began not only to say Mass for the Catholics in the colony but also to carry the gospel to the Indians of the region. The religious toleration they enjoyed under their Catholic governors soon lapsed when others took over the control of the colony, but their efforts did not falter. Occasionally arrested and imprisoned or shipped back to England, these Jesuits continued to care for the faithful and to receive converts from among their non-Catholic neighbors.

Thus in the end of the colonial period the Catholics of Maryland, Virginia and Pennsylvania were cared for chiefly by what remained of the

THEY·COMFORTED·THE·DYING·NURSED·THE·WOUNDED·CARRIED·HOPE·TO THE·IMPRISONED·GAVE·IN·HIS·NAME·A·DRINK·OF·WATER·TO·THE·THIRSTY

TO THE MEMORY AND IN HONOR OF
THE VARIOUS·ORDERS·OF·SISTERS
WHO GAVE THEIR SERVICES AS NURSES ON BATTLEFIELDS
AND IN HOSPITALS DURING THE CIVIL WAR

A monument to the memory of all of the orders of Sisters who worked as nurses on the battlefields of the war.

Jesuit missionaries, helped occasionally by Franciscans from England. But political interference in European religious affairs again brought about the suppression of the Society of Jesus in 1773. The Jesuits submitted honorably and formed among themselves a clerical body to maintain themselves. This Select Body of the Clergy received from the Vicar Apostolic of London, their nearest religious superior, the appointment of Father John Lewis as their superior and continued their services to the Catholics in these colonies.

After the American Revolution had ended English rule, the clergy in Maryland worked under Father Lewis until Rome appointed Father John Carroll the Prefect Apostolic and later the first Bishop of Baltimore. They served the bishop well while hoping that Rome would allow them to reorganize as Jesuits again. With the Sulpicians, they were still the main support of Catholicity in the United States. They were permitted to reorganize in 1805.

The story of the growth of American Catholicism in the 19th century is not like that of the spread of Catholicism in the conversion of Europe in the early Middle Ages. While it is true that there were conversions, the greatest growth of American Catholicism came from Catholic immigration. Bishop John Carroll had to bring priests from Europe to care for the growing Catholic population.

Among the refugees from the French Revolution were many learned and devoted French priests, including the Priests of St. Sulpice in Paris, whose chief work is the training of candidates for the priesthood. The Sulpicians are secular priests bound together by promise. Since they had few candidates for their seminary when they arrived in 1791, they helped the new bishop by working as missionaries in Kentucky, in the Illinois country and in Detroit.

There were many other noted secular priests who came to help Bishop Carroll. In addition, during the first years many individual members of various religious communities came to his aid. There were the Dominicans, Fathers William and Matthew O'Brien in New York, and later Father Edward Dominic Fenwick in Kentucky. Fathers Matthew Carr and John Rossiter established a province of the Augustinians in Philadelphia in 1797. There

BLACKFOOT
BLOOD
ASSINIBOINE
FLATHEAD
OJIB
CHIMAKUAN
CHINOOK
CAYUSE NEZ PERCE
S I O U
ARIKARA
HIDATSA
MANDAN
CROW
CHEYENNE
SANTEE-
-DAKOTA
TAKELMA
BANNOCK
YANKTON
SHOSHONI
WIND RIVER
SHOSHONI
TETON - DAKOTA
PONCA
SHASTA
TO
YANA
OMO
YANA
WAPPO
WASHO
OMAHA
IC
UTE
PAWNEE
OTO
ARAPAHO
PAIUTE
CHEYENNE
KANSAS
UTE
MONO
NAVAJO
HOPI APACHE
KIOWA APACHE
KIOWA
WICHITA
SUPAI
WALAPAI
MOHAVE
YUMA
SAN CARLOS
COMANCHE
CHIRICAHUA
PAPAGO
MESCALERO
TONKAWAN
KARANKAWA

Blackfoot Profile
"Mun-Shot"

Sobomoxo
("Crowfoot")
Head Chief of the Blackfeet.

KNIGHT & HILL
GENERAL STORE

BLACKFOOT TEPEE

Fredric Remington

were the Capuchins, Fathers Charles Whelan and Andrew Nugent, in New York. Father Charles Maguire, a Franciscan, worked in western Pennsylvania. Two Capuchins, Fathers Charles and Peter Helbron, were in eastern Pennsylvania, and the Trappists in Missouri and Kentucky.

Wherever the Catholic Church flourishes one can always expect to find dedicated Catholic ladies carrying on three great works of zeal—caring for the sick, teaching the ignorant and praying for the success of the apostolic mission of the Church. These religious women were not long in manifesting themselves in the United States. As early as 1729 French Ursulines had come to French Louisiana where they founded a hospital, besides carrying on in their own way the instruction of girls in the colony and prayers for the Church. And it is also significant that among the earliest actions of the first American Bishop of Baltimore was the establishment of the convent of the Carmelites at Port Tobacco, in Maryland, on August 7, 1790, and the setting up of the community of Visitation Nuns near Georgetown in 1799. These communities were set up first to pray and then to serve the pioneer American Church.

Shortly after the turn of the century the devout widow, Elizabeth Seton, began under priestly guidance to gather a band of heroic women who devoted themselves to Christian education. A few years later they became the Sisters of Charity and started what has been considered the first effort at a Catholic parochial school. She established her convent and academy at Emmitsburg. More than any other of these early communities this was an American foundation. In time the Sisters of Charity convents were founded in New York, in Cincinnati and in other communities where Catholics could establish schools and hospitals.

Two other communities of American origin made their appearance on the Kentucky frontier in the next decade. Around Mary Rhodes, Christina Stuart, and Nancy Havern, Father Charles Nerinckx formed in Kentucky in 1812 the Friends of Mary at the Foot of the Cross, better known now as the Sisters of Loretto. Working first among the English Catholic settlers near Bardstown they grew and sent out branches, especially into the Southwest and West, becoming one of the major communities in American Catholic education. At approximately the same time at Bardstown a group of Catholic women under the lead of Catherine Spalding and the guidance of Father John B. David formed the community of the Sisters of Charity of Nazareth, which sent teachers into many other American Catholic settlements.

In 1818 the Religious of the Sacred Heart came to Missouri to help Bishop William DuBourg. Under the leadership of the saintly Mother Philippine Duchesne, they settled in St. Louis and in Grand Coteau, Louisiana. About the same time the Third Order of Dominican Sisters was organized in Kentucky and sent missions into Ohio under the direction of Father Fenwick and Father Thomas Wilson. The multiplication of these communities of women and their growth in membership were the best hopes for the quality of later American Catholicism.

For Bishop John Carroll the most important problem was the perpetuation of the priesthood, especially since his own community, the Jesuits, could not expand after their suppression. The first to come to his aid were the Sulpicians who, while not a religious order in the technical sense, live mostly in communities devoted to the education of priests. More than any other community or organization in the United States they have formed the public image of the American Catholic priest—one faithful to his work of sacramental sacrifice, to preaching the word of God, and to Christian instruction. Their first institution was St. Mary's Seminary at Baltimore.

In 1817 the Fathers of the Mission, better known as the Vincentians, likewise noted for their dedication to the training of priests, came with Bishop William DuBourg to make their headquarters in Missouri. Their first leader was Father Joseph Rosati, later Bishop of St. Louis. Other prominent Vincentians were Bishops John Timon of Buffalo and John M. Odin of Galveston. These, with many other zealous religious, directed seminaries in various parts of the country. They were also very important missionaries in Texas and Illinois.

The Jesuits were reorganized as an order in America in 1805 and began at Georgetown that remarkable educational activity that has produced over 28 collegiate institutions in the country. The American Bishops begged them to go again into the Indian missions in the South and West. Their heroic activities as Indian missionaries, which they shared with many others, such as the Benedictines, have been glorified by the accounts of Father Peter J. De Smet and Bishop John Baptist Miege.

Another community noted for its devotion to the liturgy as well as its devotion to education was the Benedictine Order, which came to Pennsylvania

St. Regis Seminary in Florissant, Missouri. The two story frame building in the center is the Indian school.

First log cathedral in St. Louis. Note cemetery at right and bishop's house behind the primitive church.

An early sketch of the second Catholic church built in St. Louis in 1819. This was the start of the college.

in 1846, then to Indiana and Minnesota and many other states.

Of the religious devoting themselves mostly to preaching missions and renewing the fervor of the established parishes, the Jesuits had such heroic figures as Fathers Francis Weniger, Arnold Damen and William Pardow.

A community very active at first among the Germans and later throughout the nation has been the Redemptorists. Coming in 1833 they opened their first monastery in Pittsburgh in 1839. They were the counselors of some of the most noted American converts. From the Redemptorsts in part came the Paulists, the first American community of priests, founded by Father Isaac Hecker in 1858 and devoted especially to the conversion of America. Similar in activity were the Fathers of the Precious Blood, who established their centers in Ohio and Indiana.

In 1841 the newly formed Congregation of Holy Cross from LeMans, France, sent Father Edward Sorin with six Brothers of Holy Cross to Vincennes, Indiana. They settled first near Montgomery, Indiana, and the following year (1842)

The founder of Notre Dame University, Father Sorin

199

St. Ferdinand's Church in Florissant, Missouri, was the home of Blessed Mother Rose Duchesne. On the right is the convent where Blessed Sister Rose lived and worked through her years as a missioner on the western frontier. The famous church and grounds have been preserved through the hard work of the Florissant Historical Society.

A statue in the Church of St. Louis, King of France

The dining room of
Blessed Sister Duchesne

A relic of St. Valentine is buried under the altar of the church.

The log cabin chapel of Notre Dame. The University was founded on land owned by the missionary, Father Badin.

Father Moreau, founder of the Holy Cross Fathers

moved northward and founded the University of Notre Dame on land once owned by the pioneer missionary Father Theodore S. Badin. Sorin was soon joined by other priests, Brothers and Sisters. A few miles away, in 1843, Father Sorin set up the community of the Sisters of the Holy Cross from LeMans, which blossomed under the direction of Mother Angela Gillespie into St. Mary's Convent and Academy and later St. Mary's College. In southern Indiana, Father Sorin met the Sisters of Providence from France, who had settled near Terre Haute in 1840 under the leadership of a fellow Breton, Mother Theodore Guerin.

The multiplication of Sisters' communities followed local needs and there was no national pattern. Some were diocesan, some were branches of European communities. In 1829 the Oblate Sisters of Providence was formed in Baltimore for the care of Negroes. That same year the Sisters of Our Lady of Mercy came to aid Bishop John England at Charleston.

An aerial view of the University of Notre Dame. This renowned Indiana University was founded by Father Sorin.

The Sisters of Charity of the Blessed Virgin Mary were founded by five Irish women who came to Philadelphia in 1833 to form a religious community. Under Father Terrence Donaghoe they began their community with Bishop Kenrick's approval in Philadelphia, but in 1843 transferred the center of their activity to Dubuque.

In 1836 the Sisters of St. Joseph came from France to assist Bishop Joseph Rosati in St. Louis. Although their first teaching was at the old village of Cahokia, their real motherhouse was established at Carondolet, near St. Louis. From Carondolet the community spread to many other dioceses, established many other convents, one of the more noted of which was that in St. Paul. The Sisters of Notre Dame de Namur came to Cincinnati in 1840 and have since spread throughout the country. The Sisters of Mercy began in Pittsburgh in 1843. Their good work in hospitals and schools has since become nationwide. When the Civil War began, the religious priests and Sister served loyally as chaplains and as nurses in the hospitals and for the armies.

Of all the religious who have given of themselves as workers to maintain the charitable and spiritual works of Catholicism, the least known are

203

St. Joseph's Academy in Emmitsburg, 1845

Arnold J. Damen, S.J., founder of Loyola University

the auxiliary Brothers of the various communities, such as the Jesuits, Dominicans, Franciscans, Augustinians, Redemptorists, Holy Cross and similar communities. Their labors took the place of money and other worldly riches needed for growth. With the spread of the Catholic school system, Brothers dedicated to the classroom also became a serious need. The Brothers of the Congregation of Holy Cross arrived in 1841, taught at Notre Dame and in many parochial schools during the 19th century and in more recent times in high schools. The Brothers of the Christian Schools were introduced into New York by Archbishop John Hughes in 1846 and now have schools and colleges throughout the country.

Under the direction of Father Leo Meyer, S.M., the Marianist priests and Brothers began their teaching apostolate in Cincinnati and later at what is now the University of Dayton. They have since opened many high schools in various parts of the country. Similar work has been carried on since 1854 by the Xavierian Brothers of Bardstown, Kentucky, and by the Brothers of the Sacred Heart since 1847.

By the outbreak of the Civil War the convents of sisters and the monasteries of priests and brothers had become so numerous that a full account of their growth and multiplication in this short space would be impossible. Many other communities of religious came into the country during the following century and there were new extensions of the older communities. They came not only to look after the older immigrants, but also to care for the heavy immigration of Catholics who came from eastern and southern Europe from the end of the Civil War to the 1920's, when a limit was placed on this kind of immigration. Generally the newer communities devoted themselves to the care of the later immigrants, but their work as well as that of the previously established communities was modified by the changes in living conditions in the United States. . . .

In estimating the role of religious priests, brothers and sisters in the present position of Catholicism in the United States, the statistician must understand that the religious, more than perhaps any other group, have had to make up for the cultural and economic deficiencies of the Catholic population. They themselves have not had a plenitude of either wealth or cultural tradition on which to base their work. Under the circumstances their accomplishments constitute the religious wonder of the 20th century. But it is also well to note that the religious, by the very public character of their services, were not protected from criticism and are not blind to their mistakes. Constructive criticism must also see that such tremendous accomplishments have been the result of a confidence based on deep faith in Providence and a cheerful optimism that has paid off, so far.

As can be seen from this advertisement, steam transportation had progressed rapidly by 1845. This took place in less than fifteen years after the initial successful trip of the steamer, "De Witt Clinton."

NEW HAVEN AND NORTHAMPTON
DAILY
CANAL BOAT LINE,
AND
STEAMBOAT TO CHEAPSIDE.

The New Haven and Northampton Canal Transportation Line have extended their line of Boats to Cheapside, by adding a Steamboat to run from Northampton. They have also a Steamboat running in connection with the above line from the Basin Wharf in New Haven to New York.

By this arrangement Goods shipped from Albany and Boston by the Western Railroad via Westfield Depot, and from New York and the South via New Haven, will arrive at Cheapside with safety and regularity in the best deck Canal Boats.

The Steamboat Franklin will leave Northampton for Cheapside landing, on MONDAY, WEDNESDAY, and FRIDAY. Returning, leave Cheapside landing on TUESDAY, THURSDAY, and SATURDAY. The Steamboat SALEM will leave the Basin Wharf in New Haven for New York, every MONDAY and THURSDAY at 9 o'clock P. M. Returning leave Old Slip, New York, every TUESDAY and FRIDAY, at 5 o'clock P. M. For freight or passage inquire of *J. & N. BRIGGS*, No. 40 South Street, New York, or of *N. A. BACON*, New Haven, or of the Captain on board.

Freight from Boston and Albany will be delivered daily at the Brick Depot, Westfield, and transhipped without delay in the canal boats for Northampton and Cheapside landing, near Greenfield, and in connection with

BEECHER'S DAILY LINE FROM NEW HAVEN,
the present arrangement affords facilities and dispatch hitherto unenjoyed.
The rates of freight generally have been reduced, and Flour from Albany via the Western Railroad, will be delivered at Northampton, *for 34 cents per barrel,* and from Albany to Cheapside landing for 40 cents.
For further particulars inquire at the store house west side of the Deerfield Bridge, at Cheapside, of JOHN R. BOYLE; HENRY BEECHER, New Haven; J. & N. BRIGGS, No. 40 South Street, New York, or of the subscriber at Northampton.
JOSEPH L. KINGSLEY, General Agent.

Northampton, April 1, 1845.

John Lancaster Spalding

John Lancaster Spalding, the great Catholic educator

JOHN Lancaster Spalding is sometimes referred to as the Father of American Catholic Education. The title can be argued. However, there can be no informed argument about the role Bishop Spalding played in education and that in many of his ideas he was far ahead of his time. Neither will anyone quarrel with another title: Father of the Catholic University of America.

The life of Bishop Spalding was a bridge between the pioneer Church in pioneer America and the coming of age of both. John Lancaster Spalding was born in Lebanon, Kentucky, in 1840, the first of nine children. His early schooling was given by his mother. When he was 17, he entered St. Mary's College, Emmitsburg, Maryland, but lasted less than six months. Along with some other students, he was expelled for protesting a faculty decision.

Deciding to study for the priesthood, John Lancaster spent two years at Mt. St. Mary's of the West in Cincinnati. His uncle, Martin John Spalding, had become Bishop of Louisville and he persuaded his brilliant nephew to journey to Belgium to complete his philosophy and theology at the University of Louvain, where he was ordained in 1863. He then went to Rome for a year of postgraduate studies.

By this time Martin John Spalding had become Archbishop of Baltimore. His nephew did not join him in the Mother See of the United States but returned to Louisville where for the next seven years he filled many diverse roles. He was an assistant at the cathedral parish, secretary to the bishop, principal of the Cathedral school, editor of the diocesan newspaper and chancellor of the diocese. It was during this period that he began arguing for a national Catholic university.

Following his uncle's death in 1872, he went to New York to write his uncle's biography. Archbishop Spalding's papers had been entrusted to Father Isaac Hecker, founder of the Paulist Fathers, and Father Spalding worked closely with this scholarly convert. In 1877, Father Spalding was nominated as the first bishop of Peoria, a newly created diocese in southern Illinois.

As a bishop, Spalding intensified his campaign for a Catholic university. Under his urging the Third Plenary Council of Baltimore (1884) appointed a committee to study the possibility of a university. It was a great triumph for him when in 1888 he preached at the cornerstone-laying of the new university which was to be founded in Washington, D.C. But his interest in education was not confined to the University alone. He led a fight in Illinois to repeal a law which discriminated against Catholic schools and he promoted education for women, including the establishment of a Sisters' College at the new University.

A revealing insight into Bishop Spalding's thinking came in his clash with Archbishop John Ireland. Although the two men were personal friends, this did not deter them from differing in public. Catholic schools in those times had many of the same difficulties that plague the system today, largely a problem of financing. Archbishop Ireland developed a plan, that has its modern echoes, whereby parochial schools would be leased to the public school system, the Catholic teachers would be paid out of public funds, and religion would be taught after regular school hours; through this plan Archbishop Ireland sought to avoid any conflict with the First Amendment.

Bishop Spalding argued from American traditions and a very keen perception of non-Catholic sensitivities. He wanted government kept as far as possible from interfering in Catholic education and said that to accept any government assistance meant opening the door to government supervision and direction. He also argued against decreasing the religious atmosphere in the classroom.

Among Bishop Spalding's contemporaries there were many giants but he ranked as their equal. He had a tremendous influence in the life of the Church and its educational policies. Outside the Church, he was regarded as an authority, and this scholarly and cultured man was held in esteem and respect. Columbia University awarded him an honorary degree and President Theodore Roosevelt enlisted his skills in arbitrating a coal strike. Bishop Spalding died in 1908 after a series of strokes, truly a bridge between the old and the new, between pioneer America and the modern United States.

Bishop Martin John Spalding, Baltimore Archbishop

A reproduction from the Book of Hymns of the Dead Sea Scrolls

Five Profiles

ONE of the first statements made in this book is that Catholic roots exist in every part of the United States, even in areas thought of as Protestant oriented. To this end we have seen various beginnings and contributions. No attempt has been made at a systematic or logical history of the Catholic Church in America, nor has an attempt been made to thoroughly dissect any one region or place. Many people who should come to life in the pages of history have been overlooked and many events worth retelling have not been recorded. To do so would take more than this one volume.

We have tried to present highlights and describe features of interest in the hope that the reader will go on to private explorations. We have not tried to make any hierarchy of balance as to length or position. On some areas, such as the Spanish contribution, we have been more detailed because we believed more should be known, the facts having been hidden behind the curtain of history for one reason or another.

Because there will be many areas or personages not treated, we thought there might be some advantage to pick a representative group and let them stand for all those who are missing. Accordingly, the next section presents five short profiles: first, that of a diocese, Columbus; a bishop, Benedict Flaget; a priest, Isaac Hecker; a Religious community of women, Sisters of Charity of Nazareth; and a layman, Angelo Noce. Few readers will know much about all of these selections; and many will not even have heard of some.

These five will stand for all the past Catholics of the United States, for the Unknown, who nevertheless deserve to be saluted and blessed.

CONTAINER CORPORATION OF AMERI

Mahatma Ghandi's definition of "University"

I do not want my house to be walled in on all sides and my windows to be stuffed. I want the culture of all lands to be blown about my house as freely as possible.

Mahatma Gandi

Columbus — Into Its Second Hundred

One day in 1808 Father Edward Fenwick, O.P., a missionary in Kentucky, founder of the Dominicans in America, and destined to become the first bishop of Cincinnati, was riding his horse through the forests of Ohio, making missionary rounds. He was deep in thought, although what he was thinking about is not recorded. Perhaps it was about the great Gallipolis land swindle of a few years earlier in which five hundred Catholic Frenchmen were persuaded to come to the New World and settle in an idyllic colony on the Ohio River. A prospectus distributed by land speculators Joel Barlow and William Playfair (!) painted this rosy picture:

A climate wholesome and delightful, frost even in winter almost entirely unknown, and a river called by way of eminence, the beautiful, and abounding in excellent fish of a vast size. Noble forests, consisting of trees that spontaneously produce sugar and a plant that yields ready-made candles. Venison in plenty, the pursuit of which is uninterrupted by wolves, foxes, lions or tigers. A couple of swine will multiply themselves a hundredfold in two or three years, without taking care of them. No taxes to pay, no military service.

What Messrs. Barlow and Playfair forgot to mention, apart from their exaggerations, was that the land was in the posession of Indians who were willing to protect it with their guns, that the "noble forests" had to be cut down, and that it is one thing to hunt or fish for pleasure and quite another when they are necessary to sustain life.

While Father Fenwick rode along with his thoughts, he suddenly became conscious of the sounds of an axe. Wondering who could be in this part of the desolate woods, he turned his horse in the direction of the sounds. Thus was discovered Jacob Dittoe and his family who since 1802 had been petitioning Bishop Carroll in Baltimore for a priest. Dittoe took Father Fenwick to the homes of two other Catholic families, those of John and Joseph Finck. None of them had seen a priest in ten or twelve years. Next morning, Father Fenwick offered Mass in the home of Mr. Dittoe, and

The first bishop of Cincinnati, Edward Fenwick, O.P.

thus was born the Church in Ohio.

At that time, Ohio was a part of the Bardstown, Ky., Diocese, newly erected and with its first bishop, Benedict Joseph Flaget—one of the truly great Catholic pioneers. Bishop Flaget's diocese embraced Kentucky, Tennessee, Indiana, Illinois, Ohio, Wisconsin and Michigan. In 1812, on his way to the council in Baltimore, Bishop Flaget visited Christian families in Somerset, Lancaster, Maysville and Chillicothe, urging the people in each place to build a chapel and a residence for a priest. The first church was finally built in Somerset in 1818, and Father Fenwick dedicated it, accompanied by his nephew, Father Nicholas

Young, O.P. For a long period they were the only two priests in all Ohio.

Father Nicholas Young, at the time of his death in 1878, was the oldest (85) priest in the United States. Father Young was a man of personal wealth which he used for his work. He claimed to have traveled 50,000 miles by horseback throughout Ohio. In 1819 he established the first Catholic church in Cincinnati. That same year he said the first Mass in what is now Zanesville. He persuaded a hatter turned tavern-owner, named John Dugan, to build a church there for the nineteen Catholics. In 1821, Ohio was made into a separate diocese, Cincinnati, and Father Fenwick named its bishop.

In 1825 Father Young journeyed to his hometown of Baltimore to meet his uncle who had gone to France and Italy on a begging tour. The three men started back to Ohio by way of Washington where they were joined by the famous Father Gabriel Richard of Detroit, the only priest to ever serve in Congress. The group started out, following a road that ran along the Potomac River. It was dark when they reached the mountains around Cumberland. Something frightened the horses and

John Baptist Purcell became bishop of Ohio in 1833.

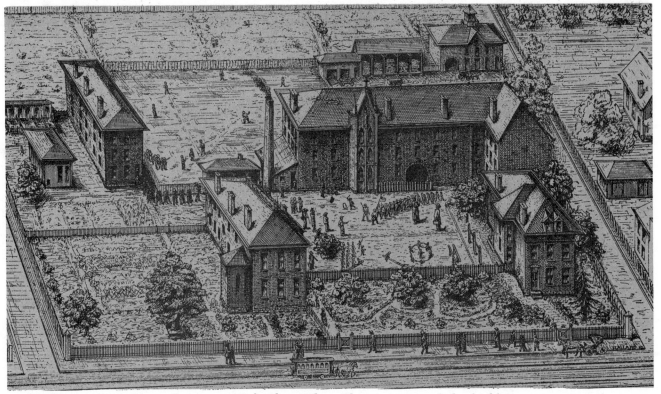

A sketch of St. Joseph's orphanage in Columbus, Ohio. This is a view of the building as it appeared in 1886.

The old canal system — this development which linked the east and west was largely a result of Irish labor.

they bolted. The passengers in the wagon were thrown out and John Dugan received a fatal injury, dying in Bishop Fenwick's arms. The priests brought his body back to Zanesville and John Dugan was buried beneath St. Thomas Church, whose property he had bought and donated to the diocese.

When Bishop Fenwick died, John Baptist Purcell was appointed the new bishop for Ohio (1833). It is one of the marvels of Providence that there were a large number of unusually competent, intellectually gifted and tremendously dedicated men that the young American Church could call upon for leadership. When the small number of priests from which they were drawn is considered, the fact is all the more remarkable. For some it is a sign that God has great expectations of the American Church.

Ohio was still pretty much a wilderness when Bishop Purcell took office. He took possession of seventeen churches, fourteen priests, and seven thousand Catholics. When he died fifty years later, his diocese had become an archdiocese out of which two new dioceses had been created, Cleveland and Columbus; Ohio had five hundred churches, almost the same number of priests, and a half million Catholics.

Bishop Purcell was an extraordinary man. Born in Ireland in 1800, he emigrated to Baltimore

James Shields, American Catholic general and senator

213

as a youth where he worked and saved money to enter Mount St. Mary's College, Emmitsburg, Md. Deciding to become a priest, he went on to Saint Sulpice Seminary in Paris which had given so many priests to America. He was ordained in Notre Dame Cathedral in 1826, returned to teach at the Mount, became vice-president, and then at the ripe age of twenty-nine, president of both college and seminary. It was from this post he was made bishop and sent to Ohio, where the former scholar took to the saddle as if born in it. It is said that Bishop Purcell never spent more than two weeks at a time in his See city but was forever moving about his vast diocese.

Like so many other American bishops, he had to depend upon Europe for help. The United States was a mission territory and would be for many more years. In 1839 Bishop Purcell went to France and signed up seven volunteers for his territory. Two of the priests became extra famous because they were immortalized in a novel by Willa Cather, "Death Comes for the Archbishop." They were Fathers John Baptist Lamy, who was to become the first Archbishop of Santa Fe, and his long time friend and companion, Joseph Machebeuf, who was to become the first bishop of Denver. They served the Ohio parishes of Danville and Lower Sandusky, respectively.

The big change to central Ohio began in 1825 when the legislature approved the extension of the Erie Canal into the state. The canal not only brought many Irish as workers but developed commerce and industry. When the canal was approved in 1825, Columbus had 2,500 inhabitants. By the time the Civil War came the city had grown to 18,-000. The usefulness of the canal ended with the Civil War and railroads took over the haulage. Today a few locks and some ditches remain, but in its time the canal was largely responsible for developing interior New York, Ohio and Indiana.

One of the more interesting figures that strode through the history of the Columbus diocese was Father Edward Fitzgerald, an Irishman who had his own mind. When he was appointed to be pastor of St. Patrick's Church in Columbus in 1857, the announcement even precipitated a riot among parishioners who wanted to retain their old pastor. The *Catholic Telegraph* described it this way: "When the Archbishop announced his intention of changing the Pastor, a number of ignorant and violent persons, who seemed to have been well trained in low groceries, proceeded with vulgar brawling and gesticulations, to strike the doors with their clenched hands, insisting that the appointment of the Pastor and the control of the church belonged only to them."

After a few days of disturbance, Father Fitzgerald finally took possession of his parish which he immediately proceeded to develop, bringing in Brothers and Sisters as teachers. He also began to build a new parish church which was to become the diocesan cathedral. During the Civil War, Father Fitzgerald was unwavering in his loyalty to the Union, flying the American flag from the tower of his church. He organized an Irish-American military unit which was among the first to volunteer for service. But he was a priest first, and was a regular visitor at Camp Chase, a prison for Confederate prisoners. He administered to these unfortunate men, and also lectured them about their "mistaken" sympathies.

After the war, Father Fitzgerald was appointed bishop of Little Rock, Arkansas. He attended the First Vatican Council in 1870 and gained his

Clarence Elwell, Bishop of Columbus, died in 1973

RNS PHOTO

footnote in history by being one of two bishops who held out to the bitter end against papal infallibility. After he left for Little Rock, a new pastor was appointed to his parish—Bishop Sylvester Rosecrans, auxiliary to Bishop Purcell.

It was Bishop Rosecrans who became the first Bishop of Columbus when the area was made a diocese on March 3, 1868. Bishop Rosecrans was a native of Ohio and an alumnus of Kenyon College. When his brother, Army Lieutenant William Rosecrans, entered the Church, Sylvester followed him. He transferred to Fordham University (then St. John's College) in New York and it was here that he decided to become a priest. He was ordained in Rome in 1852. As Bishop of Columbus he began a seminary at which he taught and brought in new teaching orders. He built the present cathedral, dying on its day of dedication. He is buried in the cathedral.

He was succeeded by scholarly Bishop John Watterson, who had been president of Mount St. Mary's Seminary. Under his administration, the diocese underwent considerable expansion. He developed Catholic schools and saw approximately sixty new churches built. During his administration, the famous Josephinum, a seminary to provide priests for German-Americans, was begun by Monsignor Joseph Jessing, which in 1892 became a pontifical seminary, directly subject to Rome. The Josephinum trained many excellent priests, many of whom are at work in the Mid-West.

The third bishop, Henry Moeller, only spent a few years in Columbus before moving on to Cincinnati and he is known chiefly for lessening the huge debt left by his predecessor's building campaign. The fourth bishop, the saintly Bishop James J. Hartley, was a native of the diocese who was consecrated in 1904. He had been a pastor of proven administrative ability. Bishop Hartley wiped out the debt on the cathedral, built several score new churches, doubled the number of schools, and founded St. Charles Borromeo Seminary. He was known nationally for his support of the Catholic Press. The Catholic Press Association was founded in his diocese and held its first convention there in 1911. He also began *The Columbus Register*, now published under the name of *The Catholic Times*. The good bishop died in 1944.

The next bishop was a proven organizer and administrator, Bishop Michael J. Ready, who for many years had been general secretary of the National Catholic Welfare Conference. He centralized diocesan agencies, organized many lay activ-

Cardinal Carberry of the Archdiocese of St. Louis

CATHOLIC TIMES

Bishop Rosecrans, brother of the Civil War general

The Church of St. Augustine in New Stratisville, Ohio, as it celebrates the 100th anniversary of its founding.

ities, created eighteen new parishes, and was particularly strong in giving support to social action movements. He was succeeded upon his death in 1957 by Bishop Clarence G. Issenmann, a large, jovial, competent man who had studied in Fribourg and Rome where he earned degrees in theology and philosophy. Upon his return to the United States, he made special journalism studies at the *Register* system in Denver, Col., and then became an editor of the Cincinnati *Telegraph*. As a bishop, he was appointed by his fellow bishops to head the NCWC Press Department and for many years was honorary president of the Catholic Press Association. He is known in Columbus for his progressive social works, his educational development, and for his great kindness to his priests and people. He was transferred to Cleveland in 1964.

The new bishop who came to Columbus was a man of many parts. A native of Brooklyn, New York, he had been pastor and professor there, as well as president of the Canon Law Society of America. For a time he served on loan as a chancellor in Trenton. He was John J. Carberry, who at the time of his appointment to Columbus, was

Bishop of Lafayette, Ind. He assumed the task of translating the decisions of Vatican II into practice and soon won the respect and admiration of the priests, faithful and non-Catholics of Columbus. He was transferred to the Archbishopric of St. Louis in 1968, and shortly was named a Cardinal. He was succeeded by Bishop Clarence D. Elwell, who had been an auxiliary bishop in Cleveland. Bishop Elwell brought an impressive background in educational administration to his new diocese, having served many years as an official of the National Catholic Educational Association. He died suddenly in early 1973.

This then is a quick thumbnail sketch of one American diocese, its development and some of the people that brought it to its present position within the American Church. Columbus was selected not for any particular reason, other than it is typical. It has a story that could be repeated in varying form for most other sections of the country. It is the story of a growing Church in a growing America. It is peopled by dedicated men and women whose actions and deeds proved their love for their religion and their nation.

My Old Kentucky Home

Bardstown is a quiet, little place of five thousand souls that sits astride a road junction in north central Kentucky. The Blue Grass Parkway bypasses the town and devotees of the Sport of Kings no longer go through the town on the way to Churchill Downs but use the new superhighways. The only attention most tourists pay to Bardstown is to use it as an exit to reach "My Old Kentucky Home" not far away. Outside of its classic colonial former cathedral, now a national treasure, there is little to interrupt their sightseeing. Yet Bardstown was once the center of Catholic life for the Old West and more celebrated and famous priests walked its streets than any other town its size can boast, al-

Bardstown was the center of mid-western Catholicism.

Father Charles Nerinckx was a Kentucky missioner

though Vincennes, Ind., comes a close second.

When Bishop John Carroll asked the Holy See in 1804 to divide his diocese of the United States because it was just too unwieldly, Rome finally obliged in 1808 and created the dioceses of New York, Boston, Philadelphia and Bardstown, and raised Baltimore to an archdiocese. Bardstown had been the center for Catholic activity west of the Alleghenies. Some great and mighty priests had worked out of there: Stephen T. Badin, John David, Anthony Salmon, Charles Nerinckx, Edward D. Fenwick and Benedict J. Flaget. It was the last named who was called from his post to become Bardstown's first bishop.

Flaget, along with Badin and Simon Bruté, was a product of the French Revolution. He had come to this country with Badin and David and offered his services to Bishop John Carroll. All

217

RNS PHOTO

"Giving thanks before the meal." The life of the early settlers was tedious and comforts and luxuries were rare.

Father Benedict Flaget was to be the first bishop of Bardstown. He, along with Badin, had fled from France.

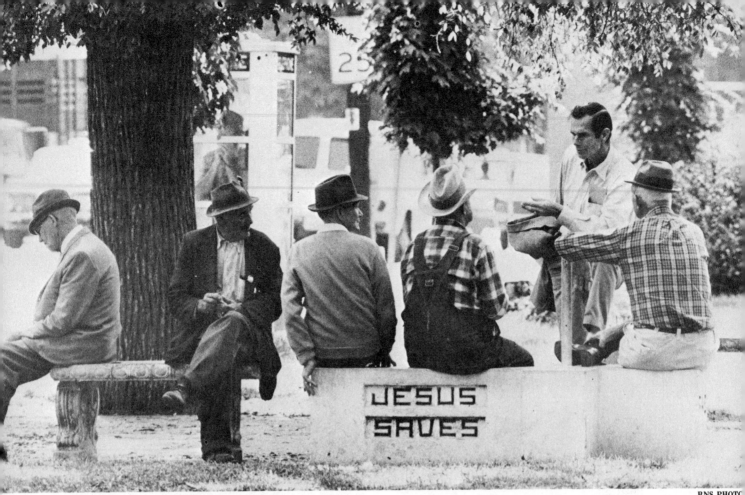

Mountainmen pass the time while sitting on a rock marked "Jesus Saves" which is in Pineville, Kentucky. Religious signs are popular in this area which saw the immigration of so many missionaries.

three were accepted, although Badin was not yet ordained. Bishop Carroll took care of that problem by raising Badin to the priesthood in the first ordination in the United States. Badin was assigned to Kentucky and Flaget to Indiana. For the next fifteen years Badin carried the Church on his small shoulders, virtually alone. Those who met him always wondered how so small and seemingly frail a man could be such a tireless giant who actually spent as much time on the back of his horse as he did off.

Along with his request for the division of his diocese, Bishop Carroll suggested that Bardstown be created the Western See. He even suggested names for its bishop: Nerinckx, Badin, Flaget and Samuel Wilson, a Dominican. Rome chose Flaget who at the time was teaching in St. Mary's Seminary in Baltimore. Father Flaget had good qualifications: he was a devoted Sulpician, with all that that implied in the way of spirituality, scholarship and historicity; he had had three years experience

on the Vincennes frontier, no easy task in itself; he had taught at Georgetown and St. Mary's and worked for a short period in Cuba.

Like the humble man he was (Bruté was to act the same way when his elevation to the hierarchy came), Father Flaget believed himself a most unlikely candidate for the episcopate. He spent three months assailing Bishop Carroll with all the reasons he could muster why he was not the man for Bardstown. Failing, he went to see his Sulpician superior in Paris to enlist his aid but that worthy gentleman had already been briefed and told the unwilling candidate that he had no choice: the pope wanted *him*. So he accepted, and then with French practicality used the occasion of his visit to raise funds for the Western mission and gain recruits; two of those who returned with him to the United States were future bishops—Simon Bruté and Guy Chabrat.

Flaget was consecrated by Bishop John Carroll in Baltimore, November 4, 1810, the sixth

American bishop. In the spring of the following year he was installed as bishop of his diocese in the log chapel Badin had built in Bardstown. His territory would have frightened any man—Kentucky, Tennessee, Ohio, Indiana, Illinois, Wisconsin, Michigan, and parts of Arkansas, Missouri and Minnesota; everything that lay in the United States between the Alleghenies and the Mississippi.

The job Flaget did is amazing. He created new dioceses, brought in religious, encouraged the foundation of native communities, built churches and schools. Although on the frontier, he was a national figure and was to consecrate three Archbishops of Baltimore and four Western bishops of dioceses he fashioned from his own. Seldom was a man loved for his own goodness as this humble Frenchman of such great talent. The story is told that the first time he met the literary Bishop John England, he exclaimed: "Let me kiss the hands of one who has written so much about the Church!" To which Bishop England, in a revelation of his own greatness, replied: "Let me kiss the hands of one who has *done* so much for the Church!"

Bishop Flaget was not a stay-at-home ordinary. He was forever moving about his diocese, always with an active pastoral sense. Nothing gave him greater pleasure than to find a group of Catholic families who had long been without a priest; he would stay with them administering the sacraments and offering Mass. Usually a man in authority makes enemies among those he must discipline, among those who are jealous; but Bishop Flaget had no enemies, even those he had to chastise were captivated by his humility, charm and unaffected grace.

Flaget founded educational institutions that were to have a lasting effect on the American South and West because of the men and women trained in them. St. Joseph's College, St. Mary's College, his seminary—each played an important role in building the Church in the West. The classic cathedral at Bardstown, with its soaring wooden columns, its Grecian proportions and stately tower, was of his design and stands today as a national monument to his genius. But he was not jealous of his perogatives. At his suggestion, Cincinnati was created as a diocese and he consecrated Father Fenwick its first bishop. His own secretary, Father Francis Fenwick, became Bishop of Philadelphia at his suggestion. So did Bishop Bruté in Vincennes and the first Bishop of Nashville. Father Chabrat was consecrated as his coadjutor, and a half-dozen other of his priests became bishops.

Stephin Badin — known as the "Apostle of Kentucky"

After a long trip to Europe and at the age of 75, Bishop Flaget rode horseback over the entire state of Kentucky to check on his diocese. Younger priests who accompanied him, freely admitted that they could not keep up with his pace. As a result of this trip, he recommended that the center of his diocese be moved from Bardstown to Louisville; he saw no future for his beloved see city and realistically realized the potential of Louisville. The Holy See agreed and the last nine years of his life were spent as Bishop of Louisville. He died there at the age of 87 on February 11, 1850. He had been sixty-two years a priest and forty of them a bishop on the American frontier.

Man Out of Season

Father Isaac Hecker — founder of the Paulist Society

IF Bishop Spalding can be called a bridge, Isaac Thomas Hecker might be referred to as the first man on the other side. Actually, although Hecker and Spalding were contemporaries, Hecker was the older and he died twenty years before Bishop Spalding was to retire. Both men grew to maturity along with the American nation. But the effects of the works of Hecker are still having their impact while those of Bishop Spalding are more difficult to assess.

Isaac Hecker was born in New York City on December 18, 1819. His family was attached to no particular church and the boy grew up without religion. Although he had a sharp mind and keen sense of observation, he left school while still a boy to join his brothers in the family bakery. It was a life that held little appeal to his restless intelligence and he sought escape. As he grew into young manhood, he thought that politics might be a good outlet. He associated himelf with Tammany Hall but soon discovered that what went on behind the political facade was not to his liking.

Hecker found that the world held little appeal to him and he might have been headed for the isolated path of Thoreau, except that he consulted Orestes Brownson, an independent thinker and incisive writer. Brownson advised him to get away from his normal surroundings and think. He suggested a social community experiment that was just starting in West Roxbury, Mass., called Brook Farm. Brownson advised him to go there and pray. Hecker went to Brook Farm and met there many of the leading literary lights of the day.

The young New Yorker was still not satisfied. He continued to correspond with Brownson, explaining the turmoil and uncertainty within him. Brownson led him gradually to an examination of religion, showing him that more than human power was needed to solve the problems of the world. Hecker began an investigation of Protestantism and then Catholicism. His search brought him in contact with many of the religious leaders of the day. Finally, he came to the conclusion that there was only one true Church and that he must become a Catholic. Friends tried to dissuade him from this step but he was adamant. On August 2,

Archbishop J. McCloskey — the first American cardinal

1844, he was received into the Catholic Church by Bishop McCloskey of New York.

But Hecker believed he had not gone far enough because he felt that something was still lacking. "Providence calls me," he wrote, "to convert a certain class of persons amongst whom I found myself before my conversion." He was not clear how he was to do this but as a first step he decided to become a priest. He joined the Redemptorists and in 1851 was ordained. He was assigned to the Redemptorist mission band to give missions to Catholics. But he was still restless. He believed that his particular mission was to non-Catholics. As a former companion of intellectuals he concluded that he knew what mental blocks they had that prevented an objective consideration of the claims of Catholicism; he believed these friends were men of good will who were seeking truth, including the Supreme Truth, and he knew how to show it to them.

To test his ideas, Father Hecker wrote two books: *Questions of the Soul* and *Aspirations of Nature*. The books aroused considerable attention, particularly among non-Catholics, many of whom entered into correspondence with the young priest. Now a new problem arose. The work of the Redemptorists was largely among German immigrants or their descendants; many of their missions were conducted in the German language. The Germanic intellectual outlook had no appeal for the Anglo-Saxon non-Catholic. Hecker sought to persuade his congregation to establish a wholly English-speaking branch. He discussed his idea with Archbishop Hughes of New York and Bishop Bayley of Newark. Both men encouraged him and suggested that he go to Rome to explain his idea to the superior of the Redemptorists.

Somewhere along the line wires became crossed or perhaps Father Hecker thought he had all necessary clearances from his religious superior when he didn't. At any rate one of those unpleasant, but in the long run providential, contretemps took place that have influenced too much religious history. In Rome his Redemptorist superior castigated him for making the journey without all the necessary permissions and then with the abruptness all too typical of religious superiors of the day, expelled the young American from his community. Stunned, Father Hecker appealed to the Holy See. After much documentation and investigation, Pope Pius IX decided that the best solution all around was to release Father Hecker and his associates (he had the support of other Redemptorists from the mission band) from their Redemptorist vows and suggest that they begin a new community.

It was a happy solution. The Redemptorist General had his authority supported and Father Hecker was left free to give the new work the direction he felt it needed. Three other former Redemptorists, converts like himself, joined him to begin the new community. They agreed to continue their parish mission work but defined the goal of the new society, the Paulists, as the conversion of America. Father Hecker did not want to restrict the new society (the first original American foundation for priests) to aims that might change. He stated that the society should "meet the needs of the Church as they arise." The Rule was approved by Archbishop Hughes on July 10, 1858, and the headquarters were based in New York.

Over the years, Father Hecker's wisdom has been proved time and time again as the Paulists changed emphasis to meet current conditions. While the Society has never had spectacular growth in numbers, its influence has been disproportionate to its size, and its priestly contribution to the American scene has been outstanding, presenting such men as Fathers Burke and Gillis to the work of the Church.

From lecture platform and pulpit, Father Hecker began preaching his message. He was an ecumenist before the word was known. He believed that Protestant beliefs should not be assaulted, rather they should be led from those points held in common with Catholics to a legitimate inquiry of differences. In a day of acute religious polarization, when most pastors looked upon Protestants as enemies who were schismatics at best and heretics at worse, Father Hecker pioneered a form of apologetics far in advance of his time.

Father Hecker was a believer in the use of social communications and he took advantage of those available to his day. He began the *Catholic World*, insisting that it meet the highest quality in standards; the magazine is still being published and is the dean of Catholic magazines in the United States. He started a pamphlet program which developed into the Paulist Press. He also began *The Young Catholic*, an important magazine of its time with a prestigious circulation; it is no longer published.

Father Hecker became one of the most important clerics of his day. He was friend, confidant and advisor to bishops all over the country. He had a major role of influence at the Second Baltimore Council in 1866. One bishop described

Paulist Press has continued the work of Fr. Hecker.

Paulist Press headquarters in Glen Rock, New Jersey

his talks there as "Pentecostal fire." The more practical New York *Tribune* noted, "There is an electric influence about him which sets everybody in motion," and added that he would give "his colleagues plenty to do and think about." In one speech he advocated greater use of the laity to counteract an idea "in the minds of the public that lay Catholics had nothing to do in their religion."

The pace at which his zeal drove him, finally proved too much for his constitution and Father Hecker had to withdraw from active work. From England, Bishop (later Cardinal) Vaughan wrote telling him to conserve his strength because "I would rather hear that five Archbishops of the United States had gone to receive their reward than learn that you had." In his last days, he set his community's affairs in order and on December 22, 1888, he went to anticipate Christmas in Heaven.

Sisters Come to Help

The year after his arrival in Bardstown, Ky., (1812) Bishop Flaget was heartened by the foundation of two new communities of Sisters, distinctly American. Father Nerinckx, with the assistance of Mary Rhodes, began the Sisters of Loretto, which today has grown to a strong community, staffing schools from primary to college. These Sisters are credited with receiving the first Negro postulants in America in 1824. In December of that same year, Father John David founded the Sisters of Charity of Nazareth. The story of these latter Sisters is set down here as representative of the many communities of American women who have served their Church and country so well.

From the moment he came to Bardstown, Bishop Flaget wanted a group of devoted women who would supplement his efforts. He lacked the funds to bring Charity Sisters from France, and realized that the answer would have to be found locally. He approached the Sisters of Charity (Mother Seton's foundation) in Emmitsburg, Md., but they were just getting started themselves and could spare no Sisters for Kentucky.

The bishop spoke about the problem to his old friend, Father David, who located two young women who agreed to try to begin a Sisterhood.

Those ladies were Teresa Carrico, who admitted "she could never get anything out of books," and Elizabeth Wells, who was called by Father David "a pure and noble soul but somewhat eccentric in her ways." Their convent was two rooms in a log house. A few weeks later, they were joined by energetic Catherine Spalding, who although only nineteen, was chosen as superior, a post she was to hold for the next quarter of a century. By Easter, the group had grown to six and the Sisters moved to a log cabin with two rooms on the ground floor, kitchen and common room, and an attic used as a dormitory.

"We were so poor," Sister Teresa recalled years later, with a suggested complaint so common to our own days, "that many a time I did not know what to put in the kettle. But something always came. And now the young Sisters can't imagine

Mother Catherine Spalding of the Sisters of Charity

what it used to be."

The Sisters named their new log cabin "Nazareth," and thus they became known as the Sisters of Charity of Nazareth. They were not yet ready to begin work, however. They needed training for themselves. Mother Spalding set up a program of manual work, some social action such as caring for the sick, and several hours of classroom work each day. Things were not ready-made on the frontier and the Sisters had to spin and weave, knit and sew; bake their own bread, grow their own vegetables and even make their own candles. When they went to church each day, they carried their shoes to save them, only putting them on when they were about to enter.

Soon the Sisters started their academy and by 1815 had thirty-four boarders. They adopted the rule of the Daughters of Charity of France; took as their motto, "The charity of Christ urges us"; and designed a religious dress. They began a day school in Bardstown and another in Union County in Western Kentucky. When they learned that they did not have a clear title to their land, they finally settled on the present site. Under Mother Catherine's direction a school was started in Scott

Sisters of Charity of Nazareth begin the work started in Bardstown, Kentucky, by three women.

County and then the Presentation Academy was opened in Louisville.

There was a devastating cholera epidemic in 1833 and the Nazareth Sisters closed their schools until it should pass. But they did not spend the time in mere waiting but began nursing the sick in Bardstown and Louisville. One of the results of the cholera epidemic was the creation of orphans but Mother Catherine met this challenge by opening an orphanage in Louisville for twenty-five youngsters. In the same building, they set aside a few rooms in which to care for the sick; this infirmary was the beginning of St. Joseph's Infirmary, one of the largest hospitals in the South.

When Mother Catherine Spalding died in 1858, the Sisters of Charity of Nazareth was a well established community with strong foundations which she had set in place. In the history of the early Church in America male figures dominate, but working quietly and without fanfare, often making a bishop or pastor look good for the records, were devoted women of the calibre of Mother Spalding.

In 1860 Nazareth Academy in Bardstown counted a hundred pupils from Louisiana and half that number from Mississippi, plus Kentucky girls. But then the Civil War came and parents from Arkansas and Texas sent their daughters to Nazareth while many Sisters went off to nurse Union and Confederate soldiers. One interesting memento at the Nazareth motherhouse is a Presidential Order signed by Abraham Lincoln which directs that "no depredations be committed" on the Sisters property. The nursing Sisters cared for soldiers in Bardstown, Louisville and Paducah, and were asked to staff several military hospitals.

When the war ended the Nazareth Sisters began a school in Mississippi. They originated works in Maryland, Virginia and Massachusetts. In 1920 Catherine Spalding College was begun in Louisville. It is now a fully accredited college of four years. One of its greatest contributions to Kentucky has been in the large number of excellent nurses it has produced.

In the post-Vatican II years, the Sisters of Charity of Nazareth have had reverses suffered by all communities as the Church renews itself. Vocations fell off. In 1966 Nazareth Academy was discontinued. Where the Sisters will develop in the second half of their second hundred years is anyone's guess. But with the strong roots they have, the pioneer spirit of Mother Spalding will find radical solutions. One thing is quite certain. The Sisters will not have to carry their shoes to church.

A Layman with an Idea

The United States was built on the efforts of many nations: The Poles (whose Orchard Lake Seminary alone trained hundreds of priests), Hungarians and Slovaks, Germans and Lithuanians, and many others. This book is not big enough to recount all their contributions. Therefore, we have selected one Italian immigrant, unknown to most Americans, as typical of the other unsung millions.

Angelo Noce was born in Genoa, Italy, in 1848. Two years later, his parents joined the steady march of immigrants to the United States. They settled on the east side of New York City, faced with problems met by every new immigrant family: language and work. Giacomo Noce, the father, was determined to make his way in this new land. He worked at a series of odd jobs and when he came home at night he heard fellow immigrants in the streets talking about the fortunes in gold that were to be made in California.

For a man who had pulled his roots up once, a second time was more easy. Bidding his wife and children a tearful farewell, Giacomo set out to California. There is no record of his difficult journey overland but he did reach the gold fields and from his earnings there the Noce brood in New York was able to survive—along with the part-time jobs of Mama Chiara. Finally, Giacomo had enough money to go home and bring the family to California, which he justifiably preferred to New York's crowded tenements.

Thus the Noces set out for the Golden West. They sailed to Panama, crossed the isthmus by donkey, and took passage on a steamer to San Francisco. Everybody helped and it wasn't long before they were able to put a down payment on a house in Jackson. Angelo went to school there and it was there that he learned about Christopher Columbus and was surprised to find out that America's discoverer came from his own hometown, Genoa.

The story of the Noce family is the story of thousands of European immigrant families. They learned that America would share its largesse with

Angelo Noce, we owe a holiday to this man's dream.

those who worked hard for it and saved. By the time Angelo was in his upper teens and ready for college, his father was able to send him to the newly founded St. Mary's College in San Francisco. After he had finished there, he took more courses at Santa Clara. He had been working part time as a printer and reporter, and decided to make these his career.

Angelo took stock of opportunities. San Francisco was a port city, always crowded with more men than jobs. He had heard that Denver, Colorado, was going to boom because of the mining industry in the Rockies. So he pushed on to Colorado where he began a successful printing business. He also accepted civic responsibility and served as deputy sheriff, a county assessor, a constable and a clerk in the Colorado legislature. He married an Italian girl in Denver and before long was the father of four sons and two daughters.

In Denver, Angelo identified with the Italian community and was pleased when the Italians had a fiesta on October 12 to honor his fellow Genoan, Christopher Columbus, on the date of his discovery. But why, he asked himself, should it be only Italians who honor Columbus, after all his discovery benefited every American? Cristoforo's day of discovery should be a holiday for all Americans. But how was this to be done?

Angelo went to see a friend in the Colorado House of Representatives and spoke to him of his idea of having October 12 declared a holiday in Colorado. The friend, probably welcoming Italian support for his own future candidacy, promised he would have a bill prepared for the House, but he must also have liked the idea because he persuaded a colleague in the Senate to introduce a similar bill in that body.

Angelo did not rest there. He began a campaign with every one he met to get behind the idea. He visited the newspapers throughout the state and obtained editorials of support. He sent his own wife around to see women. He buttonholed senators and representatives seeking their support. The Governor (Jesse F. McDonald) was so persuaded by all the arguments that he issued a proclamation declaring Columbus Day throughout the state. Finally, the bill passed and was signed by the Governor in a public ceremony on the capitol steps in which Angelo Noce played a prominent part. Thus, through the efforts of one man, Colorado became the first state in the Union (1907) to observe Columbus Day as a state holiday. When October 12 came that year, flags flew and there were parades all over the state.

Most of us would have stopped there, considering our job well done. But not Angelo Noce. Columbus belonged to all Americans, not just to those in Colorado. He traveled from state to state speaking to religious leaders, mayors, governors, to anyone who would listen. Gradually the idea of this Catholic immigrant spread. When he died in 1922 at the age of 74, Angelo Noce had seen his idea adopted by thirty-five states. So next Columbus Day when you drive off to the beach or mountains, remember the little man who started it all and gave you a holiday through the democratic process he came to love, Angelo Noce of Genoa and Denver.

In 1905, the first signing declaring "Columbus Day" in Colorado. Angelo Noce's dedication to this project was the inspiration behind this worthy proclamation.

III. THE CHURCH COMES OF AGE

The Legacy of Cardinal Gibbons

THE golden age of the Catholic Church in America is said to have begun with the elevation of Archbishop James Gibbons to the cardinalate. Historian Peter Guilday says of Cardinal Gibbons, "In a sense, the history of the Church in the United States from 1870 down to our own day is largely a biography of his episcopate."

From 1886, when Archbishop Gibbons was appointed a cardinal, until his death in 1921, the Church in the United States had a phenomenal growth—from 7 million Catholics to 20 million; from 7,000 priests to 20,000. During this period the number of bishops doubled; 200 orders of women and 70 orders of men, including teaching and nursing Brothers, began work in the United States. Some were native American foundations, others from Europe.

The Age of Cardinal Gibbons was an era in which America underwent tremendous social changes. It was the time when the term "social justice" came into being, when labor unions began, with Cardinal Gibbons defending and protecting the Knights of Labor. It was the period when the encyclical of Leo XIII, *Rerum Novarum* (Of New Things), rocked the social structure of the world. It was the period in which the battleship *Maine* was sunk in the harbor at Havana, setting the stage for war between the United States and Spain, the war that resulted in giving the United States control of the Caribbean Sea, Guam and the Philippines. It included the years of the first and terrible World War. The Age of Cardinal Gibbons was the time when the Church in the United States ceased to be a mission Church and became itself mission-sending, with the establishment of the Catholic Foreign Mission Society of America (Maryknoll).

Cardinal Gibbons was born in Baltimore in 1834. As a boy he studied in Ireland, then returned to America to live in New Orleans. He decided to become a priest, entered Saint Charles College, and matriculated to Saint Mary's Seminary. He was ordained in 1861 and for the next seven years held various pastoral and administrative posts in the Baltimore Archdiocese. At the age of thirty-four, in 1868, he was consecrated a bishop and appointed Vicar Apostolic of North Carolina.

The new bishop's territory embraced the entire state of North Carolina, in which there was a total of three churches, two priests, and a widely scattered Catholic population of one thousand souls. Bishop Gibbons traveled from one end of the state to the other and is said to have met every adult Catholic in his care. He opened a school, in which he himself taught, built six churches, brought in Benedictine monks to establish an abbey at Belmont, and persuaded the Sisters of Mercy to take over two schools in Wilmington. All this he accomplished in only four years, for in 1872, Bishop Gibbons was transferred to the see of Richmond, Virginia.

During his years in North Carolina, Bishop Gibbons had spent his time while riding horseback throughout the state in planning a book of apologetics he intended to write. The completed volume, *Faith of Our Fathers*, was to sell many hundreds of thousands of copies, break down prejudice, and introduce many people to the Church. Bishop Gibbons had seen the Church survive the "Know Nothing" assault, and he hoped his book would explain the Church to non-Catholics of good will that they might better understand the Catholic religion.

The national Catholic population at that time was five million in a nation of forty million. There were seven archdioceses, fifty-three dioceses, and seven vicariates. Bishop Gibbons was to see these figures grow. At the time of his death in 1921 there were fourteen archdioceses, one hundred dioceses, two vicariates, twenty-one thousand clergy, seventeen thousand churches, and a Catholic population of eighteen million. Catholics were represented in the highest professions, and more than a representative number occupied various posts in national, state and local government.

Bishop Gibbons did much to develop the Diocese of Richmond. In 1877, he was transferred to Baltimore as coadjutor to Archbishop James Roosevelt Bayley. When Archbishop Bayley died later that year, Bishop Gibbons was appointed his successor, head of the first archdiocese in the United States. From that time on he was a national figure, the most influential American in the growth of the Church. He was the youngest member present when he attended the Vatican Council, the oldest, surviving member when he died. He headed the Third Plenary Council of Baltimore, which produced so many important decisions, particularly those related to the establishment of the parochial school system. It was this Council that recommended the establishment of the Catholic University, a project in which Archbishop Gibbons had been interested for a long time.

Pope Leo XIII was so satisfied with the way Archbishop Gibbons had handled the Third Baltimore Council, and so pleased with the stature the Archbishop was gaining in America that in 1886 he named the Archbishop to the college of cardinals. As the leading churchman in America, Cardinal Gibbons was often called upon for counsel, particularly in settling thorny problems. During his period as Archbishop of Baltimore, a number of controversies arose. One was the famous school dispute over the role that the state should play in parochial schools. Another was the attack on the Church by Frenchmen who accused Catholics in the United States of "Americanism"—compromising doctrine to adapt to a pluralistic society. Cardinal Gibbons made his views known to the Holy Father, and the controversies subsided.

Cardinal Gibbons believed very strongly that the Holy See should have representation in this country, despite the fact that there was much feeling against it by anti-Catholics. When Archbishop Bedini, Papal Nuncio to Brazil, visited the United States in 1853 there were raucous demonstrations against him, threats of death, denunciations in the press, and hangings in effigy. When he left the United States the archbishop boarded his ship secretly from Staten Island rather than provoke a possible riot at the Manhattan pier. Twenty years later, in January of 1893, the Apostolic Delegation was opened in Washington with Archbishop Francis Satolli as delegate. The anti-Catholic American Protective Society (A.P.A.) said that the Archbishop's presence was the greatest stimulus to membership it could receive. Nevertheless, the delegation was established, and anti-Catholic attacks on it have long been forgotten.

During the first World War, Cardinal Gibbons was an example of tireless patriotism. He gave his active support to the newly organized National Catholic Welfare Conference, now the present Conference of Catholic Bishops. Through this organization Catholic war efforts were coordinated.

In 1918, Cardinal Gibbons celebrated his golden jubilee as a bishop, the first American-born prelate to reach this mark. Pope Benedict XV sent a special message, and testimonials and congratulations poured in upon the grand old man of American Catholicism. Cardinal Gibbons died quietly on March 24, 1921, having lived a life span that encompassed the greatest period in the development of the United States and of the Church in the United States.

The third Plenary council of Baltimore, headed by Cardinal Gibbons, was convened in 1884.

James Gibbons, he was the youngest delegate at Vatican I. He was also the last living member of that Council.

Catholics in Two World Wars

IN 1914 a fanatic fired several shots into an archduke in distant Sarajevo. The repercussions of the incident were felt all over the world. The outbreak of international war in Europe had direct effects in the United States, and the Catholic Church here did not escape unscathed. The Church in the United States had its main foundations in two great immigrant movements—German and Irish. (The Italians were to come later.) It was natural to expect that Americans of German ancestry should side with Germany in those days between 1914-1917 when America was supposedly neutral. The Irish in the United States did not sympathize with Germany so much as they opposed England. The nationalistic movement in their Irish homeland had much support in the United States, and the unsuccessful 1916 Easter Week rebellion in Ireland intensified feelings against Great Britain.

Like the majority of other Americans, Catholics hoped that the United States could keep out of the conflict that was raging in Europe. America itself was not threatened but American interests were at stake; and as the war progressed, the United States was drawn closer and closer to an hour of decision. Finally, President Wilson, who had recently been re-elected "because he kept us out of war," went before Congress and asked for a declaration of war against Germany. The archbishops of the United States, who were preparing to hold their annual meeting in the Catholic University at Washington, immediately made known the Catholic position, the first religious body to make a statement.

"Our people, as ever, will rise as one man to serve the nation," declared the archbishops. "Our priests and consecrated women will once again, as in every former trial of their country, win by their bravery, their heroism, and their service, new admiration and approval. We are all true Americans, ready as our age, our ability and our condition permits, to do whatever is in us to do for the preservation, the progress and triumph of our beloved country."

Overnight, the Catholic faithful moved into line behind their bishops. Irish and German Catholics remembered that first they were Americans, and the entire Catholic body gave itself wholeheartedly to the war effort. The hierarchy established the National Catholic War Council in Washington to coordinate the Catholic contribution, and the Catholic parish became the basic unit for action. The Knights of Columbus organized a broad program of aid to the servicemen and of rehabilitation for the devastated countries. In an initial war-fund drive, Catholics raised 5 million dollars. Later they participated in a drive for over 107 million dollars, of which 30 million went to the National Catholic War Council. Cardinal Gibbons wrote to all members of the hierarchy, asking their full support to make these drives successful.

Although Catholics at that time numbered 17% of the total population, it is estimated that the proportion of Catholics in the armed forces was much greater. It is difficult to pinpoint exact figures, because of the way records were kept. Michael Williams, the editor of the *Commonweal* and a Catholic writer of note, estimated that between 25% and 35% of the Army was Catholic, and that almost 50% of the Navy was Catholic. By the end of the war, about a million Catholic men were under arms.

There are a number of reasons why the Catholic contribution to the armed services was higher than its proportion to population. Because patriotism was taught to Catholics as a virtue many Catholic young men joined the services without waiting to be drafted. A large percentage of draftees from the Protestant South were discovered to be suffering from pellagra, a disease caused by undernourishment but which in those days was thought to be communicable. These men were excused from service. Medical examinations also turned up a high percentage of social diseases, which had a lower rate among practicing Catholics and Protestants than among persons who belonged to no church or practiced no religion.

Catholic chaplains were in great demand, and

Catholics served in World War I contrary to the rumors that their faith would prevent them from being patriotic.

Rev. Francis Duffy with Col. "Wild Bill" Donovan

1,026 of them served in various branches of the service. At first the role of the Catholic chaplain was misunderstood. To some officers, a chaplain was supposed to be merely a booster of morale, a sort of commissioned Red Cross worker. When it became apparent, however, to officers that the priest was willing to risk his life to aid a soldier, the Catholic chaplain was much sought after. Michael Williams tells of one instance in which five Catholic priests were assigned to Camp Sivier in South Carolina where there were only 600 Catholics among 32,000 men. When an attempt was made to transfer three of these chaplains, the commanding general protested, saying that he wanted to retain those priests and take them overseas with his divisions.

Father William O'Connor was chaplain of the 120th Field Artillery of the 32nd Division. Six times in twenty-two days he was cited for bravery. Where shells fell thickest, there Father O'Connor was to be found ministering to the wounded. Captain Ren L. Holsclaw, a non-Catholic member of the same regiment, has left us a description of Father O'Connor at the front that might fit so many chaplains. He describes how the men of his regiment were gathered under a group of trees waiting to attack when Father O'Connor (referred to as "Bill" in Captain Holsclaw's account) made a sudden appearance.

"I was not at all surprised," related Captain Holsclaw, "to see Bill remove his tin hat and begin to talk. What did puzzle me, however, was how he was ever going to make himself heard. On the left a little back, the 121st Regiment of heavies was pounding away, firing on the bridges across the Vesle. Farther back some heavies were blasting the sky, while the foe was ripping up Chamery. It was just before the general attack on Fismes, and it sounded like all the noises of the world rolled into one place and let loose. As the night drew near, the sky was covered with what resembled sheet lightning from the flashes of the guns.

"I think Bill started to talk about seven o'clock. He didn't say much. Only told the story of Jesus going from some place and being stopped by lepers who seemed to know Him and prostrated themselves before Him, exclaiming as they did so, 'Jesus, Master, have mercy!' . . . Then after he had repeated 'Jesus, Master, have mercy' till it echoed in every heart, Bill asked us to sing. He read over a few lines of 'Lead, Kindly Light.' By this time the darkness had so settled in that the flashes of the guns lighted up the sky at each burst and

Reverend Francis P. Duffy conducts the graveside service for Quentin Roosevelt in France on August 9, 1918.

the little town of Chamery looked like the home of hundreds of glowworms flashing in the dark. So in this sort of setting, the battalion sang, 'Lead, Kindly Light amid the encircling gloom, lead Thou me on.' When we had finished Bill asked every one to repeat to himself the words, 'Jesus, Master, have mercy!'

"Whether the story and song helped or not, I cannot say, other than the battalion took the hill a half hour later in one assault, and occupied a position four kilometers (12,000 feet) forward before dawn of the next day. And, too, I nor any other present will ever forget the message or the man that gave it."

Probably the best-known chaplain of the first World War was Father Francis P. Duffy, of the famous "Fighting Sixty-Ninth," the Irish regiment from New York City. Father Duffy had a motion

picture made about him after the war, and today his statue stands at the north end of Times Square. It is an heroic bronze replica that portrays him as a chaplain. Though Father Duffy survived the war, many chaplains did not. According to the *National Catholic Almanac*, the first army chaplain killed was a Benedictine priest, Father Timothy Murphy; and the first Navy chaplain killed was another priest, Father Simon O'Rourke. Father Edward Wallace, of the Brooklyn Diocese, was stricken with poison gas while aiding wounded on the battlefield, and died in a hospital a few weeks later. Father John B. De Valles, of Boston, the first chaplain decorated in the war, died in 1920 from wounds received in action. Father O'Flaherty, of the 28th Infantry, was killed by a shell while gathering dead from the battlefield. Father William Davitt, of the 125th Infantry, was killed when a

Many Americans were angered by President Wilson's methods as can be seen by this newspaper headline.

fragment of enemy shell pierced his heart. He died on Armistice Day, just one hour and a half before hostilities ended. Thus the first and last chaplains to die in the war were Catholic priests.

There were eleven Catholic major generals and fifteen Catholic brigadier generals in World War I. The Chief of Staff for the American Expeditionary Force was a Catholic, Major General James McAndrew. The Chief of Naval Operations was also a Catholic, Admiral William S. Benson. One of the popular heroes of World War I, and also one of the most decorated soldiers, was Colonel William Donovan, affectionately known to his men and the American public as "Wild Bill." Colonel Donovan won all four decorations of the Army: the Congressional Medal of Honor, Distinguished Service Cross, Distinguished Service Medal, and the Purple Heart.

The *National Catholic Almanac* lists the following firsts in World War I that went to Catholics: first soldier wounded, first army officer killed, first sailor killed, first nurse wounded, first American to die on enemy ground, first prisoner of war, first to shell the enemy, first to meet the enemy in air, and first commander of an American division to capture important enemy positions. The following first awards were also made to Catholics: first Distinguished Service Cross, first posthumous Distinguished Service Cross, first women's award of the Distinguished Service Cross, first Navy award of the Congressional Medal of Honor, and first Army Aviation award of the Congressional Medal of Honor.

After an interval of nearly a quarter century, World War II found Catholics once again render-

Pope Leo XIII was the author of "Rerum Novarum".

236

ing heroic service to their country. The hierarchy organized the National Catholic Community Service, which became an official part of USO (United Service Organizations) and which established canteens, social centers, and hostels wherever American troops went, and provided for the serviceman a home away from home. The hierarchy also began Bishops' War Relief to aid victims of the war, which remains today as Catholic Relief Services. This organization has mounted the largest nongovernmental relief operation in the world. Catholic priests again volunteered as chaplains, and 3,036 priests served with the armed forces, of whom 83 died during the war.

The Chief of Army Chaplains during the war was Brigadier General William R. Arnold, who was consecrated a bishop and after the war became head of the military ordinariate. A Catholic chaplain, Father Aloysius Schmitt, died in the opening battle of the war. He was among those who went down with the USS *Oklahoma* at Pearl Harbor. The first Congressional Medal of Honor ever given to a chaplain in the armed forces was awarded to Father Joseph T. O'Callahan, S.J., who risked his life to aid servicemen on the aircraft carrier *Franklin* when that ship was set ablaze in a kamikaze attack.

A commemorative postage stamp was released by the United States Post Office some years ago to commemorate four chaplains who voluntarily gave their lives when the troopship *Dorchester* was torpedoed in the North Atlantic on July 5, 1943. They were a Jewish rabbi, a Methodist minister, a Dutch Reformed minister, and Father John P. Washington, of Arlington, N.J. The *Dorchester* was carrying troops to Europe when it was struck. The chaplains assembled on deck with the soldiers for evacuation, and then it was discovered that there were not sufficient life jackets aboard. The chaplains took off their own life jackets and gave them to soldiers. As the ship went down, the four chaplains were seen with hands joined, singing "Nearer My God to Thee."

Not all priests who served the armed forces were commissioned chaplains. In the Orient many missioners driven from their posts by the Japanese served as contract chaplains. They held no rank but rendered the same service as the regular chaplain. One priest who volunteered was Father William T. Cummings, a Maryknoll missioner from San Francisco. Father Cummings was working as a missioner in the Philippine Islands when the war broke. He immediately offered his services to the

In New York, ceremonies are conducted for Fr. Duffy.

237

Army and was accepted. He was to make an heroic record, serving the soldiers, through the terrible siege of Bataan, the infamous Death March, and finally to his death aboard a Japanese prison ship.

During an Easter sermon on Bataan, Father Cummings originated the famous statement of World War II, "There are no atheists in fox holes!" Brigadier General Carlos Romulo, aide to General MacArthur, was present at the Mass and heard the sermon. Later, when he escaped from Bataan, he sent the phrase flaming around the world. A nurse, Juanita Redmond, also escaped, and told the world of the heroism of Father Cummings under fire when enemy planes bombed a base hospital, despite the fact that it was plainly marked.

"Right in the middle of the bombing," reported Lieutenant Redmond, "Father Cummings, the Catholic chaplain, came into our ward.

" 'Boys, that was tough,' he said, 'but let's pray to God they don't come back.'

"He stood there praying with his hands in the air. He prayed for about five minutes, and then another wave of bombers struck. One bomb fell only a few yards from him, and a piece of it broke his arm and cut his shoulder, but he never stopped praying and his voice didn't falter. It wasn't until the last bomb fell that Father Cummings finished his prayer. Then he turned to another chaplain who had come in, and said: 'All right, partner, take over. I'm wounded.'

"He certainly saved a great many lives that day, because if he had not come in and told the boys to stay by their beds, a good many more would have run out into the open and been machine-gunned."

Father Cummings was back at work the next morning, and he remained with his soldiers through the terrible days ahead, until starvation and exhaustion cost him his life.

One out of every four members of the armed forces in World War II was a Catholic. It is estimated that the distribution of Catholics was higher in the Navy and Marine Corps than in the Army. By the time the war came to an end, the names of 67 Catholics had been added to the distinguished winners of the Congressional Medal of Honor, the nation's highest decoration given for heroic service over and beyond the call of duty. Of the Catholic winners, 48 were in the Army, 10 in the Navy, and 9 in the Marine Corps. Captain Richard E. Fleming was the first Marine officer, and Sergeant John Basilone, the first Marine enlisted man, to receive the Congressional Medal.

Carlos Romulo, Philippine Foreign Affairs Secretary

One of the earliest heroes in the war was Major James P. Devereux, the Marine commander on Wake Island. Major Devereux and his 400 Marines held off a powerful Japanese landing force for two weeks. His men sank one Japanese cruiser and three destroyers, besides shooting down many Japanese planes before the defenders were overwhelmed. Taken prisoner, Major Devereux spent the rest of the war in a prison camp. After the war, he was elected to Congress from Maryland.

Catholics held important command posts in World War II. General Alfred Gruenther planned the invasions of North Africa and of Italy; he was a right hand to General Eisenhower. He later served on the Joint Chiefs of Staff, as commander of NATO and still later became president of the Red Cross. Admiral William Leahy was a chief advisor to President Roosevelt, with whom he attended important Allied conferences. General Walter Bedell Smith was Eisenhower's Chief of Staff and played a major role in the invasion of France. General Anthony C. McAuliffe delivered the most-quoted expression of the war. When his 101st Airborne Division was surrounded by the Germans at Bastogne, his terse reply to a German order to surrender was the single world, "Nuts!" The 101st held out until reinforcements arrived.

General William Donovan, the World War I hero, was the spymaster of World War II. He headed the secret and important Office of Strategic Services. Peppery General James Gavin commanded paratroopers in Sicily, Salerno and Holland, and after the war became Ambassador to France, and an outspoken critic of the Vietnam War. General Joseph Lawton Collins made a brilliant war record that included the capture of Cherbourg. Later he was head of the Joint Chiefs of

Greunther later became president of the Red Cross.

Staff, the top military man of the United States. Other Catholic general officers who had outstanding records include Generals John M. Devine, Alonzo Patrick Fox, Geoffrey Keyes, Walter Muller, Martin F. Scanlon, and Donald Frank Stace—all of the Army; General Arthur Thomas, of the Air Force; General C. R. Sanderson, of the Marine Corps; and Admirals William Callaghan, D. V. Gallery, John B. Heffernan, and Vincent R. Murphy.

Early in the war, the entire United States mourned with an Irish-Catholic family. The family was that of Tom Sullivan, a freight conductor on the Illinois Central, who lived in Waterloo, Iowa. Mr. and Mrs. Sullivan had five sons in the Navy: George, Frank, Joseph, Madison, Albert. The boys served aboard the light cruiser, *Juneau*. In the Battle of the Solomon Islands, the Japanese sank the *Juneau*, and the five Sullivan boys went down with their ship. It was a tragedy that touched the heart of every American family. The Vice-President of the United States sent a telegram to Mr. and Mrs. Sullivan calling the loss "one of the most extraordinary tragedies which has been met by any family

Gen. A. C. McAuliffe with a cartoon depicting his famous reply

239

An artist's rendition of the death of four World War II chaplains who perished on the troopship "Dorchester"

in the U.S." The heroic manner in which the parents bore their great loss was an inspiration to all Americans. "Christ had five wounds too," Mrs. Sullivan told reporters. A motion picture was later made of the story, and a warship was named for the Sullivan brothers.

This same spirit of heroism and acceptance of God's will was again exhibited to the country when a letter from Marine Lieutenant Anthony Turtora was published in the press. Lieutenant Turtora's letter arrived at his home in the Bronx after his parents had received word that he had been shot down over Guadalcanal. To Tony Turtora's parents his last words seemed like a summary of his

life: "Always pray, not that I shall come back, but that I will have the courage to do my duty."

Tony Turtora's prayer was the spirit Catholic servicemen brought to the challenge of World War II. They died in every part of the world, on land, in the sea, and in the air. They stood shoulder to shoulder with their fellow Americans of all faiths —and fought bravely for the country that was their homeland. Some of them became heroes, like Lieutenant Colonel Francis Gabreski, who shot down thirty German planes; others fought the war in unsung roles, ordinary GI Joes, who met the enemy from their foxholes and so fulfilled their American destinies.

After Pearl Harbor, American troops engaged the enemy all over the world.

General (Bishop) William R. Arnold signed the first certificate of award to the Churches on July 23, 1943.

Patriotism, love of one's country, has been a virtue that the Catholic Church has taught its followers. It was Christ who said that a person should give his country its due and Saint Paul wrote that the Christian should be obedient to authority. Vatican Council II called upon citizens to have a loyal devotion to their country and taught that they "should practice true and effective patriotism." Patriotism is a cousin of justice which compels us to pay our debts to our country. It is an ally of charity which demands that we love our fellow countrymen.

But the Church has never inculcated blind patriotism or patriotism carried to excess. These are other names of nationalism, an inordinate affection for one's own country to the detriment of the rights of other nations. Nationalism is really a false religion in which the State has been substituted for God. It is opposed to the unity of the human race. In our own times, nationalism disguised as Nazism, Fascism and Communism has wrought great havoc in the world and taken the lives of many young Americans.

The contribution of Catholics in the various wars of the United States have been delineated up and through World War II. Two more recent wars —the Korean conflict and the war in Vietnam— will not receive the same documentation because we are too close to them and too many are still alive to make final judgments. Suffice it to say, that Catholics did their share in these wars, alongside all the other peoples who make up America. They had their share of leaders and heroes.

In researching material on patriotism, the question arose about how many chaplains won the medal of honor, the nation's highest decoration which is presented in the name of Congress for "conspicuous gallantry and intrepidity at the risk of life above and beyond the normal call of duty." Investigation revealed that only four chaplains have received this medal—and by coincidence the four happen to be Catholics. This is not said in any way to impugn the patriotism and heroism of non-Catholic chaplains, of which there are many examples. But this book happens to be about Catholics in the United States and for this reason the deeds of others are not recorded here.

Although the Medal of Honor originated with the Civil War, it was not until World War II that it was first bestowed upon a chaplain. That first recipient was Chaplain (Commander) Joseph T. O'Callahan of the Navy. Father O'Callahan was a Jesuit from Boston, Mass., who was a chaplain aboard the aircraft carrier *Franklin*. The ship was attacked by kamikaze (suicide) squads of Japan, just as it was getting ready to launch its planes. In moments the huge vessel was an exploding in-

ferno. Father O'Callahan went among the explosions and fires to minister to the dead and wounded. When he had taken care of the spiritual needs of his men, he organized firefighting crews, directed the jetisoning of ammunition and bombs, played a hose on hot bombs that were rolling about the deck—all of this in spite of heat, smoke and immediate danger to life. After the war he returned to Holy Cross College in Worcester, Mass., where he died in 1964.

The second medal went to an Army chaplain in Vietnam, Father Angelo J. Liteky, of Jacksonville, Fla., a member of the Missionary Servants of the Holy Trinity. Father Liteky was serving with an Army light infantry unit when it was ambushed in 1967. Despite heavy fire, he crawled within yards of an enemy machine gun to reach two wounded soldiers and drag them to safety. Although wounded in the neck and foot, Father Liteky personally carried over twenty wounded men to a landing zone for evacuation. Father Lite-

Funeral procession of Bishop Arnold, the first Catholic chaplain to be buried in Arlington National Cemetery.

Congressional Medal of Honor, the highest military decoration of the United States

ky is alive and at this writing is still an Army chaplain.

Another medal winner was Maryknoll Father Vincent R. Capodanno from Staten Island, N.Y. He was a Navy chaplain attached to the 1st Marine Division in Vietnam. He was in the Company Command Post when he learned that a platoon was trapped by enemy fire. Without thought of his own safety he braved heavy gunfire to reach the trapped Marines. He moved about the battlefield, giving the last rites to the dying and aid to the wounded. An exploding mortar inflicted many painful wounds on his arms and legs and severed part of his right hand but he refused medical aid himself and refused to evacuate the area while Marines were in need. Seeing a wounded hospital corpsman in the line of enemy fire, he went to his aid. Just as he reached the wounded man, a machine gun burst caught him in the head, neck and chest and

Chaplain Angelo J. Liteky, Medal of Honor recipient

Chaplain Joseph O'Callahan, USN, receives Medal of Honor from President Harry S. Truman on January 23, 1948.

Father   Capodanno

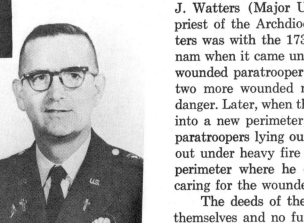

Father Watters

he was killed. Father Capodanno had spent his whole life as a priest in the Orient, working first in Taiwan as a Maryknoll Missioner, and then his last several years in the mud and sweat of Vietnam as a chaplain. He was an American who loved his country and who loved all of God's children, even those who took his life.

The fourth chaplain to win the Medal of Honor, like Father Capodanno, came from within sight of Manhattan Island. He was Father Charles J. Watters (Major USA) of Jersey City, N.J., a priest of the Archdiocese of Newark. Father Watters was with the 173rd Airborne Brigade in Vietnam when it came under attack. First, he carried a wounded paratrooper to safety; then he recovered two more wounded men and pulled them out of danger. Later, when the Americans were forced back into a new perimeter, he spotted several wounded paratroopers lying outside. Three times he crawled out under heavy fire to drag injured men into the perimeter where he cared for their needs. While caring for the wounded, he was killed himself.

The deeds of these Catholic priests speak for themselves and no further comment on patriotism is needed.

In the wilderness on the outskirts of Chancellorsville, a cross marks the grave of an unknown Union soldier.

The cloud of war has cleared from the sky over Europe but the memory of those who fought and died lives on.

In Europe, a monument dedicated to all of the men who died while fighting for their countries in two world wars.

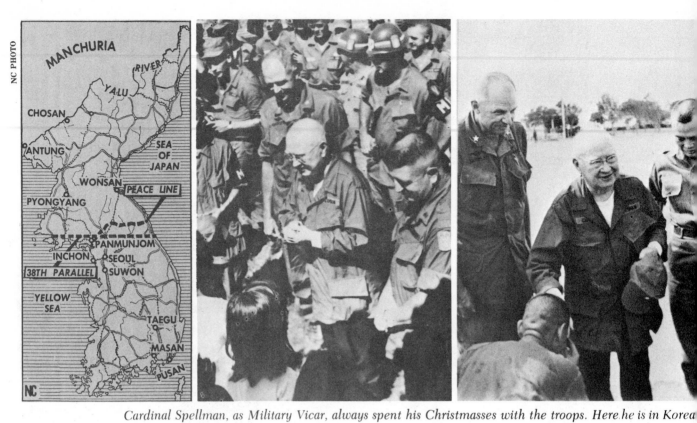

Cardinal Spellman, as Military Vicar, always spent his Christmasses with the troops. Here he is in Korea

The homeless and the orphans. The war in Korea touched the civilian in many ways as can be seen from these faces.

KOREA

Korea and Vietnam

A quiet vigil for an American soldier far from home.

Newly ordained Korean priests. They are seen as they give their first blessing to their fellow religious.

American troops as they fight in Korea in 1950. The United Nations declared North Korea as the aggressor.

United Nations forces are greeted by civilians as they enter a local village in the early months of the war.

The American soldier in 1950

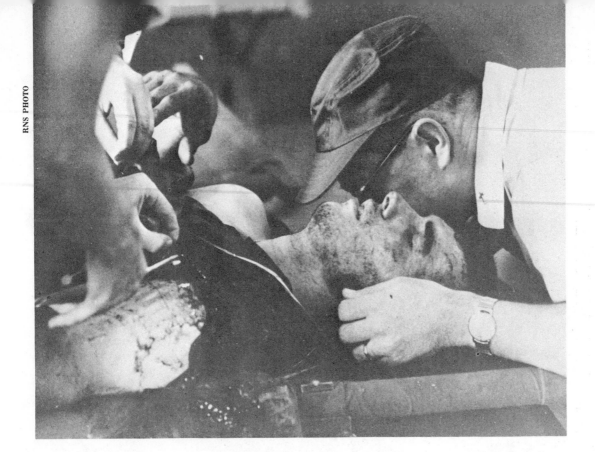

254

VIETNAM

General Creighton Abrams, the top U.S. military commander in Vietnam, recently converted to Catholicism.
(Bottom) A 25th Infantry Division soldier is removed
from a battle zone outside of Nui Ba Den in Vietnam.

(Opposite page)
(Left) A Chaplain comforts a badly wounded soldier.
(Lower left) Cardinal Terence Cooke visits Vietnam.

And
Deliver
Us
From
Evil

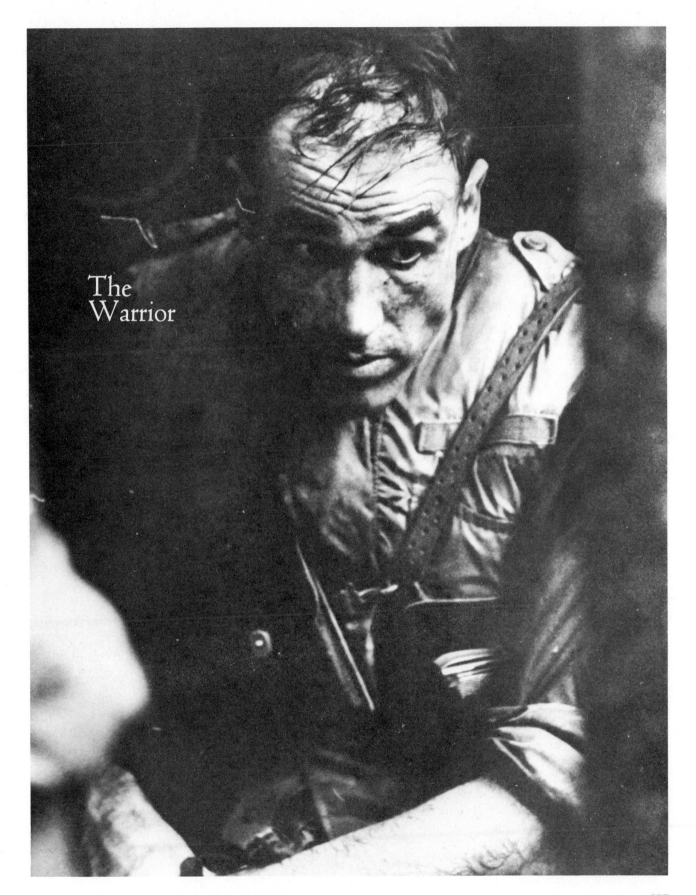

The
Warrior

The United States and the Mission Movement

ALTHOUGH Catholicism had been introduced in America by missioners, and although those heroic priests were among the foremost pioneers of our country, advancing always with its frontiers, the Church in the United States before the twentieth century had very little interest in apostolic work outside its own borders. This was not because religious leaders here did not wish to fulfill their essential vocations as Christians — namely, the evangelization of the world — but because the religious leaders were faced with so many immediate and urgent problems within the United States that work for the foreign missions had to be put off until another day. Europeans, particularly the French and Spanish, were left with the task of preaching the Gospel.

The Church in the United States was itself a missionary Church. The jurisdiction for the Church in the United States rested in the Sacred Congregation of Propaganda Fide in Rome, the missionary congregation. Moreover, Europeans were inclined to think of the United States as a mission field to which they must send men and money. Large bodies of European clergy came to the United States to do mission work among the Indians and also among their own nationals who had come to this country as immigrants.

Over the years there were a few Americans who worked in the foreign fields, but they were notable only because of their rarity. In most instances, these priests were members of a religious order or congregation that had its headquarters in Europe. They were not part of an American mission effort. This lack of broad vision and dedication was of serious concern to a few American priests who wanted to do something to remedy it. The first step was the introduction of the Society for the Propagation of the Faith into the United States in 1897; but even this Pontifical fund-raising agency was adopted only in a few of the larger dioceses.

The Boston S.P.F. Director, Father James Anthony Walsh, who had assumed his office in 1903, was one of the men in whom an interest in for-

eign missions was deep and abiding. He believed that America should contribute more than money to the mission apostolate, but he knew that the Catholic people needed to have a greater understanding of mission work if they were to offer their lives to it. He gathered a few priest friends about him to discuss the problem in practical terms. The result was that in 1906 the Catholic Foreign Mission Bureau was established for the stated purpose of preparing and publishing books on mission personalities and mission topics. The following year, the group brought out America's

Mother Mary Joseph was teaching at Smith College before entering the Maryknoll Missionary movement. She founded the Sisters.

Father J. A. Walsh was the Superior of Maryknoll until his death in 1936. He was a cofounder of with Father T. Price of North Carolina

Father Thomas Price, the other cofounder, was to head Maryknoll's first mission band in 1918. This dedicated man was to die in 1919.

American missions in the world. An artist's rendition of the headquarters of the Catholic Foreign Mission Society.

first national missionary magazine, *The Field Afar*. The SPF was publishing the *Annals of the Propagation of the Faith*, a translation of the French *Annals*, but it was French oriented. The announced purpose of the new magazine was to spread knowledge of foreign missions, but the group had recorded that its real aim was "to prepare the way for a Catholic Foreign Mission Seminary in this country." The plan was to have one of the European societies, such as the Mill Hill Society in England, establish a branch in this country.

There was another American priest interested in foreign lands and in getting a society to train Americans as missioners. He was Father Thomas Frederick Price, a native of North Carolina and a veteran of twenty-five years of mission work in the Tar Heel State. Father Price had accomplished many works — among them the founding and editing of the magazine *Truth* and the establishment of an orphanage — but he was still filled with a divine unrest. Then, by one of those strange arrangements of Providence, Father Price met Father Walsh at a Eucharistic Congress in Montreal in 1910. The two priests discovered that they were very much alike in their thinking, and before they left Montreal they had decided to work for the foundation of a foreign mission seminary.

There were subsequent meetings, and a plan was drawn up. It emphasized that the sole purpose of the foundation was to give the United States representation on the foreign mission fields by training American youths to be foreign missioners. The seminary was to be closely identified with the American clergy, because its mission priests would be their representatives. The Apostolic Delegate, Archbishop Falconio, advised that the hierarchy should be asked to back the project as representative of the American clergy and people, otherwise the new society would be just another organization with its future growth restricted. The best time and place to have the project adopted by the hierarchy would be the annual meeting of the archbishops in Washington.

Father Price went to see Cardinal Gibbons whom he had known for many years. The cardinal had once been his pastor in North Carolina, and as a boy Fred Price had served Mass for the future Archbishop of Baltimore. Cardinal Gibbons received the plan warmly and promised to give it his full support. He wrote to all the archbishops in the United States, outlining the project and asking them to consult with their suffragan bishops. The cardinal pointed out the need for such an organiza-

tion and stated that while requirements at home were great "the surest way to multiply our own material means for work at home, is by not limiting the expansion of charity and by not paralyzing the zeal of self-denial." He added that American Catholics could not delay participation in foreign missions "lest our own faith should suffer."

The archbishops met at the Catholic University towards the end of April, 1911. They unanimously approved the plan for a national foreign mission seminary, and they instructed Fathers Walsh and Price to proceed to Rome without delay to get all necessary authorizations to make the plan a reality. On June 29 the Sacred Congregation of Propaganda announced that it had decided favorably on the proposal. The two American priests were given formal authorization to open a house and recruit students. Thus the Catholic Foreign Mission Society of America came into being.

When Fathers Walsh and Price returned to the United States, they decided to establish the new Society in the vicinity of New York City. A site in Westchester County was purchased. Later a better property overlooking the Hudson River was bought, and the Society moved there. The new property was on a hilltop, and Father Walsh named it "Maryknoll," a title that was to become the popular name for the Society. Father Price scurried about the country, trying to find recruits for the new seminary. The first to join was Francis X. Ford, a New York seminarian. He was destined to become a bishop in China and to meet death at the hands of Chinese Communists. In Cumberland, Maryland, Father Price recruited James Edward Walsh, who was also to become a bishop in China, and who was to receive what was thought to be the equivalent of a life sentence in a Communist prison.

Many Europeans predicted that the new Society would not succeed, because American youths were too luxury-loving and did not have the stamina necessary for foreign-mission life. The year of 1913 gave the critics cause to think their prediction right, for not a single new student was enrolled at Maryknoll. The tide turned in 1914, with new students joining and the first priest, Daniel McShane, being ordained. By 1917, when the first mission field was obtained in China, the Society numbered eleven priests, twenty-five major seminarians, and thirty-five minor seminarians. The first mission band left for China the next year. It consisted of four priests: Fathers Price, Walsh, Ford and Bernard Meyer. From then on the

The first four missioners of the Catholic Foreign Mission Society of America to leave for China in 1918 were: (front) Fathers James E. Walsh, Thomas F. Price, Francis X. Ford and (standing) Father Bernard F. Meyer.

Kansas' Fr. Kapaun died in Korea. *Bp. Patrick Byrne died in N. Korea.* *Bishop Ford died in a Chinese jail.*

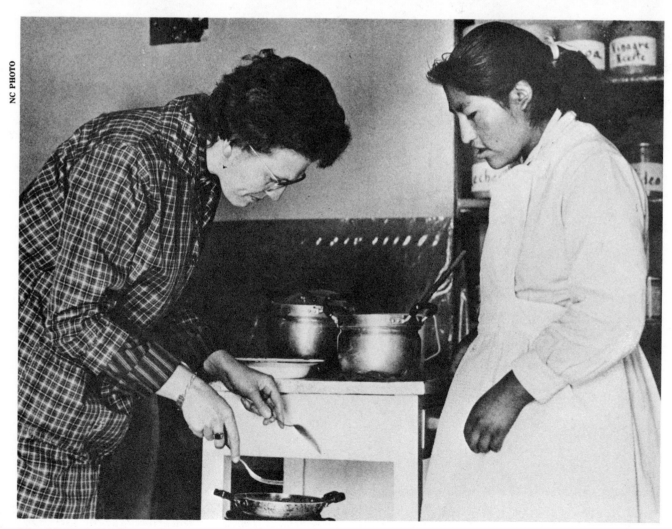

Mia Mermans, who works as a lay apostle, has started a training center for young women in Potosi, Bolivia.

Bishop James E. Walsh listens to the National Anthem as he is welcomed home to his boyhood town of Cumberland, Maryland, upon his return in October, 1970. Bishop Walsh was a prisoner for twelve years in Communist China.

Fr. Charles Nolan as he conducts a "man on the street" interview in the Philippines. He is a Columban father.

Two American missionary nuns were killed in the earthquake which struck Chimbote, Peru, in the Spring of 1970.

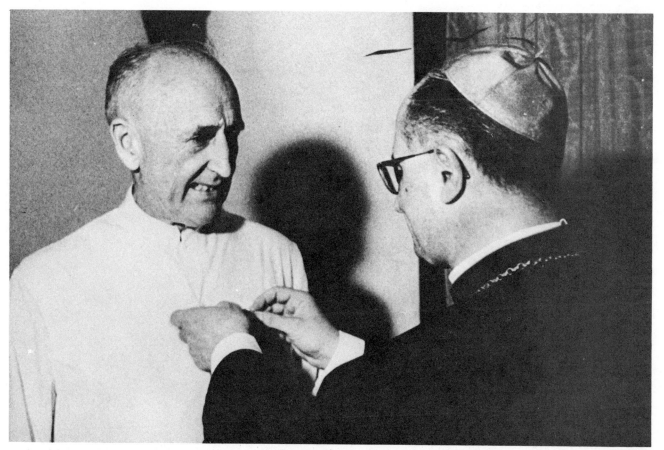

Columban Father Patrick O'Connor receives the Papal Cross Pro Ecclesia et Pontifice from Archbishop Palmas.
He has learned much from missioners.   A young man makes his living amidst a large amount of coconuts.

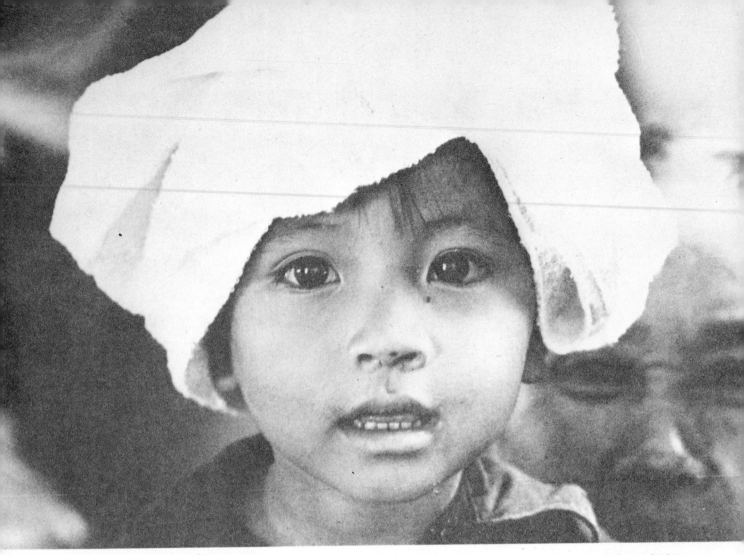

A refugee left homeless by the war in Vietnam. Many of these children are aided by Catholic Relief Services.

growth of the new society was steady.

Today Maryknoll priests are spread throughout the world. They have built a fine record of service and devotion to mankind. Some Maryknollers have given their lives for their cause—death by bandits, from Communists, through accidents. Many more Maryknollers have known prisons and persecution. They have proven that American youth can answer the challenge of Christ to "go into the whole world." But Maryknoll's contribution has not been solely in foreign fields. Through the work of the Society, the Catholic people of the United States have become more mission conscious and have acquired a greater understanding of the essential role the salvation of the world must play in their own spiritual lives.

Today there are approximately 8,000 American priests, Brothers, and Sisters working in the mission fields abroad. Based on statistics released by the former Mission Secretariate, the ten leading institutes of men, including Maryknoll, are Jesuits, Franciscans, Redemptorists, Divine Word Missionaries, Oblates of Mary Immaculate, Marianists, Capuchins, Sacred Heart Fathers, Holy Ghost Fathers. The leading institutes of women are Maryknoll Sisters, Sisters of St. Anne, Marists, Medical Mission Sisters, Dominicans, Servants of the Immaculate Heart of Mary, School Sisters of Notre Dame, Religious of the Sacred Heart of Mary, Franciscan Missionaries of Mary, Ursulines. The United States is now the major financial contributor to the missions of the world.

Not to be overlooked are Father Thomas Judge, founder of the Trinitarians; and Mother Drexel, whose Sisters worked with Indians.

A significant development in recent years has been the lay mission movement. Young men, young women, and married couples have left America for Africa, Asia and Latin America to work in critical areas as part of the Church's world-wide movement. Organizations have been established for the training and support of lay missioners.

The Catholic Near East Welfare Association supplies aid to the victims of the Arab-Israeli conflict.

Catholic Near East Welfare Association

Many shelters have been established to serve the homeless. Many children have spent their entire lives in the camps.

Catholic Relief Services sent food, clothes and medical supplies to assist on both sides of the Israeli war.

Pope Paul receives Msgr. John G. Nolan, president of the Pontifical Mission which has delivered one hundred million dollars in aid to the refugees of the Arab-Israeli wars. Pope Paul's personal gifts have now surpassed the one hundred thousand dollar mark. Catholic Charities has expanded from its early beginnings in the United States to the extent of being considered as one of the largest private charitable organizations in the world.

The Largest Private Relief Organization in the World

IT began as a light, late summer rain—and then without warning it turned into disaster. The rain became heavier and heavier, until it poured down in torrents. Winds mounted, and lightning flashed. For thirty-six hours the storm lashed west-central Taiwan, during which period thirty inches of rain fell. Streams became gorged, and swelled to five times their normal size. Bridges were swept away; dikes and dams trembled from the pressure and then crumbled, sending an avalanche of water through towns and villages, inundating rice fields, carrying away human beings in its headlong dash to the sea.

When the storm abated, the Taiwan Government assessed the loss at a staggering $100-million, but that figure gave no indication of the human loss: thousands of dead and injured, homes destroyed, crops washed away. What followed is a story not known to many Americans, but one in which every American can take pride.

A gigantic relief operation was mounted. Using Catholic missions serving as field bases, Father Francis J. O'Neill—of Woonsocket, Rhode Island —Catholic Relief Services director for Taiwan, began shipping tons of supplies by helicopters rushed in by the United States Marines. Cargo planes of the Chinese Air Force were loaded with more supplies for the stricken area. During a ten-day period, more than 1,850,000 pounds of relief goods were moved to seventeen drop points.

The typical way this material was used is revealed in a report from one American missioner: "This is what we did. From August 9 to August 22, we took care of 1,360 families in Yuan Lin, supplying them with 60,700 pounds of flour, 47,700 pounds of corn meal, 12,530 pounds of rice, and 5,432 boxes of powdered milk. There were times when we thought we were going to pass out from fatigue. The long lines of people waiting for food never seemed to end. . . ."

The organization responsible for this massive relief operation is Catholic Relief Services—the largest private, voluntary, overseas, person-to-person relief program in history. For many years, it alone accounted for almost half the total annual

Catholic Relief Services helps throughout the world.

amount of relief supplies distributed overseas by more than fifty American agencies registered with the International Co-operation Administration. Because of the vast mission organization of the Catholic Church, CRS can count on the assistance of more than 1,250,000 volunteer workers in sixty-four countries where the program operates.

Catholic Relief Services was established by the American hierarchy in 1943, as a division of the National Catholic Welfare Conference, to provide relief and rehabilitation to victims of World War II. It executed tremendous operations in Europe and Asia after that war ended. Wars in Korea and Indo-China further increased the load that CRS was carrying. The program was enlarged to encompass two-thirds of the world's population— human beings who suffer from poverty, hunger, disease, and homelessness.

Since its foundation, CRS has distributed more than six billion pounds of relief goods valued at over $900 million, to unrecorded millions of needy persons, without regard to race, creed, or

270

To serve the constant needs of the poor and the homeless is the never ending concern of Catholic Relief Services.

Huacho, Peru, was virtually destroyed in 90 seconds by a massive earthquake. Catholic Relief was on the scene.

color. The supplies are given on a continuing basis in such depressed areas as Korea, South Vietnam, Hong Kong, Spain; in the latter country, two million children participate in a CRS feeding program for school pupils. In addition, crash programs are put in effect where necessary. The instance in Taiwan, already cited, is one example. Chilean and Peruvian earthquakes and the Hungarian uprising are others. When Fidel Castro caused several hundred thousand Cubans to flee their homeland, CRS set up headquarters in Miami, Florida, to administer relief.

CRS aid goes to where it is most needed and is not distributed on a religious basis. When an earthquake struck Agadir in Moslem Morocco, CRS rushed a half million pounds of clothing for distribution among its victims. Six million people in India have been aided by CRS. A family-feeding program has been established in Turkey. Arab refugees in Jordan have received food and clothing from CRS; and when a recent outbreak of influenza threatened those refugees, CRS flew in 60,000 vials of influenza vaccine. In Hong Kong, CRS has built 1,044 cottage-type houses for refugee families, and donated seventy boats to refugee fishing families. CRS representatives traveled by train, boat, jeep, and foot to reach the Tibetan refugees in their camp at Missamari, India, and there the representatives told those victims of Red terrorism that quantities of food were on the way from the CRS Calcutta warehouse and that fifty thousand pounds of men's clothing had already been shipped from New York. The story of truly Catholic help given by CRS would make a book in itself.

In a single year, CRS gives aid to more than 40 million people in over sixty countries. CRS administers relief and resettlement programs, the total value of which is well over $100-million. It resettles upwards of forty thousand refugees in new homes and new jobs. It ships more than a billion pounds of relief goods annually—clothing, medicine, hospital supplies, and U.S. Government surplus food. This is an amount equal to 29,411 carloads, or a freight train 278½ miles long. It dis-

Bishop Edward Swanstrom is thanked by the Koreans.

patches a shipment of relief supplies on an average of every nine hours, throughout the year. It ships usable clothing at the rate of two thousand bales a day from four ports in the United States.

"The accomplishment behind these figures," says Bishop Edward E. Swanstrom, CRS executive director, "is a great tribute to the generosity and Christ-like concern of the American people for the poor, hungry, needy, and sick, in less-fortunate areas of the world."

And it is the Catholic people of America who make this gigantic relief effort possible. The funds for the operation of CRS come from United States Catholics through their parishes. Two drives are conducted each year. On Laetare Sunday, a collection is taken up in every parish in the United States; and during Lent, the children in Catholic schools are asked to make sacrifices to help needy children overseas. The second drive is held immediately preceding Thanksgiving, to obtain usable clothing and shoes. This Thanksgiving drive has produced 135 million pounds of clothing, shoes, and blankets, which have a value of $160 million—

a truly remarkable record of generosity.

While to date CRS has been largely concerned with necessary and urgent immediate aid, it has also developed programs for long-term help, and these programs are being expanded. Bishops all over the world have asked CRS for assistance to establish their Catholic social programs. CRS is also setting up institutes where local people will be trained in technical know-how. This type of program can have a very helpful effect on individual and national economies, and future years will see a tremendous expansion in this phase of CRS aid.

Moreover, American Catholic aid to the needy of the world goes beyond CRS. The Catholic people of the United States generously support many mission societies that are working overseas and rendering assistance to the poor and sick: hospitals, schools, and technical institutes have been built with funds provided by the American people. There are also a number of private relief projects. The National Council of Catholic Women distributes thousands of dollars through its Madonna Plan, which aims at aiding mothers overseas: in a single year, substantial grants have gone to hospitals and mother-and-child clinics in Austria, Algiers, the Congo, Tanganyika, India, Pakistan, Korea, Taiwan, the Philippines, Dominica, Mexico, Puerto Rico. The Feed-a-Family program of the NCCW operates in Trieste, Germany, Lebanon, Pakistan, India, Thailand, Viet Nam, Hong Kong, Korea, Japan, Puerto Rico.

The Catholic Daughters of America conduct a Relief-for-Peace program. Catholic women in Philadelphia work for overseas aid. A recent report of this group reveals that it shipped 594 cases of relief goods, weighing 162,498 pounds and valued at $343,298. A group of Catholics in Detroit—the World Medical Relief—specializes in collecting drugs and equipment for medical-missionary groups overseas. In a single year, shipments have been made to Catholic hospitals and clinics in Korea, Hong Kong, Taiwan, Viet Nam, India, Pakistan, the Philippines, Burma, Thailand, Malaya, Laos, Liberia, Chile, British Honduras, Greece, Italy, Trieste, Spain. Also to be added are the contribution of individual Catholics such as the late Doctor Thomas Dooley and Doctor Walsh, Project Hope Founder, who out of Christian concern have devoted their personal efforts to helping their fellowman. It is impossible to arrive at any accurate figure of this private type of relief, but undoubtedly it runs into many million dollars a year.

Food, clothing and medical supplies are rushed to an area that has been struck by an earthquake.

The Catholic Spirit in America:
Catholics in Industry and Commerce

IT is an accepted truism in America that a man's worth is determined by his own merit, and that religion or nationality or heredity is not a barrier or passport to success. The actual fact is that Catholics have not in the past achieved the proportion of business recognition that other elements of our population have achieved. In one early sociological study, there were listed 859 Catholic and 18,369 non-Catholic business executives, and the proportion of success based on over-all population was four to one; .083 per cent of the general group attained business distinction, while only .019 per cent of the Catholics acquired similar recognition. However, three studies made since the turn of the century show definitely that Catholics are moving into top corporate positions.

In 1949, William Miller published a survey on 181 presidents and chairmen of the boards of business corporations active from 1900-1910. In 1927, William S. Ament wrote a paper called "Religion, Education, and Distinction" which was based on a survey of *Who's Who in America*. Again, in 1945, C. Wright Mills analyzed 1,464 biographies. In comparison of these studies, certain facts become apparent. In 1927, 2.1 per cent of the successful businessmen were listed as Catholics, but the 1945 survey showed 4.4 per cent; this is a gain of more than double. But when the 1945 survey is compared to that of 1900-1910, an increase of 250 per cent is found for Catholic top executives. The trend, therefore, is for Catholics to play increasingly greater roles in the industrial world.

In his book, *Men Who Are Making America*, C. Wright Mills remarks, "More likely, poor immigrant and poor farm boys who become business leaders have always been more conspicuous in American history books than in the American business elite." Nevertheless, they do get to the top, and among them are Catholics who usually prove very generous in sharing their good fortune.

John Mackay located the famous Comstock Lode.

John W. Mackay was born in Dublin, Ireland, in 1831. His parents emigrated to America when he was nine years old. The boy went to work in New York shipyards, always dreaming of making his mark in his land of adoption. The 1849 gold strike in California fired John's imagination. At the age of twenty, he went west in search of fortune. But luck was elusive; he failed first in California, then in Nevada. He continued prospecting and mining in Nevada for twenty years. The discovery of the Comstock Lode led him to Virginia City, and there in 1872, he and his partners—

William Russell was the founder of the Pony Express.

J. Peter Grace, Catholic president of Grace Company

James Fair, William O'Brien, and James Flood—located the fabulous Bonanza Mine. Mackay owned a two-fifths share and became a very wealthy man.

After he had a stake, John Mackay showed his talent for business, proving once again that money makes money. With his partners, he founded the Bank of Nevada, and he became its president for years. Because of his dislike for Jay Gould, who controlled the Western Union Telegraph Company, Mackay joined forces with James Gordon Bennett to found the Commercial Cable Company and the Postal Telegraph Company. In a long rate war, he defeated Western Union. When he died, he was one of the richest men in America.

William R. Grace also was born in Ireland, one year later than Mackay. He went to Callao, Peru, as a clerk in the office of a shipping company. His brother Michael joined him, and the two formed Grace Brothers and Company. William Grace then came to New York and opened W. R. Grace and Company. Contacts he had made in Peru brought him contracts to obtain the supplies for

Peru's railroad-building program. The money made on this transaction enabled Grace to begin the New York and Pacific Steamship Company, and later the Grace Steamship Company. He was twice elected mayor of New York City.

The Grace Company became a power in South America, particularly among the west coast countries. Grace's son, Joseph Peter, took over the business and expanded it into mining, farming, retail trade and banking. Today it is operated by a grandson, J. Peter Grace, and is one of the leading corporations in the United States; it has diversified its holdings and specializes in chemicals, paper factories, and many subsidiaries. J. Peter Grace, who directs the sprawling international empire, has also served as director of the following organizations: the National City Bank of New York, Ingersoll Rand Company, Kennecott Copper Company, and others. He is a trustee of Notre Dame University, Saint Vincent's Hospital, and other charitable works. He is also a Knight of Malta and a Knight of the Holy Sepulchre.

277

Charles M. Schawb, the giant of the steel industry

Thomas Ryan, financier and owner of Seaboard Railway

Charles M. Schwab worked as a clerk in a grocery store, and later found employment as a stake driver at a dollar a day in the Carnegie Steel Company. By his talent and dedication, he rose to become president of the Carnegie Steel Company, president of the United States Steel Company, and president of the Bethlehem Steel Corporation. He gave large bequests to Catholic institutions.

Thomas Fortune Ryan left his home in Lovingston, Virginia, at the age of seventeen, and spent three days walking the streets of Baltimore before he found work in a dry goods firm. Later he went to New York and obtained employment in a broker's office. Eventually, he became one of the leading financiers in the United States and **owner** of the Seaboard Railway. Ryan in his day was reputed to be the only man who ever donated an entire cathedral to the Church. (Others have done so since.) He gave the cathedral in Richmond, Virginia, together with all its furnishings.

Another American success story is that of Amadeo P. Giannini, who was born in 1870 in San Jose, California. He was the son of immigrant Italians who began life in America by operating a fruit-and-produce store. Young Giannini went into the business with his father and, by the time he was nineteen years old, was a full partner. He developed the produce business until he had the largest firm of its kind in San Francisco; then at the age of thirty-one he retired. But a Giannini could not remain idle. In 1904, Amadeo organized the Bank of Italy to help people of small means obtain loans. His business acumen was revealed during the panic of 1907; other banks in San Francisco were failing, but the Bank of Italy paid depositors dollar for dollar. When Giannini retired, at the age of seventy-five, his company was entitled "The Bank of America," and it had 517 branches in California and other branches in European and Asiatic countries. It had become one of the most important banking institutions in the United States.

Other Catholics in America have built up large fortunes. Patrick Cudahy, founder of one of the largest meat-packing concerns in the United States began his rise to a huge personal fortune when he started as a twelve-year-old delivery boy. Generoso Pope started with an Italian newspaper in New York but extended his activity to become one of the largest sand-and-gravel dealers in the country. John A. Coleman began work as a page

278

The accomplished mayor of Chicago, Richard J. Daly

Frank Folsom, industrialist and Catholic head of RCA

Thomas E. Branniff, founder of a great airline

boy on the New York Stock Exchange and eventually became chairman of its board of governors.

Michael Morrissey worked as a paper vendor in Massachusetts, rose to general manager of the American News Company, then became president and chairman of the board of the Union News Company, whose newsstands are found in railroad stations all over the United States. Morrissey also served as a director of the Pullman Company, Commodore Hotel, Irving Trust Company, and Emmigrant Savings Bank. John Raskob built a personal fortune as an executive of the DuPont Company. He was a close friend of Al Smith, contributing heavily to the latter's political campaigns. When Raskob died, his fortune was administered by a foundation for charitable causes.

William F. O'Neil began work in his father's department store; then in 1909, recognizing the importance of the automobile, he became associated with the Western Tire and Rubber Company,

where he rose to president. He then became owner of the General Tire Company in Akron, Ohio, and he and his family diversified their interests by buying control of the Yankee Radio Network in New England, the Mutual Broadcasting System, R.K.O. Pictures, and finally of Aerojet General, a company that produces rockets, rocket engines, and aircraft material.

Ben Duffy began work as an office boy in Batton, Barton, Durstine and Osborn, a firm that is a byword for advertising. Duffy became its president and the most respected man in the advertising industry. Andrew Haire was the founder of one of the largest business-magazine publishing companies in the United States. Patrick Frawley made one fortune as inventor of the Paper-Mate pen; then sold out, and took control of the Shick Razor Company and Technicolor, Inc. Bing Crosby, generally known as an entertainer, has a complexity of business interests controlled through his

Joseph P. Kennedy, diplomat and father of a president

Bing Crosby Enterprises. They include a race track, a baseball team, and extensive holdings in many corporations. Conrad Hilton parlayed a Texas boarding house into an international hotel chain.

Joseph P. Kennedy, father of the late president of the United States, made a fortune in real estate. Thomas P. Murray became a millionaire through his industrial equipment company, served as director of the Bank of New York and the Chrysler Corporation, and later was apppointed an Atomic Energy Commissioner. Justin Henry Oppenheim was president of the New Idea Farm Company, producer of agricultural equipment. Robert L. Houget was head of the United States Lines; Daniel Creeden, president of Libby, McNeil and Libby; William M. Jeffers, president of Union Pacific Railroad; Cornelius Kelley, chairman of board, Anaconda Copper Mining Company; John D. Reilly, president, Todd Shipbuilding Company; Frank J. Sensenbrenner, chairman of board, Kim-

The outstanding singer and actor, Bing Crosby

Ben Duffy, president of a New York advertising firm

Connie Mack will always be remembered in baseball.

berly-Clark Corporation; Walter O'Malley, owner, Dodgers baseball team.

All the names mentioned in this section have been selected at random, as representative of Catholics who have succeeded in the world of finance, industry and commerce. They have been chosen to show that American Catholics have attained places of eminence in the business world. While most Catholics remain in the middle and lower classes, many do rise on the basis of achievement. Undoubtedly, in the years ahead, the proportion of American Catholic executives will come further into line with the proportion of Catholics in the general population. The Catholic Church in the United States is now reaching its maturity, even the last wave of Catholic immigrants—the Puerto Ricans—are beginning to climb from the ghettos. However, as a group the Puerto Ricans and their older cousins, the Mexican Americans, have a long way to go to reach the status of the descendants of the old waves of European immigrants. But if history is a criterion, they will make it.

Patrick Cudahy, leader in the meatpacking industry

Catholics in the Labor Movement

Cardinal Gibbons, he worked for the goals of labor

T.V. Powderley, Grand Master of the Knights of Labor

BECAUSE the Catholic immigrants in the United States made up a substantial proportion of the working force, America's Catholic hierarchy have always been seriously concerned about laboring conditions and social reform. In the days of the development of the labor movement, the Catholic Church faced the dilemma of protecting from capitalistic abuses the economic rights of its members, and at the same time safeguarding them from exploitation by socialistic and atheistic forces.

The first stirrings of organized labor took place in Philadelphia, in 1827, with the creation of the Mechanics' Union of Trade Association. Two years later that became the Workingmen's Party. The party was accused of being anti-religious, and its New York unit advocated abolition of tax exemption for Church property. Even before these groups were organized, however, Catholic voices had been heard. Matthew Carey, the Catholic publisher, who had arrived in Philadelphia in 1784, was one of the earliest to speak out in defense of the workingman. Archbishop Norbert Blanchet reminded the Hudson's Bay Company of its spiritual and temporal obligations to its workers. The Catholic *Freeman's Journal*, in 1845, called for a just wage that would meet the necessities of life, and rejected the law of labor supply-and-demand as justification for setting wages.

In October, 1929, the stock market crashed. In a short time thousands of men were out of work as the country began to feel the effects of a depression that would last for over ten years. This man is forced to sell apples for a living.

In July, 1932, the "Bonus Army" met U.S. troops after being ordered to disperse in Washington. These World-War I veterans are seen as they give up their position in a partially demolished building on Pennsylvania Avenue.

The battle starts on the South Chicago field on June 31, 1937 as a fatal clash between striking steel workers and police began. On the right, a patrol wagon waits to carry out victims and those of the strikers who may be arrested.

The beginnings of the "Bonus Army" arrive in Washington to spend the night on the lawn of the Capitol building. The men had come with bed rolls but police, beginning the harrassment, refused to allow the veterans to use them.

President Eisenhower addressed a Labor Day crowd on the White House lawn upon the issuance of a commemorative labor stamp. He is flanked here by Catholic Labor Secretary James P. Mitchell and labor leader George Meany.

The labor movement fought a long and hard battle to overcome many social injustices.

The skilled worker in the United States has at last assumed a position commensurate with his talents.

Two young priests try out a new idea. While still performing their priestly duties they have taken jobs "on the side." Father Betram is employed as a sales clerk while Father Yaroch works part time as a cab driver.

While labor fought for the position it has gained today, the Catholic Church was right with them. Many of the Catholic hierarchy, especially Cardinal Gibbons and Bishop Ireland, gave their full support to labor.

In 1970 an agreement is reached between striking farm workers and owners. The National Conference of Catholic Bishops helped bring the sides together.

Catholic social attitude toward the labor movement was firmly stated in Leo XIII's encyclical, "Rerum Novarum." Instrumental in Leo XIII's favorable attitude was the leadership and arguments of American Cardinal Gibbons.

Each Labor Day Americans pause to realize the benefits of each worker and the hard years of struggle necessary to bring about the favorable position and equitable wage that is now guaranteed by Federal Law.

The first really successful attempt to unite workingmen was made in Philadelphia in 1869, with the organization of the Knights of Labor. That was a secret, ritualistic group, which united workers of all types. Its secrecy disturbed some American bishops. Years earlier, the Holy See had condemned all secret societies — with the Freemasons particularly in mind, and about the secret societies, the American bishops at the Fourth Provincial Council of Baltimore (1840) had warned: "As far as we can discover, the pretext is their own protection, but the practice is monopoly, blasphemy, insubordination, drunkenness, idleness, riot and terror of the vicinity." In 1850, a query to Rome, about secret societies, was simply referred to earlier rulings, which condemned them.

Yet as the labor movement developed, and the Knights of Labor grew in strength, some members of the Catholic hierarchy were gravely disturbed. Terence V. Powderly, the influential Grand Master of the Knights of Labor was a Catholic, and a considerable proportion of the organization's members were Irish Catholics. The problem was complicated by the fact that anarchistic and socialistic groups were trying to take over the labor movement for their own ends. Was the Church to condemn the labor organizations, ignore them, or give them support and assistance to grow and to keep out harmful elements?

Bishop Martin J. Spalding had taken one strong position, which was revealed in private correspondence released after his death in 1872. He wrote: "In our country capital is tyrant, and labor is its slave. I have no desire to interfere with the poor in their efforts to protect themselves, unless it is proved that these societies are plotting against the state or the Church."

The matter came to a head in the year 1887. The Canadian bishops had obtained from the Holy See a condemnation of the Knights of Labor, and that was being used by employers in the United States as a weapon against labor unions. Cardinal Gibbons was greatly disturbed by developments, because he saw the Church in the United States being maneuvered into a position where it was being presented as "a friend of the powerful rich and the enemy of the helpless poor." He announced that he would not desert the poor and weak classes in their hour of need.

The Baltimore cardinal arranged a meeting with President Cleveland and Terence Powderly. The cardinal then called a meeting of all the United States archbishops, to hear Mr. Powderly.

Martin Spalding sympathized with the labor movement.

Dorothy Day was a socialist who converted to Catholism.

Working conditions were unhealthy and very dangerous. It was a long and arduous day for these coal miners.

Bishop Ireland, supporter of the labor movement

That leader explained the Knights of Labor: he stated that secrecy was enjoined by a simple pledge and not an oath; that this secrecy was approved only insofar as it was necessary to keep the business of the knights from their enemies, and that there was nothing in this secrecy that would prevent members from manifesting their consciences in the Sacrament of Penance. The archbishops then took a vote. Only two of the twelve archbishops were for condemnation of the Knights of Labor. The others agreed with the opinion of Cardinal Gibbons, that the hierarchy must do all in its power to prevent a censure of the Knights of Labor in the United States.

Cardinal Gibbons had received strong support

Rev. Dennis J. Comey talked these dockworkers into going back to work during this attempted wildcat strike.

from Archbishop Ireland, and the two ecclesiastics prepared a long document that was to be submitted to the Holy See. The document made a detailed examination of the organization of the Knights of Labor and their secrecy; it considered all the objections that could be made to the knights, and offered rebuttal; and it concluded with a series of reasons why the Knights of Labor should not be condemned. Cardinal Gibbons took the document with him to Rome in 1887, when he went to get the red hat of his cardinalate. Success crowned his efforts.

Not only did Pope Leo XIII not condemn the Knights of Labor in the United States but he also released, in 1891, his now-historic encyclical, *Rerum Novarum*, which deals with the condition

In 1891 Pope Leo XIII issued the historic "Rerum Novarum." It stands today as the basis of social Catholic doctrine.

of the working class. *Rerum Novarum* set forth the eternal principles of social justice. Although it was attacked as socialistic when it was released, it stands today as the basis for Catholic social doctrine.

When the Columbian Catholic Congress met in Chicago, during the World's Fair in 1893, the Catholic laymen attending gave serious study to the encyclical and its application to the United States. Archbishop Ireland presented the theme of the congress when he declared, "It is an age of battlings for social justice." From that time on, priests and bishops were to play increasingly important roles in the struggle for workingmen's rights.

In the great anthracite coal strike of 1902, Father John Curran, known affectionately as "the miners' friend," worked ceaselessly to bring together the mine owners, the Morgan interests, and John Mitchell, the labor representative. Father Peter Dietz became closely associated with the American Federation of Labor and traveled about the United States, attempting to awaken the social consciences of Catholics. Father Dietz made his "Labor Mass" a feature of every A.F.L. convention that he attended between 1909 and 1922. He addressed the A.F.L. Convention of 1910, announcing that the American Federation of Catholic Societies, representing over three million men of all nationalities, "holds out to the trade-union movement the hand of fellowship and support." At that convention, he organized the Militia for Christ, whose officers included top Catholics in the labor movement: Peter McArdle, president of the Amalgamated Association of Iron, Steel, and Tin Workers; Thomas Duffy, president of the National Brotherhood of Operative Potters; James O'Connell, president of the International Associa-

The working conditions of these coal miners were of constant concern to a great many of the Catholic hierarchy.

tion of Machinists; Frank Duffy, international secretary of the United Brotherhood of Carpenters and Jointers; and the prominent labor leader, John Mitchell.

Two Catholic leaders who played an important role in the formation of Catholic social thought were Monsignor John Ryan and Father Joseph Husslein, S.J. Monsignor Ryan was a professor of moral theology at the Catholic University, and Father Husslein was associate editor of *America* and a teacher at Fordham University. Both priests were prolific writers, and articles and books on social teachings came steadily from their efforts. Monsignor Ryan was the author of the prophetic *Program of Social Reconstruction*, which was released by the American hierarchy in 1919. This document, far in advance of its times, called for housing for working classes, reduction in the cost of living, a legal minimum wage, social securi-

ty, labor participation in management, the end of child labor, and the abolition and control of monopolies. The document was attacked as "socialistic," but all of its programs urged in it by the United States hierarchy have since been generally adopted.

In the same year (1919), the National Catholic Welfare Conference was formed from the old National Catholic War Council. One of its divisions was the Social Action Department, which was given the express injunction to promote the social teachings of the Catholic Church and to interpret, to the Catholic people of the United States, the application of that social teaching to the complex problems of the country. Monsignor Ryan was chosen as the first director. He was later succeeded by Father Raymond McGowan, another pioneer in social action. Another director was Monsignor George Higgins, also known for the weekly labor

Dennis Comey was the Director of the Institute of Industrial Relations at St. Joseph's College, Philadelphia.

Gibbons worked long and hard for the rights of labor. Here he meets with President Theodore Roosevelt.

column he writes for many Catholic newspapers.

Other priests have played key roles in the social-action programs over the years. The recently deceased Monsignor John Monaghan was one of the founders of ACTU (Associated Catholic Trade Unions). He served as mediator in many strikes. Father Benjamin Masse, S.J., an editor of *America*, became a prominent labor authority. Father William Smith, S.J., founder of the Crown Heights Labor School, was willing to take on either labor or management if he believed either had a wrong position. Father Philip Carey, founder of the Xavier Labor School, served on the War Labor Board and also as an arbitrator for the American Arbi-tration Association. Father Carey became prominent in his fight to clean up racketeering in the waterfront labor movement.

Catholic laymen also have contributed their efforts to the development of labor unions. Martin Durkin, president of the United Association of Journeyman Plumbers and Steamfitters, became Secretary of Labor of the United States; as did another Catholic, James Mitchell. Philip Murray brought the gigantic Steelworkers' Union to the height of its power and was a key factor in the creation of the C.I.O. George Meaney is the present head of the A.F.L.-C.I.O. The late Heyward Broun founded the American Newspaper Guild.

Eisenhower's Secretary of Labor, James P. Mitchell   *Martin Durkin was also Labor Secretary for "Ike."*

Msgr. John A. Ryan, an exponent of social justice   *J. A. Beirne, president of the communication workers*

Cesar Chavez, head of the United Farm Workers Organizing Committee, led the famous grape boycott in 1969.

George Meany, president of the AFL-CIO, receives a papal decoration from Cardinal O'Boyle in October, 1969.

Joseph Bierne is president of the powerful Communications Workers of America, and has also found time to render much public service. John Brophy, George Delaney, Joseph Curran, and James Carey are other Catholic leaders in the labor movement. The list could be continued at considerable length.

Some day the complete story of the role of the Catholic Church in shaping the development and policies of the American labor movement will be fully told and documented; it can only be indicated here. The effect of the opposition of the Catholic Church to the infiltration of socialism into the labor movement has not yet been fully assessed. The role of the American hierarchy—particularly that of Cardinals Gibbons, O'Connell, and Farley—played an important part in bringing the social message of the Church to the attention of labor leaders. The hostility of the Catholic Church to the formation of a political labor party was an important element in preserving the essential, democratic system. Of all the Churches in America, it was the Catholic Church that has best identified itself with the welfare of the laboring man and that pioneered along the uncharted paths of social justice.

James P. Mitchell places a wreath on the memorial of Cardinal Gibbons in recognition of his service to labor.

Three Modern Politicians

ONE thing this book doesn't want to do is pass judgments on people who have not yet gone to their reward; even the Lord waits His decision until the customer arrives at the Pearly Gates. Many a Catholic editor has made the mistake of canonizing a living Catholic, only to discover at a later date that their raptures were over a man with feet of clay. Not that the people in this volume are all saints; but an attempt has been made to select Catholics who were representative of their Faith, who practiced that Faith, and whose actions and

finished St. James Parochial School at fourteen, he went to work. As soon as he was ready to vote, he joined his district Democratic club and within a year had his first political jobs as a clerk and server of jury duty notices. Despite his educational handicap, Smith had high native intelligence, was a master of detail, and had the gift of remembering what he read. When he was thirty, he was elected to the New York State Assembly. He studied and mastered state government and in ten years was the Speaker of the Assembly.

thoughts were influenced by their religious convictions. Even many who would meet this test we have omitted because they are too recently gone and history and perspective have not given an indicative judgment.

In selecting three typical Catholics whose careers were in politics, a wide selection is available. The men selected are ones for which the reader can stand back a bit to make judgment; yet they are contemporaries of many who still enter the booth on election day.

Alfred E. Smith

Brief mention has already been given to the distinguished Governor of New York, Alfred E. Smith. Smith lost the presidency because he was a Catholic but he was not a man who would deny that his religious beliefs influenced his judgments. Yet he could never imagine himself leading a Catholic party. He was a two-party believer.

Alfred E. Smith was born in the shadow of the Brooklyn Bridge in 1873. A poor boy, when he

In 1918 Al Smith and his brown derby moved into the governor's mansion where he remained for four terms. His record as governor was imaginative, enlightened and competent, surviving the test of time without blemish. He was defeated for the presidency in 1928, as already detailed. Although he initially supported Franklin D. Roosevelt, he broke with him in a disagreement over economic policies. He died in 1944 during World War II which he foresaw.

Like John Kennedy many years later, Smith was attacked on religious grounds that he could not be loyal to the Constitution and the Catholic Church at the same time. In the *Atlantic Monthly*, Smith gave his credo: "I believe in the absolute separation of church and state in the strict enforcement of the provision of the Constitution that Congress shall make no laws respecting an establishment of religion or prohibiting the free excise thereof." Kennedy was able to prove that a Catholic could give his full allegiance to his country; Smith never had the chance.

Despite the attacks made on him because of his religion, Al Smith never tried to hide it or play it down. It was something of which he was proud. He accepted positions on Catholic committees, was seen frequently with members of the hierarchy and let it be known he was a good friend of Cardinal Hayes, and did not avoid being named a Papal Chamberlain or a Knight of Malta. Smith's philosophy was an open one: take me as I am or forget me.

He strongly favored the social position of the Church and it was his religious convictions and not expediency that made him such a champion of the poor. He declared on one occason: "We have been in a great hurry to legislate for the interests. . . . We have been slow to legislate along the direction that means thanksgiving to the poorest Man recorded in history—to Him who was born in a stable in Bethlehem." Smith pushed through laws of social welfare that benefited the poor, widows, child welfare and working people. He had the popular title of the "Common Man."

Although there was disappointment among Catholics when he was defeated by Herbert Hoover for the presidency, in retrospect it was the best thing for the Church. Hoover inherited the greatest financial collapse the country has ever known and the start of the Great Depression. Had Smith been president, his religious beliefs would have in some way been blamed for the tragedy which touched every American. Instead, Smith is remembered in New York State as one of its greatest governors, a man of progressive social legislation, and one who conserved the scenic resources of the state with his acquisition of parks and beaches and then built the first good network of roads so that the common man might get to them.

WORLD WAR ROOTED IN THE VATICAN

Telegram From Bavarian Minister at the Vatican Made Public in France.

How in the world the following dispatch ever got by the Knights of Columbus censors may never be explained. But it got by—that's the thing to realize.

The responsibility for the World war, in which so many American soldiers laid down their lives, and [ ]he whole of Eu[ro][ ]y, has at last authoritatively [s]houlders of the [mo]ving to the New [ ]confirms the pre-

16-YEAR OLD GIRL PREFERS DEATH TO ROME'S JAILS

ANOTHER VICTIM OF H. O. G. S.

Girl Killed While Trying to Escape From Papal Den in Roxbury, Massachusetts.

Boston, Oct. 18.—Anna E. Sposito, a 16-year-old girl of Newton, was

The anti-Catholic publication the "Menace" provided the reading public with "facts" such as these. Many of the attacks on the Church were based on the evidence supplied by "ex-religious" many of whom were found to be never part of the Catholic religion.

ABSOLUTE PROOF THAT ROMANISM DESIRED DEATH OF PRESIDENT ABRAHAM LINCOLN

AGED EX-NUN ATTACKS ARCH-CRIMINAL ROME

Edith O'Gorman Auffray, in Her 82nd Year Fearlessly attacks Roman Catholic Church Exposing Wickedness and Immorality of

Abraham Lincoln had been shot by John Wilkes Booth, a pervert to Romanism. A plot for his removal had been hatched for months in the home of John Surratt on H. street, and a far-reaching Jesuit conspiracy with headquarters in Canada had at last reached its ultimate purpose

time is spent in mumbling Latin offices, drinking wine or whiskey "punch" and making merry on the fat of the land.

"While in the Paterson convent and orphan asylum, I had opportunity of witnessing much cruelty and abuse of the poor orphans there. On

Frank Murphy

There are undoubtedly many Americans today to whom the name Frank Murphy will be meaningless, yet in his day he played important roles on both state and national scenes. Frank Murphy was born in the little Lake Huron town of Harbor Beach, Michigan in 1890. Like Al Smith he was born poor and had to leave school early to work in a factory. But Murphy had a drive for formal education and through a variety of jobs was able to put himself through the University of Michigan and then get his law degree two years later (1914).

An intellectual by nature he was a cavernous reader and was seldom without a book in his hands. His quest for knowledge took him to advanced studies in London and Dublin. Back in Detroit, he practiced law by day and taught at the Catholic University of Detroit Law School by night. In 1919 he accepted an appointment as a United States Attorney for the Eastern District of Michigan. Two years later he returned to practicing and teaching law.

In 1930 he was persuaded to run for Mayor of Detroit and won. From that time on the name of Frank Murphy was projected on the national scene. He played an important role in the Democratic Convention of 1932 which nominated Franklin D. Roosevelt, whom he supported instead of Al Smith who also sought the nomination. When Roosevelt was elected, Murphy was named Governor General of the Philippines where he worked for the transition of that colony to commonwealth status. He was tremendously popular in the Philippines and not one of the least reasons was his Catholicity. (Before Murphy, Filipinos thought that all American officials were Masons.) Mass was celebrated daily in the Governor's Palace, except on Sunday when he made it a point to hear Mass in a different Filipino church with the Filipino people.

Murphy returned to the United States to run for governor of Michigan in 1936. He was elected but had a difficult term, mainly caused by the famous sit-down strike at General Motors. Murphy refused to use troops to eject the men who had occupied the G.M. buildings. He won great

Frank   Murphy,   Michigan   governor,   1937-1938

liberal support but was attacked in the press; the Dies Commitee, a Congressional power, accused him of being a Communist. His championship of the new Congress of Industrial Organizations (CIO) did not help him. As a result he was defeated in his bid for re-election.

In 1939, President Roosevelt appointed him Attorney General. Among those he successfully prosecuted was the mentor of Harry Truman, Tom Prendergast, a Democratic political power in Kansas City, Mo. He also went after various Communist fronts. The next year, Roosevelt appointed him to the Supreme Court. Here he was known as a "civil rights liberal." He was a close friend of Justices Black and Douglas, who were constantly under attack for their liberal views. Actually, Justice Murphy was following principles upon which he had acted consistently all his life. He died while on the Court, July 19, 1949.

Like Al Smith, Frank Murphy never hid his Catholicism. He was a daily communicant and led a very abstemious life in which he neither drank nor smoked. He never married. He also never denied that Christianity influenced his decisions and believed strongly that democracy had its roots in Christianity.

Brien McMahon

Brien McMahon

One of the great mysteries of life is why God suddenly summons men to Himself just when they are coming into the blossomtime of their important careers. This was the case of James O'Brien McMahon, better known simply as Brien McMahon, who died suddenly at the age of not yet forty-nine with much work left unfinished.

Christianity revolves around two commandments: love of God and love of neighbor. Actually, only the first is necessary for if one truly loves God, he must love His creation. But Jesus gave the fullness of these commandments so that no man could miss the point. Al Smith and Frank Murphy operated from these two principles, each in his own way. So did Brien McMahon in his quest to control atomic energy and preserve the world from nuclear horror.

Brien McMahon was born in Norwalk, Conn., in 1903. He was graduated from Fordham University in New York and then received his law degree from Yale Law School. He entered private practice until 1933 when he was appointed an Assistant United States Attorney General. Later he took charge of the Criminal Division. He argued twenty cases before the Supreme Court and never lost one. He figured prominently in newspapers because of some of the cases he prosecuted, such as the McKesson and Robbins swindle, the Harlan County Coal Operators, and many others.

In 1944 he was nominated by the Connecticut Democratic Party for the office of senator and was elected. A brilliant man with a bent towards the scientific, McMahon interested himself in the then secret atomic bomb—not as a weapon but for uses in peace. He introduced and carried through the Senate the first bill on the control of atomic energy. Consequently, he was appointed Chairman of a special committee on atomic energy. He arranged with scientists working on the bomb project to give him special courses in nuclear physics so that he might be more effective. As a result he and his committee produced the bill that established the Atomic Energy Commission. Congress, realizing the importance of atomic energy and its dangers, yet knowing very little in the way of actual information, decided to create the Joint Congressional Committee on Atomic Energy which would serve as a watchdog and alert the legislature. McMahon was the natural selection as its chairman.

McMahon realized the dangers in the uncontrolled power of a nuclear power. He also knew that the Russians would develop hydrogen weapons, just as we were doing. He believed that the best protection for the world was to internationalize all nuclear knowledge and put it under strict international control. He saw the United Nations as the logical body to exercise this supervision and control. He advocated open inspection under the supervision of the Security Council. By some McMahon was condemned as an internationalist and a "one-worlder." But he was honest in his quest for world peace and had told close friends that he intended to devote all his effort to establish order and peace. His untimely death ended that quest.

Three diverse men. All three had different reactions in their approaches to politics, yet basically all were in the same quest. Al Smith worked for the poor and needy of the world. Frank Murphy sought a reign of liberty under law within his country. Brien McMahon strove to create world peace. The accusation has been made that the Catholic Church is monolithic — if this means agreement in basic principles and beliefs, that is true. But in the application of those beliefs and principles, each individual seeks his own way and this is the opposite to monolithic. And that is what the lives of these three Catholic politicians clearly demonstrate to any man of good will.

The Comforting Hand of Charity

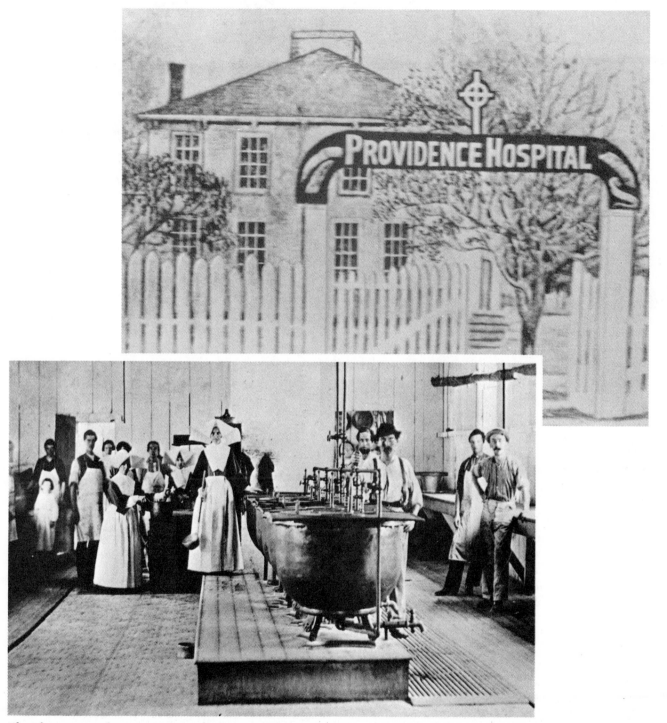

The first privately operated hospital in Washington, D.C., and the only one to care for civilian as well as military patients, was Providence Hospital founded by four Daughters of Charity from Emmitsburg in June, 1861.

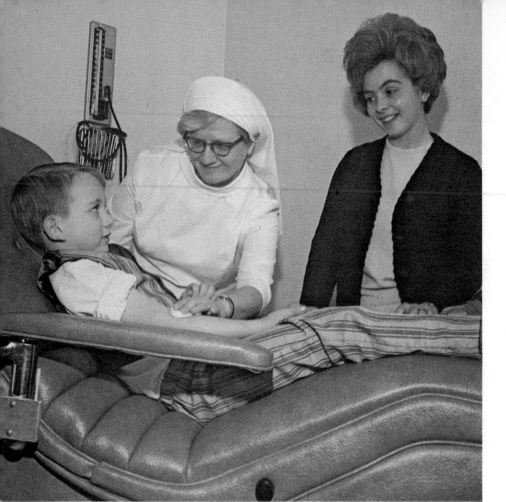

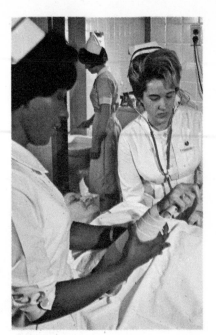

Long years of training and study have their final rewards in working for the good of all mankind.

More than anything else, the selfless works of the various orders of Sisters has contributed to the development of 814 general hospitals.

IF the Catholic Church had done nothing else in the United States but conduct its charitable works, the American people would still be deeply in its debt. The Church marched with advancing civilization, and sometimes was there beforehand. Besides the steeples of churches and cathedrals, there rose hospitals, orphanages, shelters for the handicapped, places of rest for the aged. Long before any community hospital became a part of the American landscape, Catholic hospitals were serving patients of every race and creed. In the Civil War, the Government called upon Catholics Sisters to staff military hospitals, and approximately 800 Sisters thus served their country through nursing. They were familiar sights on battlefields; and we have eyewitness descriptions of them searching for wounded at night by lantern light, and comforting the dying and treating the wounded amid the carnage of Gettysburg.

Statistics have no compassion in themselves,

but they are indicative of the extent of the Church's charity. For Catholics of the United States, the following statistics are listed: 814 general hospitals; 135 special hospitals; 14 million patients treated annually; 350 schools for nurses, training some 36,000 student nurses; 273 orphanages and infant asylums; 339 homes for the elderly. There are Catholic schools for exceptional children, and special schools for the blind. The Catholic University of America conducts the Visually Handicapped Institute, where teachers for the blind are trained.

The first school for the deaf was established in 1837, at Carondelet, Missouri, by Sisters of Saint Joseph, pioneers in this type of work. Catholic clinics for the deaf today give hearing tests and advice on the use of hearing aids. Special clinics and schools are operated for deaf-mutes, and there are some hundred centers in the United States that provide religious care for the deaf and the

Hand of Charity

A Sister must have long hours of training in various fields in order to fulfill her duties.

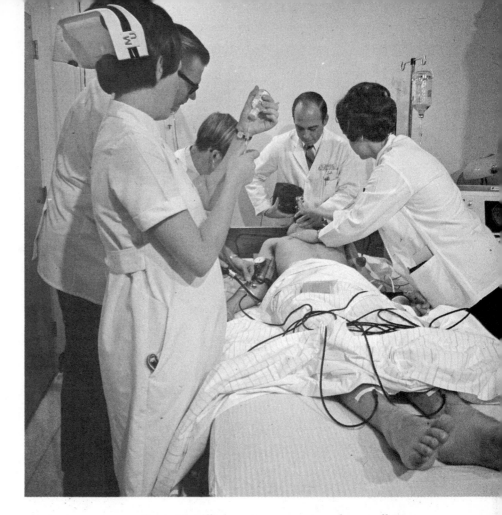

Over 14 million patients are treated annually in 949 general and specialized hospitals run by Catholic Religious Orders in the United States.

dumb. Priests and Sisters have been trained in the use of sign language, by means of which retreats and religious exercises are conducted.

The charitable work of the Church is co-ordinated in each diocese, through the organization of Catholic Charities. The first such central agency was established in 1903, and the idea spread quickly. The principal areas served by Catholic Charities are these: health services, care of the aged, child-welfare services, family-welfare services, and recreational services for youth. In the New York Archdiocese, for example, Catholic Charities co-ordinates the work of some 200 welfare agencies. In a single year (there), more than a half million people will be aided by Catholic charities at a cost of millions of dollars contributed by the Catholic people of New York.

The Catholic Charities units are co-ordinated by the National Conference of Catholic Charities founded in 1910. The Conference has a fourfold

program: to bring about an exchange of views among Catholics experienced in social-welfare work; to publish literature related to works of charity; to further the development of Catholic social-welfare work; and to assist local organizations to improve their programs. The Conference numbers about 1,500 institutional and organizational members, and several thousand individual members. This organization also represents the Catholic Church before the Economic and Social Council of the United Nations.

Another Catholic organization active in the field of charity is the Society of Saint Vincent de Paul. It is an association of laymen, dedicated by personal service to aid the poor and needy through the corporal and spiritual works of mercy. In 1845, the first group, or "conference," of this association was established in Saint Louis, and thereafter the movement spread rapidly. By 1910, there were 730 conferences; today there are approximately

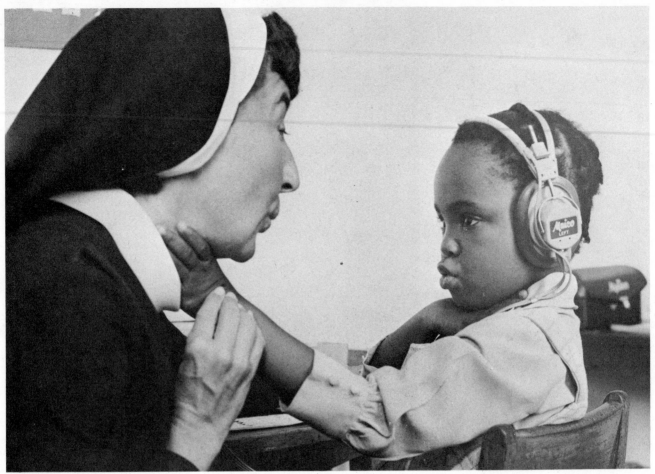

The Center House in Virginia works with the disadvantaged and handicapped to help them developed basic skills.

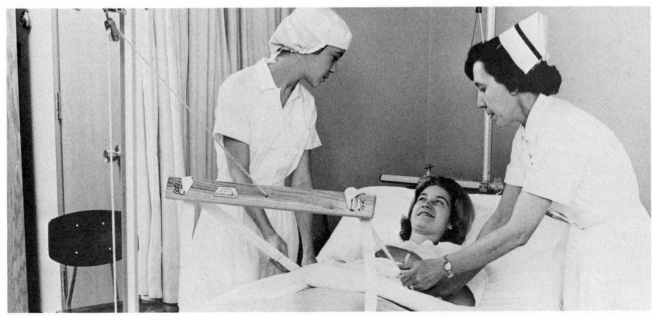

A hospital must provide more than just care. A smile and friendly conversation helps as much as the treatment.

Boys Town director Msgr. Wegner with Patrick Norton.
The home was begun in Nebraska by Father Flanagan.

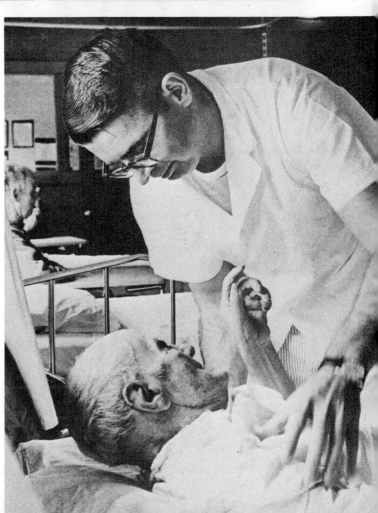

This doctor's work is not just care but also comfort.

3,500 conferences. Members of the organization visit hospitals and other institutions, to give spiritual and material aid where it is needed; they take care of poor and neglected children, sponsor summer vacations for the underprivileged, provide Christian burial for the poor, give shelter and food to the homeless, and offer legal advice to the needy. It is conservatively estimated that the Society of Saint Vincent de Paul has distributed over a hundred million dollars to the poor of the United States. Other organizations, such as the Knights of Columbus and the Ladies of Charity, also perform charitable works in behalf of the needy.

The Catholic Church has always been deeply concerned about the leisure time of young people, and as a result, many organizations have been founded to serve the young. Catholic Boy Scouts and Girl Scouts are well known. One of the most active and developed programs is that of the Catho-

For many it is impossible to leave their homes for Sunday Mass. The answer then is to bring Mass to them.

lic Youth Organization. The CYO was founded in Chicago in 1930 by Bishop Bernard Sheil as a program of spiritual, cultural, social, and physical activities. The movement spread rapidly, and today it is found in all parts of the United States. The parish is the basic unit, and the parish units are co-ordinated through diocesan councils. The youth program of the Church is federated under the hierarchy, through the National Council of Youth.

Some of the best-known priests in America gained recognition because of their charitable work. Father Nelson Baker, who founded a group of charitable institutions at Lackawanna, New York, was a man who touched many lives. When he died, in 1936, a half million people came to do him honor. There were times when the mourners, four abreast, extended for over a mile; even at two o'clock in the morning it took a half hour to reach his bier. Men, women, and children; whites

and Negroes; Catholics, Protestants, and Jews; rich and poor—all of these were in the line to pay their respects to the man who had helped so many babies, mothers, sick, orphans, and teen-agers. Father Edward Flanagan became internationally known because of his famous Boy's Town in Nebraska; and he, too, had the support of people of many faiths.

From the time the first Catholic orphan-asylum-and-hospital was established in 1727, by the Ursuline nuns in New Orleans, the charity of the Catholic Church has been a witness to all Americans of the love of God. That charity has been rendered upon the basis of need, and not religion. The Church's many relief works have grown as the United States grew; and in their growth, they have become organized. But always, on the personal level where they are implemented, the spirit of Christ shines through.

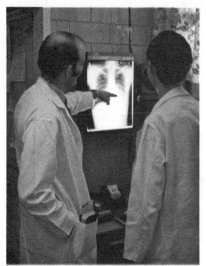

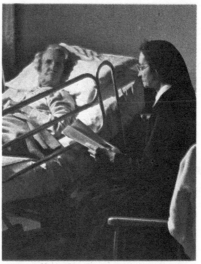

There are 135 specialized hospitals run by Catholics in America.

Not all of the responsibilities of these Sisters are technical.

Some skills which we all possess are not appreciated until lost.

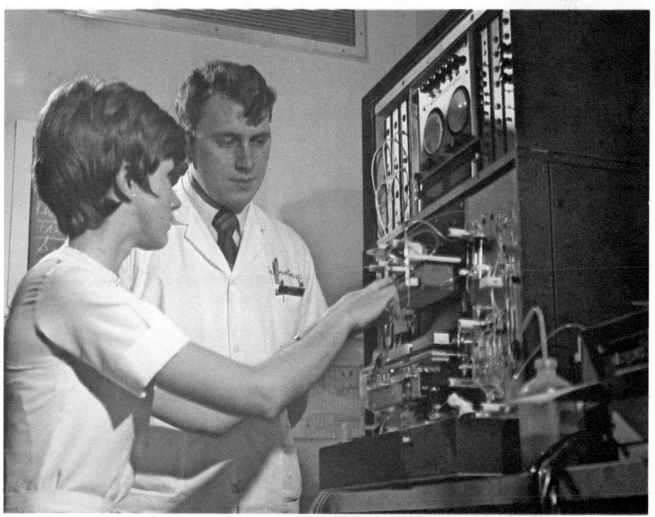

The work in any hospital requires many months of training on a technical level. To most, it is well worth it.

Catholics and Intellectual life

THE impact of Catholics on American intellectual life is yet to be felt to any great degree. The sad fact is that American Catholic scholars are conspicuous by their rarity. The names of a few priests—Cardinal John Wright, Bishop Primeau, Fathers Avery Dulles and John Tracy Ellis, the late Fathers John Courtney Murray, John LaFarge and Gustave Weigel — might come immediately to mind, but the search for prominent lay intellectuals is tedious. Some might suggest Eugene McCarthy, Pat Moynihan or Daniel Callahan, while others might challenge their selection on one point or another. Catholics have turned out a fair share of lawyers and doctors, and even college professors with their doctorates; however, general scholarship with national impact seems to present a void.

Doctor John J. Kane, the Notre Dame sociologist, made a random sampling of the *American Catholic Who's Who* some time back. His study revealed that only two per cent of the persons sampled were listed as physical scientists, and no one was listed as a social scientist. In answer to his own question about this lack of scientific scholarship, Doctor Kane came to three conclusions. First, not enough Catholics go to college. Second, of those who do go to college, only a very small number go on to graduate schools for training as scholars. Third, many Catholics go to non-Catholic colleges and are thus unaware of Catholic social thought. However, since that study, the conclusions have been in transition with more Catholics going to college and entering graduate school.

While Doctor Kane's reasons are immediate, the problem of the lack of Catholic scholars is really rooted in history and psychology. Reference has already been made to the prejudice and bigotry exhibited towards Catholics by the American culture. The result has been that in the past Catholics have tended to segregate themselves, to protect themselves by remaining apart from American cultural life. We founded our own schools, gathered together in our own associations, developed our own writers, and met with our own kind. The result has been a sort of inbreeding. The objection might be made that, in European Catholic societies, the same type of inbreeding exists; but actually the situations are not parallel. The reason for the American Catholics' withdrawal was defensive, born of an unconscious, or sometimes conscious, sense that fellow citizens regarded Catholics as inferiors.

This projection of inferiority was due to first, the Catholic's immigrant status. He had come to the United States, had begun at the bottom of the economic ladder and had developed a vague sense of not really belonging. He gave himself to his new country, only to learn that he was not readily accepted. His children who were born here found the way easier; but at the same time,

John Courtney Murray, Catholic priest and scholar

they inherited from their parents some of the immigrants, uncertainties. The process of assimilation and balancing-out was a matter, not of years, but of generations. Only today are American Catholics moving into an area of security and a consciousness of their equality.

While the immigrant Catholic desired education for his children, that education was valued for practical and economic reasons, and not from any desire for the children to become scholars. Education meant better jobs and more money, and only sufficient education to accomplish those objectives was desired. In many cases, that meant solely an elementary-school diploma, and very seldom more than a high-school one. However, as an objection to the immigrant-status argument for the lack of education among Catholics, it is often pointed out that Jews also were immigrants in relatively the same period, and that they had a much higher proportion of children in school and college.

It is true that the Jews had a greater record of scholarship. But again the cases are not completely parallel. Jewish society was much more closely knit than that of Catholics, and aid from one Jew to another was much more frequent. But the main factor was the Jewish tradition of scholarship; indeed, education is almost a tenet of Jewish religion, extending back into Biblical times. For many centuries, the Jews had been outsiders and consequently were better adapted to meet discrimination and challenge; while for most Catholic immigrants, being an outsider was a new experience.

John Tracy Ellis, America's foremost Catholic historian, in referring to the lack of scholarship pointed out that when the Catholic University was founded in 1889, the first rector was compelled to recruit the original faculty of eight from six foreign-born professors and two converts. Ellis added that this was necessary even though the rector was very conscious of the charge of "un-American" that was being leveled at the new university by the A.P.A.

One other factor militated against scholarship for Catholics, and that was inherent in American culture itself. Americans have a passion for equality; although they may not always grant it to others, they demand it for themselves. When someone gets "too big for his britches," the American tendency is to reduce him in size. Americans are also uneasy with people whom they don't understand— and this uneasiness extends to scholars. In European and Asiatic cultures, the scholar is respected;

Fr. Hesburgh, president of Notre Dame University.

317

The reknowned Catholic author Clayton Barbeau has long been an advocate of the worth of the family structure.

Cardinal Wright is a respected author and essayist.

in the United States, he is too often suspected. Americans jokingly pass off this suspicion with terms such as "egghead" or "liberal." This common attitude is perhaps one explanation why intellectuals do poorly in politics and usually enter government only by appointment.

Catholics readily absorbed this facet of American cultural behavior. Even the fact that they had their own schools did little to teach them respect for scholarship. Christopher Dawson observed: "We know only too well how little effect the Catholic school has had on modern secular culture, and how easily the latter can assimilate and absorb the products of our educational system."

There were three periods of American Catho-

William Brennan, Catholic on the Supreme Court

Orestes Brownson, philosopher convert to Catholicism

Fr. Reinert was the president of St. Louis University.

lic life when Catholic intellectuals were more reasonably proportioned to the population. The first period occurred in colonial Maryland, where culture and scholarship were appreciated. It has already been stated that Maryland's Catholic families sent their children to Europe for classical educations. In colonial Maryland, there was gentility that respected the intellect, and the English Jesuits who labored there were men of broad culture.

The second period of Catholic intellectualism

Fr. John LaFarge (right) fought for civil liberties.

in the United States began when exiled French priests came here. Simon Bruté, Jean Cheverus, Edward Sorin, Benedict Flaget, Francois Matignon, Gabriel Richard are important names of the period. The quest for knowledge, the appreciation of things intellectual, were part of those priests' way of life. Father Richard erecting a library in the wilderness was typical. Bruté hauled thousands of books over the Appalachian Mountains to build the greatest library in the West.

Champion of the conservative cause, William Buckley

Fr. Walter Ong discusses anti-Catholicism in America.

Frances Keyes wrote over 50 books in her 85 years.

But unfortunately, the French priests had little contact with each other, and the areas where they labored were the most primitive in the country. It is difficult to assay what their effect would have been if they had remained in the seaboard cities of large Catholic population.

Another intellectual movement took place in the middle of the nineteenth century, but that, also, did not come from within the native Catholic Church. It was brought about by a series of conversions of Protestant intellectuals: Orestes Brownson, Isaac Hecker, James Roosevelt Bayley, William Henry Anderson, Anna Dorsey and Joseph Chandler were scholarly, cultured people. They had some effect on their times, but it was personal and started no trends. Father Hecker did found the Paulists, a religious society that has had impact on education and things of the intellect. He also began *The Catholic World*, which became a forum for serious Catholic minds. Brownson also had a magazine where the intellectual could find voice.

That same period saw the foundations of many of our largest Catholic universities: Georgetown (1789), Saint Louis (1818), Fordham (1841), Notre Dame (1842), Villanova (1842), Dayton (1850), Santa Clara (1851), San Francisco (1855), Niagara (1856), Saint Bonaventure (1856), Seton Hall (1856), Marquette (1857), Saint John's in Collegeville (1857).

One of the most interesting phenomena in the story of the Church in America is the development of the Catholic school system. The statistics are not only impressive but encouraging. There are now some 260 Catholic colleges and universities, with double the number of students over 1945.

If the increase in Catholic college enrollments is encouraging, there is also a caution signal there: college facilities are crowded; first-rate professorial ability is eagerly sought and is spread quite thin; and expenses have no ceiling. Some Catholic colleges solve the professorial problem by hiring non-Catholics, and while this works well in certain subjects, it does dilute Catholic influence. Other colleges, hoping to get government financing to meet pressing money problems for expansion and salaries, secularize themselves to such an extent that they prostitute their very reason for being. Many in the educational field believe that there are too many Catholic colleges; that too many religious groups, provinces of religious groups and dioceses, all seek the status symbol of a college without consideration of the costs and complexities. The accusation is also made that Catholic colleges are too catholic; that they attempt to teach everything—accounting, astronomy, business administration, geophysical engineering, fashion design, prosthetics, right through to zoology; that it would be better for the Catholic college to specialize in speculative subjects that have a definitely Catholic frame of reference, and to allow the secular colleges handle secular subjects; certainly the main criterion for judging a Catholic college is on the basis of the quality of its theology and philosophy departments, and on this criterion very, very few would get a high grade.

Criticism is also made of the type of scholar the Catholic college produces. There is evidence that colleges for men are less successful than those for women. Robert Knapp and Joseph Greenbaum in their study, *The Younger American Scholar*, were unable to include a single Catholic college for men as a producer of scholars in the sciences and humanities. However, in considering origins of women scholars, Siena Heights College, Adrian, Michigan, was listed tenth. Among a sampling of small colleges for women, Nazareth College, Nazareth, Michigan, led the list, outranking the better-known Swarthmore. Aquinas College, Grand Rapids, Michigan, was sixth; and Loretto Heights College, Denver, was twelfth.

In any event the whole matter of Catholic education is under very radical scrutiny both as to its philosophical approach and its practical existence. Since the end of Vatican II, disorientation among Catholics and ever expanding costs, along with a lack of qualified teachers, have caused the closing of elementary schools, some high schools and a few colleges. There has also been a movement for consolidation, mainly on the lower levels. The problems are even more acute in seminary education and the realization has at last come that fractional operations are not only uneconomic but unproductive. An attempt has been made for the consolidation of some seminaries, others have diversified, and a few have joined with Protestant seminaries.

While critics of Catholic education have certain validity to their arguments, the situation is changing very rapidly. Most of the critics speak in the present, but base their remarks on conditions of a generation ago; and most of the surveys that show poor Catholic scholarship are a decade or more old. The fact that fifty per cent of Catholic students entered college in 1970 is in itself indicative of the change. This is an age of specialization, wherein leadership demands knowledge and intellectual ability. It took more than 170 years for Catholics to reach full political equality in the United States; now circumstances are suitable for equality in scholarship. Impatience in reaching that goal is not wrong in itself, but it does become harmful when a false image is projected to the world without adequate explanation.

Another indication of the developing Catholic intellectual level is found in the quality and growth of Catholic intellectual publications. *America, Commonweal, The Catholic Worker, Catholic World, The Critic, Thought, Worship*—these magazines are but a few that illustrate the diversity. There are others, like *Cross Currents* and *Worldview*, which while not ostensibly Catholic, are edited by Catholics. The Thomas Moore Association of Chicago has done a great deal to stimulate Catholic intellectual discussion.

When all the facts are weighed and evaluated, they indicate that American Catholics are about to make to the United States the intellectual contribution that has been for so long delayed.

Father Andrew Greeley, an author and a sociologist

American Catholics and Science

It has often been said that science and theology conflict, and in certain circles the impression has been created that the Catholic Church is opposed to science. Nothing can be further from the truth. Pope Pius XI, in his letter *In multis solaciis*, which re-established the Pontifical Academy of Science, declared: "Science, which is the true knowledge of things, never is repugnant to the truths of the Christian Faith." Indeed, science and religion go hand in hand because both have the same end: truth. Science deals with truth derived from observable phenomena, while religion deals with truth that has been revealed by God. Since all truth comes from God, and since God cannot contradict Himself, true science and true religion cannot conflict.

The Pontifical Academy of Sciences is proof in itself that the Church has no fear of science. In this institution are gathered the finest scientific minds in the world, not all of them Catholics. Doctor Alexis Carrel was a member of the academy until his death. Doctor Carrel has been called the most original physiological surgeon of the century. In 1906 he joined the Rockefeller Institute for Medical Research, and he served with the institute in New York City until his retirement in 1939.

Doctor Carrel developed a new method for suturing blood vessels, making it possible to transplant entire blood vessels. For this work he received the Nobel Prize in physiology and medicine. Doctor Carrel then went on to new discoveries, the greatest of which was the cultivation of living tissues outside the body. With Charles Lindbergh, famous trans-Atlantic flier, Carrel perfected the mechanical or artificial heart, a germproof perfusion pump. This discovery is largely responsible for the seemingly miraculous heart operations that are performed today as routine.

Despite his scientific achievements, Doctor Carrel found no conflict between his vocation and his religion. He presented his views on religion and science in a best-selling book, *Man the Unknown*. Whenever Doctor Carrel could get away from his work, he went to Lourdes, where he served on the commission that evaluates the cures obtained there.

One of the most remarkable of American Catholic institutions is the *Institutum Divi Thomae*, which was founded for the sole purpose of scientific research by the late Archbishop John McNicholas. The *Institutum* also offers special training to graduate Catholic scientists. The main laboratory is in Cincinnati, where experiments and investigations are conducted in biology, chemistry, biochemistry, bacteriology, nutrition, and physics. Another laboratory is in Florida, where aquatic and marine studies are made. There are also some

Doctor Alexis Carrel, Nobel Prize winner in medicine

CATHOLIC LIFE ANNUAL

Doctor Tom Dooley the great humanitarian of Indochina was a Catholic. He died before completing his mission.

fifteen other laboratories affiliated with the *Institutum*, and they carry on research under its supervision.

The work of the *Institutum* is very broad. It is making depth studies related to cancer, hoping ultimately to find a cure. It examines the basic problems of growth, of metabolism, and of cancer-resistant cells. Biodynes were discovered at the *Institutum;* they are substances that control cellular metabolism, and that can be used in healing wounds. Studies are being conducted on the effects of ultraviolet and infrared lights for therapeutic and sanitary ends. Agricultural research is carried on in relation to food preservation, veterinary diseases, and reclamation of waste farm products. The *Institutum* also does classified work for the United States military.

The man behind this unique Catholic activity is Doctor George Sperti, who took over direction of the *Institutum* when he was only thirty-five years old. Doctor Sperti invented the K-va meter,

Doctor William Walsh, Catholic head of Project Hope

325

A Whole New Science
Opens for Mankind

NASA

NASA

Commander of Apollo 9, James McDivitt is a Catholic.
Catholics have contributed much to the NASA program.

Reverend Msgr. Luigi Ligutti is the representative to the F.A.O. of the United Nations from the Vatican.

Father John A. Zahm, Notre Dame anthropologist

the Sperti Sun Lamp, and various light-treatment processes affecting food and bacteria. He is the discoverer of biodynes. He has been a member of the Pontifical Academy of Sciences since 1936.

One of the most distinguished Catholic scientists in the United States, Doctor Hugh Taylor, was head of the Princeton University chemistry department until his retirement. Doctor Taylor received many awards for experimental chemistry and honorary degrees from more than fifteen colleges and universities. During his active days at Princeton, chemists from all parts of the world arrived to study under him. He, also, became a member of the Pontifical Academy of Science.

To attempt a complete list of prominent

Catholic scientists would be impractical; but indications can be given of some Catholics who excelled in their professions. Peter Debrye, a member of the Pontifical Academy of Science, formerly head of the chemistry department at Cornell University, regarded as a world authority on chemistry, won the Nobel Prize in 1936. Anthropology is represented by the late Father John Cooper, founder of the Catholic Anthropological Society, and until his death associated with the Catholic University. Doctor Frank Setzler led many anthropological expeditions, authored many books and articles, and rose to be head curator of the Smithsonian Institution. In botany, Catholics are represented by Constantine Rafinesque and Edward Grant. The naturalist Louis Agassiz said of Rafinesque, "Both in Europe and in America, he anticipated all contemporaries." Grant has been referred to as one of the leading scientists of the world.

Medicine, also, receives its contribution. Doctor John Kolmer, professor at the University of Pennsylvania and at Temple University, became recognized as an expert in bacteriology and chemotheraphy. Doctor Thomas Parran turned his medical talent to public service and rose to be the head of the United States Public Health Service. Doctor Parran was preceded by Doctor Robert O'Reilly, personal physician to President Cleveland. After forty-five years of public service, Doctor O'Reilly retired in 1909 as surgeon-general of the United States Army. Doctor Eugene Geiling, professor at Johns Hopkins University and the University of Chicago, has been recognized as an authority on insulin and gland studies. The greatest surgeon in the first half of the twentieth century was generally acknowledged to be Doctor John Murphy.

Doctor Albert Zahm, once a professor at Notre Dame University, became head of the aerodynamics division of the Library of Congress. He made many important inventions that advanced the aircraft industry: among them were the three-torque control, the wire tensometer, the vectrograph protractor, the three-component anemograph, and a series of important discoveries involving aerodynamic balances. Frank Piasecki was a pioneer in the development of the large helicopter; today his helicopters are widely used in both civilian and military aviation.

Physics has received the attention of many Catholic scientists. Karl Herzfeld left Johns Hopkins University to become head of the Catholic Uni-

Julius Arthur Nieuland, famed chemist and botanist

Lloyd Bucher, commander of the ill-fated "Pueblo," was a graduate of Father Flanagan's Boys Town.

versity's physics department. He has written many monographs and has received a large number of awards and decorations for his experimental physics. Another specialist in physics research was Doctor John Hubbard, who taught at Johns Hopkins, the New York University, and the Catholic University. Thomas Killion, a physicist who made a success in business and then as an instructor at Massachusetts Institute of Technology, went into Government service and became the scientific head of the Office of Naval Research, developing the Polaris submarine program and the Navy's space program.

Many priests have contributed to America's

scientific development. The late Father Julius Nieuwland, a professor at Notre Dame University, won acclaim in the fields of botany and chemistry. He helped develop Lewisite gas, but his greatest discovery was the formula and method to produce synthetic rubber—which revolutionized the American rubber industry and saved the Allies in World War II when Far Eastern rubber plantations were lost to the Japanese. Two of the leading seismologists in the United States are Father William Lynch, of Fordham University, and the late Father James Macelwane, of Saint Louis University. These priests developed the outstanding seismological stations in the country for the accurate location of earthquakes.

Although the number of Catholic scientists is not overwhelming in proportion to the total Catholic population, the gap is being narrowed every year. Catholic universities are strengthening their science departments, and more Catholic graduates are going on for higher studies. Typical of these newcomers is Doctor William J. Thaler, still a young man but referred to as "one of the most imaginative scientists on the national scene." Doctor Thaler won his doctorate from the Catholic University and has held high posts in the Office of Naval Research.

Doctor Thaler was the architect of the historic Argus project. When he first set this project down on paper, many physicists regarded it as absurd. Doctor Thaler ignored adverse comments upon his idea, and went ahead. The Argus project involved cloaking the earth in a shell of electrons by detonating three atomic bombs at an altitude of over three hundred miles, for the purpose of gathering vital data on the earth's magnetic field and the radiation in the upper atmosphere.

Despite many attractive offers from private industry, Doctor Thaler chose to stay in public service. "Making money," he said, "is not, to my mind, synonymous with success. The thing is not what I have done materialistically, but what I have done with myself, intellectually, spiritually, and philosophically."

This is the spirit that every true Catholic scientist brings to his work.

Albert Zahm specialized in the aerodynamics industry.

Catholics Contribute to Literature and the Arts

The Catholic contribution to the American culture has been a subject long debated, and it is not the intention to go into lengthy argument here. Certainly, a strong case can be made for the influence of European Catholic artists on their American brothers. All our literature, for example, owes an inestimable debt to Shakespeare, Dante and Cervantes; in addition, many of our writers were directly influenced by Catholic authors—James Russell Lowell, who spent much time in Spain, was strongly influenced by the writings of Calderon; William Cullen Bryant has an unacknowledged debt to the Spanish poetess, Carolina Coronado; Washington Irving's writing bears the imprint of Fernan Caballero, in addition to finding many of his sources on the Iberian peninsula. In the realm of painting, Whistler, Chase and Sargent are indebted to Velasquez and El Greco; our music bears the influence of both Spain and Italy. For anyone who wishes to pursue this subject further, Stanley T. William's book, "The Spanish Background of American Literature" will make a good starting point.

But what about American Catholics? What influence have they had on the arts? Here is where evaluation becomes important. Simply put, there are areas where Catholics have made important contributions, and others where more might have been done. There is not too much of a question that the Catholic contribution has been late-flowering, but it is at last showing signs of maturity. Cultivation of the arts presumes education and time to think; and in the developing Catholic Church, there was little of either. It is perhaps permissible for Catholics to lacerate themselves over the smallness of the Catholic effort in the leading arts, but the reality of conditions under which the Catholic Church existed is a factor that tempers criticism.

Theodore Maynard, the Catholic author and critic, remarked truly of the eighteenth-and-nineteenth-century Church in the United States, "The Church was asking for priests, not poets!"

As Maynard so well pointed out in his review

Phyllis McGinley, Catholic writer of popular poetry

of American Catholicism, there was less discrepancy in culture between Catholics and Protestants in the early days of our Republic than there was later on. The Carrolls, Brookes, and Neales were European-educated and were the equals of any Protestant citizens when it comes to the civilities of life. Hector St. John Crevecoeur, a trustee of St. Peter's Church in New York City, published in London in 1782 his *Letters of an American Farmer*, regarded as the first book by a Catholic author in this country. The fiery Matthew Carey founded the *Columbian Magazine* in 1786 and, in the following year, started the *American Museum*—the first issue of which was devoted to Bishop Carroll. In 1811, Robert Walsh began the first American quarterly, the *American Review of History and Politics*; later he was to become editor of the *National Gazette*.

Ethel Barrymore, the classical actress of the stage

Joel C. Harris, author and creator of "Uncle Remus"

Thus in the early cultural history of our country, Catholics held a proportionate place. It was when the immigrant waves swept in upon our shores, when the Catholic population grew in leaps and bounds—an uneducated, working-class population—that the cultural gap developed. When people are poor, culture is a luxury ill afforded. Outside of some folk customs, the German and Irish immigrants brought with them little in the way of artistic culture. The later-arriving Italians brought a love of music, particularly opera, which did make an impact on American cultural mores. The earlier Spanish did have a profound architectural influence.

It is only in modern times—when Catholics have gained position and means, when their children are receiving college educations, when there is money to spare for other than necessaries—that we find a notable, Catholic, cultural awakening. The foregoing statements do not imply that Catholics had no cultural effect upon their adopted country even during the immigrant period. Con-

sidering conditions as they existed, the actual effect was in greater proportion than could reasonably be expected.

Father Abram Ryan, the poet of the Confederacy, wrote fair to good verse. James Randall was a competent poet, but today is best remembered for *Maryland My Maryland*. Father John Bannister Tabb, blockade runner and convert, wrote poems of simple sincerity. Agnes Tobin was a poet of considerable talent, who went to London to live in an artistic atmosphere. Francis Thompson and Ezra Pound were members of her coterie; Yeats called her the best American writer of poetry since Whitman; and Joseph Conrad dedicated one of his books to her. She made a translation to Racine's *Phedre*, now unfortunately lost, which critic Arthur Symons called "the finest ever made."

Louise Imogen Guiney would have been an outstanding poetess if she had not devoted more of her time to writing essays and criticisms than to writing poetry. She had a tremendous gift of

Actor and television personality, Joseph Campanella

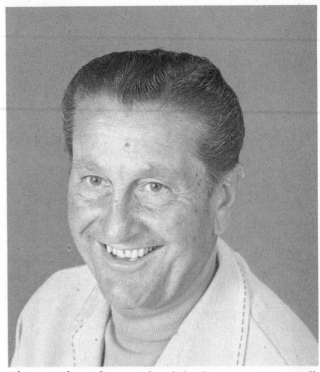

The popular television band leader, Lawrence Welk

Excellent singer and television comedian, Jim Nabors

One of America's best recording artists, Perry Como

Frank Blair, the newscaster of NBC's "Today Show"

Michael Parks was the star of "Then Came Bronson."

Hank Stram, the headcoach of the Kansas City Chiefs

Songstress and television star, Florence Henderson

335

Joyce Kilmer, poet who died in the first World War

Helen Hayes, the winner of an Academy Award

expression, coupled with a deep well of feeling. Joyce Kilmer's poetic talent was stilled in the prime of life, at his death in the first World War. T. A. Daly delighted millions with his Irish and Italian dialect verse, much of which appeared in newspapers and was later published in such books as *Canzoni, Carmina,* and *McAroni Ballads.* Joyce Kilmer's wife, Aline, published four books of poetry, as did Theodore Maynard.

In present times, Sister Madeleva—of St. Mary's College, Notre Dame, Indiana—won wide recognition as a poetess of distinction. Sister Madeleva broke away from the syrupy piety so long associated with religious poetry, and her imagery is reminiscent of Saint John of the Cross. A financial writer, A. M. Sullivan, escaped the confines of Wall Street and the investment world through his poetry. A former president of the Poetry Society of America, Mr. Sullivan published a dozen books of verse. The best-known modern Catholic poet is, of course, Phyllis McGinley, who has published many volumes, among them *A Short Walk from the Station* and *The Love Let-*

Fr. Rivers, composer of modern Catholic music

ters of Phyllis McGinley. Miss McGinley writes for some of the larger magazines for women, and her poetry is probably read by countless admirers. Father Daniel Berrigan, S.J., is an excellent poet; undoubtedly, the best priest poet in America. While one can quarrel with his activist politics (which led to jail), it is hard to fault him as a poet.

Mention should be made of William Reedy—son of a St. Louis, Missouri, police captain—who became a leader of the American literary revival. His magazine, *The Mirror*, was the show place for aspiring talent. It was Reedy who encouraged Edgar Lee Masters to write *Spoon River Anthology*. Reedy was a rallying influence for many of the Chicago intellectuals, men and women who became outstanding literary figures: among them were Carl Sandburg, Vachel Lindsay, Theodore Dreiser.

In the last half of the nineteenth century and in the early part of the twentieth, a group of Catholic women novelists made their appearance. None of them is remembered today, despite a prolific output. Anna Sadlier wrote over forty books

Vince Lombardi, perhaps the greatest football coach

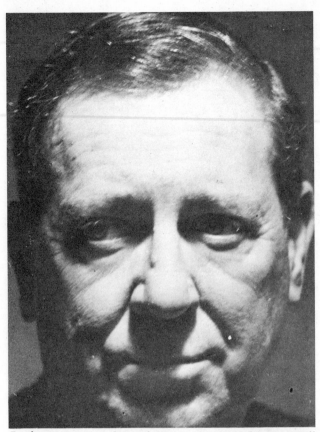

Paul Horgan, author of "Memories of the Future."

Father Abram Ryan was a fair poet of the Confederacy.

and hundreds of short stories; some of her titles are priceless: *Wayward Winnifred, The Monk's Pardon, Myles Mischief,* and *Mary Tracey's Fortune.* Christine Reid (Mrs. Frances Tiernan) was a Notre Dame Laetare medalist. Among her books were *Daughter of Bohemia, The Lady of Las Cruces,* and *A Gentle Belle.* Mary Agnes Tincker, Anna Hanson Dorsey, and Mary Waggaman were other novelists of this school. None of them equalled the quality of Pearl Craigie, who wrote under the pseudonym of John Oliver Hobbes and gave the world the witty *School for Saints* and *Robert Orange.*

One of the best-known American novelists of that same period was F. Marion Crawford, who became famous in 1882 when his first novel, *Mr. Isaacs,* a romance of India, was published. It was followed by many others, which include *Via Crucis* and *The White Sister.* Frank H. Spearman, a convert to the Catholic Church, was a very popular novelist of his day and a sought-after writer of short stories. One of his books written in 1906 was recently made into a modern television series. Stephen Fiske was equally at home in drama and in the novel. He wrote several Broadway successes, managed several theatres, originated the Actor's Fund, worked as a dramatic critic, and wrote a number of popular books.

The first of the long list of romantic novels by Kathleen Norris was published in 1911. A few of her well-known titles are *Mother, Saturday's Child, The Story of Julia Page,* and *An Apple for Eve.* Although she was an extremely popular and financially successful writer, her work cannot be termed great literature. Helen C. White, however, a professor at the University of Wisconsin, managed to combine scholarship and literary quality in her books: *A Watch in the Night, Not Built With Hands,* and *To the End of the World.* Frances Parkinson Keyes continued up to her death her long writing career with a steady output of fiction as popular as her earlier best-selling novels, *Crescent Carnival* and *Joy Street.* Mrs. Keyes also wrote Catholic chronicles and biographies—of Our Lady of Guadalupe, St. Anne, St. Catherine of Siena, and others.

Mary O'Hara, a convert, is a serious composer of music and has also written books beloved by children—*My Friend Flicka, Thunderhead,* and *Green Grass of Wyoming.* Two of the most respected Catholic fiction-writers in the United States are Richard Sullivan and J. F. Powers. Sullivan, who joined the English department at Notre Dame in 1936, and a man of great sensitivity

Ivan Mestrovic

Drama critic Walter Kerr and his playwright wife, Jean, received the Laetare Medal for outstanding Catholics.

and introspection, had his work published widely in magazines. Most of Powers' stories are written about (or against a background of) the Catholic clergy, of whom he has a great understanding. His *Prince of Darkness* is a classic, and will be included in anthologies for many years to come. A master of the short story technique, his work has been published in America's best literary magazines, such as *The New Yorker*. Of late, however, his well seems to have run dry.

In the 1920s, the frantic years of uncertainty and confusion, the vogue for writers was life on the Left Bank of Paris. Unfortunately, a number of Catholics were caught up in the restless spirit of the times, their religious life abandoned in a blind alley. F. Scott Fitzgerald, Ernest Hemingway, Theodore Dreiser, James T. Farrell and Eugene O'Neill were among the talents who fell victims to the period. Yet even though they tried to put religion from their lives, their heritage of faith could not wholly die, and its evidence is found cropping up in their work. It is one of the tragedies of the Twenties that so many authors became lost and were unable to find their way home.

Catholics engaged in the field of letters, apart from fiction and the novel, have been many. It is unfortunate that today so little is known about Orestes Brownson, whom Theodore Maynard describes as "the most remarkable mind American Catholicism has produced." Self-taught, arrogant, aggressive, Brownson was intellectually ready to take on all comers. His apologetics for the Church were written with force and candor. A contemporary of Brownson, and also a convert, was Isaac Hecker, a follower of the Brook Farm experiment. Hecker became a priest, founder of the Paulists, and editor of *The Catholic World*. He, too, had a brilliant mind, and if his writing was not as fiery as that of Brownson, it was often more persuasive. Hecker led many into the Church, and his Paulists have produced many dedicated priests, of whom Father Walter Elliott and Father James Gillis were outstanding. Father Gillis, for many years editor of *The Catholic World* and a popular columnist and lecturer, was in his own life a sort of combination of Brownson and Father Hecker.

Unquestionably, the most respected modern American Catholic literary figure is Agnes Repplier, a native of Philadelphia. As a ranking essayists in the English language, a master of the art of criticism, a model biographer, Miss Repplier was a writer's writer, and what is most satisfying is the fact that her fame rested on Catholic writings. It was Father Hecker who persuaded Miss Repplier to abandon the short story in favor of the essay. Toward the latter part of her career she shifted to biography and wrote lives of Pere Marquette, Junipero Serra and Mere Marie of the Ursulines. Miss Repplier was honored by her fellow Catholics by the awarding of the Laetare Medal. She also received the gold medal of American Academy of Arts and Letters, and honorary degrees from such institutions as Yale, Columbia, Princeton, and the University of Pennsylvania.

Paul Horgan first came to the serious attention of the literary world when he won the 1933 Harper fiction prize for *The Fault of Angels*. Since then his writing has brought him many rewards, including the much-sought Pulitzer Prize. In recent years Horgan has been mining the history of the Catholic Southwest with great profit. He has written a classical work on the Rio Grande River and one on Santa Fe. Another writer who found inspiration in the Southwest is Fray Angelico Chavez. The late Flannery O'Connor was a gifted teller of short stories. She has been recognized for her literary style as outstanding in the country.

Satire, one of the most difficult of literary forms, has received its share of attention from Catholics. A very popular writer was Finley Dunne, some of whose "Mr. Dooley" essays were read at Presidential Cabinet meetings. Dunne's satire had a strong influence on public opinion, and Mr. Dooley's remarks were widely quoted. One of the finest bits of American satire, *Mr. Blue*, was written by Myles Connolly—whose talent never duplicated that achievement. Modern satire finds an exponent in the gifted artistry of Jean Kerr ("Please Don't Eat the Daisies"), one of the nation's top humorists. The late Edwin O'Connor has shown his gift for satire in his clinical examinations of Irish-American mores in *The Last Hurrah* and *The Edge of Sadness*.

Catholic writers have come to the fore in specialized fields. It is natural to expect Catholic theologians to write on theology and other spiritual subjects; but the Trappist, Thomas Merton, brought great literary skill to his works, which have a large non-Catholic following. John Kiernan was a popular naturalist who wrote most readable articles and books; Rudolph Allers became an au-

thoritative writer on psychology; Maureen Daly directs herself to teen-age girls; Father John La Farge wrote on race relations; Walter Kerr excels in theatrical criticism; Father John Courtney Murray specialized in writing on Catholicism and the American spirit. Monsignor John Kennedy, editor of Hartford's *Catholic Transcript*, has proven a durable and competent dean of Catholic book reviewers; his criticism is informed, balanced and exceptionally readable.

Catholics have also risen to prominence in the theater. Philip Barry was one of the most gifted dramatists of the contemporary theater: he is best known for the successful and incisive *Philadelphia Story*; he also wrote *Holiday, Hotel Universe*, and the Catholic-motivated *The Joyous Season*. Emmet Lavery wrote *First Legion, Murder in a Nunnery*, and *The Magnificent Yankee*, among other plays; then he heard the call to Hollywood and devoted his writing to the screen. Eddie Dowling wrote for the stage, but is better known as an actor, producer, and director; among his successes were *The Time of Your Life, The Glass Menagerie, The Iceman Cometh, White Steed, Shadow and Substance*. George M. Cohan was not only a dramatist but also a song writer and an actor; his music is part of Americana. Jean Kerr is one of the latest Catholics to become a successful playwright; her *John Loves Mary* demonstrated a deft touch for comedy.

Catholics have long found an outlet for their talent in the theater. Augustin Daly was a prominent producer before World War I, and he introduced many performers who were to become important names in drama. Some of the Catholic actresses at the turn of the century were Eva Davenport, Paula Edwards, Maude Feeley, and Mabel Tagliaferro. Edwin Booth, perhaps the greatest actor ever to appear behind American footlights, was a Catholic. Chauncey Olcott was one of the greatest box-office names of his day. Walter Hampden made a career out of playing Cyrano de Bergerac. Mary Anderson, Margaret Anglin, Ethel Barrymore, and Mrs. Drew are names that conjure up the imagery of yesterday's great leading ladies. Helen Hayes is the grande dame of the modern theater; her talents are admired by actors and playgoers. In the 1930s and 1940s, Frank Fay was held in similar regard by the professionals.

Catholics have also played important roles in the artistic end of the motion-picture industry. John Ford has an international reputation as a director, and his pictures, such as *Stagecoach* and *The Informer*, are regarded as classics. John

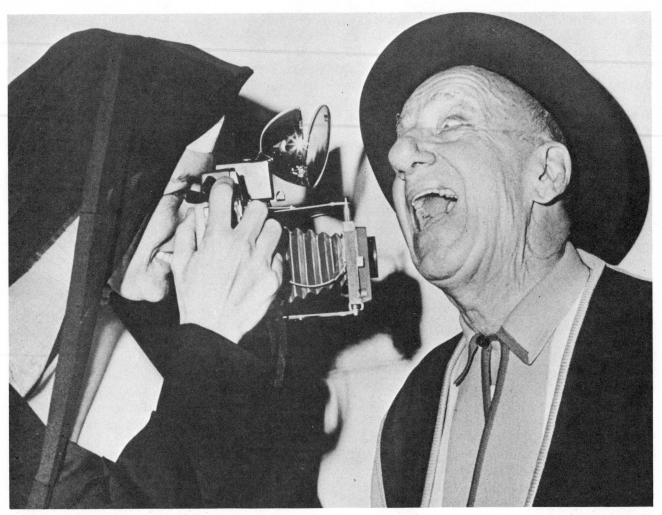

One of America's most popular entertainers has to be the great Jimmy Durante who is a practicing Catholic.

Farrow, Alfred Hitchcock, Frank Capra, Leo McCarey are other top directorial talents who made classic films. The late Dudley Nichols, Fred Niblo Jr., and Joseph Connelly give Catholic representation among top screen writers. Bing Crosby, Pat O'Brien, James Cagney, Walter Brennan, Jimmy Durante, Ricardo Montalban, Irene Dunne, Claudette Colbert, Loretta Young, and Anna Maria Alberghetti are personalities prominent in Catholic activities off the screen. The late Spencer Tracy and James Gleason were most generous to Catholic causes.

Radio in its heyday was studded with Catholic personalities. It was the daily habit for tens of millions of Americans to listen to Morton Downey, Bing Crosby, and Amos-and-Andy (The Andy—Charles Correll—of the pair became a convert to Catholicism, and the program was written by Jo-

seph Connelly who contributed much to Catholic activities). When television made its appearance, many of the leading figures of radio naturally moved into the new medium, as did many in the motion-picture business. In the first (and so far last) Golden Era of television, Catholics were represented by such familiar names as Jimmy Powers, Danny Thomas, Jerry Mathers, Lawrence Welk, the Lennon Sisters, Ted Mack, Jack Kelly, Ed Sullivan, John K. M. McCaffrey, Ann Sothern, Jane Wyatt, Macdonald Carey, Horace McMahon, Peter Hayes, Mary Healey, Terence O'Flaherty, Stephen McNally, Carroll Naish, and Don Ameche. Television, which still has little room for the experimental, did make an exception with Richard Walsh, who has produced dramatic shows that were original and advanced. Robert Crean is one of television's finest dramatists, bringing to his works a valid sense of values which devolve from his religion.

There is always a great difficulty in speaking of Catholics in the arts, entertainment and sports fields. One does not become a good singer because of a religion or a hitter of home runs because of belonging to one church. Neither does one become a good Catholic simply by being consistently under par for seventy-two holes. A Sign of the Cross before a boxing match is no excuse for not being able to counter and block. Religion is no substitute for talent, and talent no substitute for religion; and it is also true that religion and superstition can be very easily mixed. Therefore, in reading what has gone before in this section and what remains, these distinctions should be kept in mind.

There is also a further distinction to be observed: In the *creative* arts, religious beliefs and values play an important role in what a person does. An artist's philosophy will show through his writing, music, painting or design. Therefore, a critic is able to judge these artists in relation to the Catholicity; they may not be Catholic writers or Catholic painters but Catholics who write or paint, and in whose writing and painting, even though the subject may be as far from religion as one can get, religious values nevertheless have their influence, and are judicable.

In the *active* arts—entertainment or sports —Catholics are mentioned with no implication that their religion (even though it may affect their outlook) enabled them to hit a high C or run out of the pocket for a first down; but they are presented merely as bits of interesting information, as fellow Catholics who by a particular talent made a success of what they were attempting to do, and in the whole have lives that can be an example to others—and this is said without any attempt at a spiritual judgment.

Do Catholics appreciate culture? Well, the first American city to have an opera house was Catholic New Orleans, and Catholics have long been prominent in the realm of musical arts. One need only think of the great names of the past— McCormack, Patti, Martinelli, Caruso, Alda, De Luca, Tetrazzini—to realize the contribution made to American culture. The range, however, is considerably broader than opera. Singers include such diversity as Ethel Waters, Lucrezia Bori, Ann Blyth, Jessica Dragonette, Hildegarde, Mario Lanza, Marion Talley. Musical directors range from the magnificent Arturo Toscanini to the perennial Guy Lombardo. Ignace Paderewski was the leading pianist of his time. Fritz Kreisler was a composer and violin virtuoso of outstanding talent and repute. Jimmy McHugh wrote as many popular songs as any American composer. He began his writing for the Cotton Club Revues, the Blackbird Revues, and for Ziegfeld. Included in his prolific output are these well-known songs: "When My Sugar Walks Down the Street"; "I Couldn't Sleep a Wink Last Night"; "I Can't Give You Anything But Love"; "Don't Blame Me"; "On the Sunny Side of the Street'; "Exactly Like You"; "South American Way"; "Let's Get Lost"; "Diga Diga Doo."

The "father" of the modern musical was a Catholic, George M. Cohan. Mention ought to be made of the Catholic contributions to religious music. Outstanding figures in that field are: Pietro Yon, composer, organist, and teacher; Justine Ward, teacher, writer, founder of the Pius X

Fred Allen brought "Allen's Alley" into every home.

343

School of Liturgical Music at Manhattanville and the person largely responsible for the rapid acceptance of plainchant; Nicolo Montani, compiler of religious music.

Catholic art, largely influenced by Barclay Street commercialism, caused Ralph Adams Cram to observe: "Catholic art, particularly in the United States and Canada reached the lowest point achieved by any art, religious or secular, within the historic period." Even today the average Catholic taste leans to the saccharine and realistic, but there is a growing tendency to appreciate the beautiful instead of the pretty. We have had Catholics who contributed to the arts, even if they were not fully appreciated by their fellow religionists. Conde Naste was a leader in fashion and founder of a large publishing house that established American taste through *Vogue* and *Vanity Fair*. Elizabeth Nourse was a distinguished American artist, whose talent was widely praised in Europe. John and Christopher La Farge were artistic leaders of their times. Of John La Farge, Maynard said, "He could be at will either medieval or modern—that is, Catholic." La Farge gained eminence as a painter, architect and designer of stained glass.

Architecture has not received the attention from Catholics that it deserves, though there are some Catholics of recognized ability in the architectural field. Barry Byrne designed the first modern Catholic church in the United States. Edward Schulte, John Comes, and Frederick Vernon Murphy are names known to the architectural profession. John Bartolomeo has a masterful touch in his simplicity and contrasting lines. Mario Ciampi

Kate Reed, Pat Hingle and Arthur Kennedy in the television production of Arthur Miller's work, "The Price"

"First Station of the Cross" is the title of this sculpture in black German oak by artist Anton Grauel.

Bishop Nicholas T. Elko, apostolic administrator of Byzantine rite

The Catholics of the United States came from many different rites and cultures but they have contributed all of their talents to God and to the betterment of the land that has given them their freedom.

is a daring architect whose modern design is both functional and beautiful. Conrad Pickel's stained glass windows have brought him international acclaim.

A very distinguished American Catholic architectural firm is that of Maginnis and Walsh. Charles Maginnis was born in Ireland, came to the United States in 1885, and a year later opened his architectural office, later forming a partnership with Timothy Walsh. Maginnis designed the Shrine of the Immaculate Conception in Washington, D.C., the high altar of St. Patrick's Cathedral in New York City, Maryknoll Seminary, Trinity College Chapel, St. Gregory's Seminary, and buildings for Boston College, Holy Cross College, and Notre Dame University. He received many awards and honors for his work.

Catholics are finding their places in the contemporary art world. Lauren Ford has attained an international reputation for her painting of the life of our Lord as he would have lived it in the hills and valleys of New England. Leon Dabo is represented in the National Gallery and in many art museums throughout the country. William Congdon is an outstanding modernist. Corita Kent, once a nun, is nationally known for her serigraphs, but the irony is that since leaving the convent her inspiration seems to have been lost. Gerald Bonnette in sculpture and A. de Bethune in graphic arts are well known and influential. Very original are the drawings of Jean Charlot. Harold Rambusch and Maurice Lavanoux are authorities on sacred art and architecture, and promoters of good taste in liturgical decoration. Bernard Gruenke is known for his imaginative, forceful approach to interior design.

Among modern sculptors of recognized talent are Trevor Moore, Charles Umlauf, Henry Gottfried Kreis and Father Thomas McGlynn. It was Father McGlynn who went to Portugal for interviews with Sister Mary of the Immaculate Heart, who was one of the three shepherd children, and under her direction sculptured the celebrated statue of Our Lady of Fatima. In a class by himself is Ivan Mestrovic, before his death professor of sculpture at Syracuse and Notre Dame Universities, whose work has classic proportions. Mestrovic is internationally recognized as one of the world's great artists. He received honorary doctorates from leading universities, awards from many governments, and was a member of the academies of arts and sciences of many nations.

Athletes would probably protest their non-classification as artists, arguing that success in the world of sports demands unusual dedication, talent, practice and skill. So, at the risk of provoking debate, mention will be made here of Catholics in the sports world. The number of Catholics who have gained fame and popularity because of athletic prowess is so extensive that only a brief indication can be made here of their impact upon their various fields of activity. Chroniclers of the world of sports hardly less famous than those whose careers they have followed, include such names as: Jimmy Powers, Arthur Dailey, Red Smith, Bob Considine, and, one of the greatest of all, Westbrook Pegler. Catholics who have been baseball team owners, president, managers, include: John McGraw, Walter O'Malley, Gil Hodges, Birdie Tebbetts, Louis Perini, Horace Stoneham, Joe Cronin, Walter Briggs, Al Lopez, Jimmy Dykes, Connie Mack, to name but a few. Of all Catholic baseball players, the immortal Babe Ruth is in a class by himself; his fantastic records have withstood years of onslaught. Other Catholic baseball players of renown include such names as Whitey Ford, Yogi Berra, Frank Crosetti, Johnny Pesky, Jim Piersall, Johnny Podres, Phil Rizzuto, John Coleman.

Football has received generous contributions from Catholic colleges. Knute Rockne revolutionized the game, and ranks as one of the greatest football coaches of all time. Frank Leahy and Hugh Daugherty made their marks as outstanding college coaches. Joe Kuharich was named professional coach of the year. Basketball gave fame to Joe Lapchik, Bob Cousey, Walter Dukes, Dick McGuire. Track and field brought many Catholics to prominence; the names of Jesse Owens, Greg Rice, Tom Carey, Ron Delaney, are but a sampling. Boxing brings to mind such athletes as John L. Sullivan, the first heavyweight champion; Gene Tunney, the literary Marine; Jim Braddock, the Cinderella Man; Rocky Marciano, who retired undefeated; Tommy Loughran, Lou Ambers, and Tony Zale. Whatever the sport, Catholics have made their contribution. Even in rowing, there was Jack Kelly of Philadelphia; he was the only rower ever to win the coveted James E. Sullivan Memorial Trophy, awarded annually to America's most-outstanding athlete. He has one other distinction, as the brother of a former motion picture actress, now Princess of Monaco. Perhaps this fact is an indication that American culture is now exportable.

Knute Rockne was the football coach at Notre Dame when he became a Catholic. He perfected the forward pass.

The Catholic Press in the United States

THE Catholic press of the United States is second to the religious press of no other country. It is the leading religious press, not only within the nation but in the world. Despite the fact that in the years immediately after Vatican Council II, some readjustments took place—partly because some publications lost the confidence of their readers due to a lack of focus on the true changes resulting from the Council, and partly because there was a duplication where some consolidation was needed —nevertheless, the stature and influence of the Catholic press is indicated by the growing respect and attention accorded it by the secular press which has made it the subject of study both in part and in whole, and by the fact that it is made up of more than newspapers, magazines, and sundry associate publications such as directories, guides to camps and educational institutions, and so on.

In the ordinary sense, a "Catholic" publication is one that is published as an arm of some official body in the Church—a diocese, a religious order, a recognized group—has the approbation of the bishop in whose diocese it is published (at least tacitly); and is Catholic in tone, sympathy and content. General publications, although edited by Catholics, do not fall in this category. There is a gray zone of publications, which are published with the consent of a bishop and which are sympathetic to Catholic causes but the content of which is more general; it can be argued whether these are genuinely Catholic publications, but usually they are accepted as such. Then there are others with no episcopal approbation which claim the term "Catholic"; these are usually not considered part of the establishment by those in it. Finally, there are few calling themselves "Catholic" which have the actual disapproval of their bishops; these likewise are considered outside the term "Catholic press." The best guide is the annual directory published by the Catholic Press Association which not only lists members but all publications to which the consensus gives the word "Catholic."

The earliest "Catholic" publications fall into the latter categories listed above. The first such, *Courier de Boston*, a French-language weekly, made its appearance in the spring of 1789 under the editorship of Paul Joseph Guerard de Nancrede, an instructor at Harvard College; it had a short life. Mention has already been made of the *Michigan Essay and Impartial Observer*, an informative and crusading paper founded by Father Gabriel Richard in 1809. The Irish published a number of papers, such as *Shamrock* (1810) and the *Truth-Teller* (1825); but in most cases, those publications also were short-lived.

The first strictly Catholic newspaper in this country was founded by Bishop John England in 1822, and was called *United States Catholic Miscellany*. It had its ups and downs, but it lasted until the Civil War. Other papers that appeared under Catholic auspices were *The Catholic Press*,

Father Richard Gabriel, "pioneer of the wilderness"

Father James Gillis was editor of "The Catholic World."

Hartford, 1829; *Jesuit and Catholic Sentinel,* Boston, 1829; *New York Register* (1833); *Catholic Advocate,* Bardstown, Kentucky 1836; *Catholic Journal,* Washington 1833; *Shepherd of the Valley,* Saint Louis, 1832; *Catholic Herald of Philadelphia,* 1833. In studying those early publications, one is immediately struck by their readiness to defend the Catholic Faith, particularly against the onslaughts of *The Protestant,* a virulent anti-Catholic journal. Bishop England declared the objective of his paper as this: "To publish fair and simple statements of Catholic doctrine from authentic documents, to refute calumnies, and to examine and illustrate misrepresented facts of history."

The question of which is the oldest current Catholic publication in the United States is one subject to argument. *The Pilot,* of Boston, appeared under that title in 1836. However, it was the successor of a number of other papers. Bishop Benedict Fenwick founded the *Jesuit or Catholic Sentinel* on September 5, 1829. It then went through a series of confusing name changes, some names lasting only a few months. In 1834, Bishop Fenwick withdrew his approbation of the paper since it had become "an apple of discord and disunion," and for two years Boston had no official paper. *The Pilot* finally began publication in 1836, but although it had tacit approval of its ordinary, it did not become the official archdiocesan publication until 1908.

The oldest continual Catholic publication in the United States would, therefore, seem to be the *Cincinnati Telegraph-Register,* founded by Bishop Edward Fenwick on October 22, 1831. Its first editor, Father James Mullon, an ex-sailor, immediately began battle with the enemies of the Church, particularly the *Cincinnati Journal.* The paper also sought to strengthen the faith of its Catholic readers, and the first page of the first issue was given over to proofs for the existence of God. Reports from such prominent Catholics as Father Stephen Badin and Father Peter De Smet were carried in its columns.

Another of the early Catholic newspapers that have had continuous publication is the *Pittsburgh Catholic,* which first made its appearance on March 16, 1844. The paper was founded by Bishop Michael O'Connor, who turned ownership over to a group of laymen. Its first editor and publisher was Patrick Boylan. The *Pittsburgh Catholic* as early as 1859 came out for separation of Church and State, a principle usually associated with more modern times.

Over the years, several attempts have been made to found a national Catholic daily, a form of publication popular in European and Latin-American countries. The Third Plenary Council of Baltimore urged such an effort in 1884 but to date a daily publication has not been able to succeed. The first effort at a daily was made by Nicholas Gonner, of Dubuque, Iowa, a man dedicated to Catholic publishing. The *Daily American Tribune* made its appearance on July 1, 1920, carrying frankly on its masthead the words: "First Catholic Daily in English." In 1922, the paper was moved to Milwaukee, in the hope of increasing its circulation. When the *Daily American Tribune* began publishing in 1920, it had a circulation of 11,000. The circulation peak was reached in 1937, with 21,000 subscribers. Always in trouble financially, never able to get an abundance of advertising, lacking the active support that would mean subscriptions, the *Tribune* came to a limping end in 1942.

Another attempt at a Catholic daily was made in Kansas City, Missouri. *The Sun Herald* first appeared on October 10, 1950, calling itself "a Christian newspaper." The paper was published by a group of dedicated Catholic laymen and laywomen, and carried articles by many of the best-known Catholic writers. The paper began with a circulation of 2,500 and was never able to get much over 10,000. After fighting against mounting deficits, the staff surrendered to harsh economics and suspended publication with the issue of April 28, 1951. The fact is that with the acceptance of Catholics as one of the major forces in American life, the secular press began to give more and more coverage to Catholic activities, with the result that there was a diminishing need for a Catholic paper devoted primarily to news. It is a fact now beginning to be realized by Catholic weeklies which find themselves non-competitive with secular dailies in hard news and which have had to turn to interpretation and background to survive and meet a need.

There have been some successful foreign-language dailies published from Catholic orientation in the United States: *America* (Ukrainian), *Draugas* (Lithuanian), and the very successful *Polish Daily News* of Chicago. However, all of these publications became self-liquidating as fewer

and fewer descendants of immigrants retained the tongues of their parents' or grandparents' homelands. There is a successful Spanish-language paper in Miami, Florida, *Diario de las Americas*, which sometimes refers to itself as a Catholic daily, and while it is Catholic in outlook and direction, it can only use the term in its broadest application. There are some foreign-language weeklies, usually of minimum circulations, published more to satisfy some idea of their owners, than to meet any felt need.

Although there have been many brilliant Catholic editors over the years, some of whom have already been mentioned, two men in particular deserve to be singled out for their contribution to the Catholic Church and their effect on the United States as a whole. They appeared at a time when the Catholic Church did not have the status

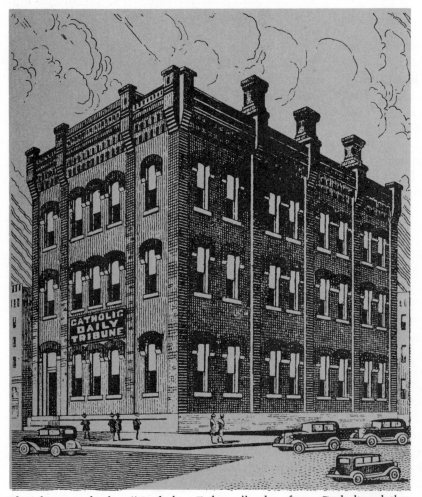

The home of the "Catholic Tribune," the first Catholic daily.

Catholic Telegraph

EDITOR:
Very Rev. E. PURCELL. V. G.

ASS'T EDITOR :-
R. F. FARRELL.

OFFICE—CORNER VINE & LONGWORTH STR'S.

Cincinnati, O., April 19th, 1865.

ASSASSINATION OF THE PRESIDENT.

Amongst all the wicked deeds which have marked with blood the history of the country, the murder of the President, by BOOTH, may be set down as the most atrocious of all. The news of the dreadful event overwhelmed the nation with affliction. Though the liberty of the press allowed the most unmeasured abuse of his Administration, though his motives were misrepresented and his person abused, and he was denounced as a tyrant, yet no one thought that any hand would be raised to shed his blood. And yet

Bishop James J. Hartley was the host in Columbus, Ohio, in 1911 when the Catholic Press Association was founded.

that it does today, and, if at times their work seems overly apologetic, it is because of circumstances under which they lived. They were vigorous, inventive and hard-hitting men, very much in the tradition of great journalists. These two were Monsignor Matthew Smith and Archbishop John F. Noll. Monsignor Smith was a short, nervously charged man of great vitality and drive who spent fifty of his sixty-nine years in the newspaper business, forty-seven of them as a Catholic editor developing an effective chain of papers.

In 1913, Smith, then a layman, was made editor of the *Denver Catholic Register*, having previously worn his green eyeshade in Altoona, Pennsylvania. Deciding to become a priest, Smith carried a full seminary schedule and continued to publish the Denver paper. He insisted that the paper have human interest and eye appeal, and that it should give all the Catholic news, even if briefly. He was ordained in 1923, and the following year started a national edition, simply *The Register*.

As the circulation of *The Register* began to reach towards a million, Monsignor Smith installed the best equipment in a modern plant, and offered his services to dioceses that would not be able to afford papers of their own. The first such paper, the *Central California Register*, appeared for the Monterey-Fresno Diocese in 1929; it was a combination of the national edition and a special local insert. The idea became popular, and editions were published for such areas of small Catholic population as New Mexico, Montana, Idaho, Utah, Nevada. For many years, *The Register* averaged about thirty diocesan editions. Even larger dioceses, able to afford papers of their own, joined the plan because of the quality of *The Register*. In more recent years, the number dwindled because of the desire of newly self-sufficient editors to take off on their own.

Monsignor Smith was not solely a good businessman; he was also a crusading editor, ready to try innovations or take up a cause. His was one of the first papers in the country to use full color on its front page. He invented new types of headlines and layout. He wrote a weekly column that was one of his paper's most popular features as well as an example of lucid and tight writing. In that column, he campaigned for better treatment of migrant workers, battled the Ku Klux Klan, protected the rights of Mexican minorities, and promoted the cause of Christian reunion. Monsignor Smith began a College of Journalism as an adjunct to *The Reg-*

ister, so that members of his own staff and those of diocesan editions could be trained. Many men who studied on *The Register* now hold important posts on Catholic and secular publications, and more than a few graduates are bishops.

Monsignor Smith died on June 15, 1960, creating a real void in Catholic journalism. Bishop Albert Zuroweste, episcopal chairman of what was the NCWC Press Department at the time, gave a tribute that found an echo in the hearts of all Catholic editors. "No individual in the history of the Catholic Press Association," declared Bishop Zuroweste, "contributed more to the spread of Christ's doctrine, to the written word of the Catholic weekly, than Monsignor Smith."

After Monsignor Smith's death, the number of diocesan editions slowly declined, as did the circulation of the giant national *Register*. The main reason for the latter was that succeeding editors brought a more and more extreme viewpoint to the paper which was not acceptable to its readers. Down to almost a tenth of its peak circulation, the Register was sold by the Denver archdiocese in 1970 to Patrick Frawley, a successful Catholic businessman, mentioned earlier, whose views were more to the conservative side. Dale Francis, who had been in Catholic journalism, in one form or another, since his conversion to the Catholic church was appointed editor. Francis has the respect of his fellow journalists and had been chosen by them for the annual Catholic Press Association award for his contributions to Catholic publishing.

Without taking away from Bishop Zuroweste's eulogy of Monsignor Smith, John F. Noll was certainly his match. This crusading editor was made Bishop of Fort Wayne in 1925, and then the Holy See gave him the personal title of archbishop in recognition of his tremendous contributions to the advancement of Catholic letters and the Church itself in the United States.

John F. Noll was born in Fort Wayne, Indiana, in 1875. His grandfather had emigrated to that outpost on the Erie Canal from Germany in 1836. His competitive spirit developed early (he had eighteen brothers and sisters). He decided to be a priest and went to a preparatory seminary conducted by the Capuchin Fathers in Calvary, Wisconsin, and then to the major seminary at Mt. Saint Mary's in Cincinnati. He was ordained in Fort Wayne, June 4, 1898, and began a round of churches, so much the part of the life of a curate. Almost from the day of his ordination, Father Noll

Msgr. Matthew Smith was one of the pioneers of Catholic journalism with his weekly. "Denver Catholic Register."

Archbishop John F. Noll (1875-1956)

Bishop Noll with Alfred Smith, governor of New York and presidential candidate in 1928, at Notre Dame in 1933.

showed an interest in helping Protestants to a better understanding of Catholics. At a time when the word ecumenism was unknown, he was cooperating with Protestant pastors, and spoke in Protestant churches long before most priests would even dream of such activity. He firmly believed in the invincibility of truth and felt that if it were known misunderstandings and bigotry would disappear. He used a magazine, *Truth*, published by Father Thomas F. Price in North Carolina, who was later to be a co-founder of Maryknoll, in his pastoral work.

It was this magazine that brought Father Noll into the Catholic press himself. The magazine did all that he wished as regards the broad spectrum of the Church but since it was a national publication, it didn't meet his local needs. With the permission of Father Price, he began putting on his own cover, called it *The Parish Monthly*, began adding more pages, and shortly was printing his own magazine. Neighboring pastors asked him to print copies for their parishes, and without realizing it, he had become a Catholic publisher.

In 1910 Father Noll was appointed pastor of St. Mary's Parish in Huntington, Indiana. The problem of transferring his printing was solved when he found the opportunity to buy a printing establishment in the city of his new parish. At this parish, Father Noll became aware of new anti-Catholic forces rising against the Church—virulent publications such as *The Menance*, *The Peril* and *The American Defender* spewed forth hatred and division—and Socialism with its materialism was growing in political strength while making a strong bid for labor support. Father Noll decided to put his printing plant to work at full capacity. He designed a new paper, named it *Our Sunday Visitor*, and issued its first copy on May 5, 1912, in a press run of 35,000. That he had hit upon a general need was evident because by the end of the first year its weekly circulation was 200,000. Based on his own personal journalism, defending the rights of the Church, and supporting the teaching of the Church, *Our Sunday Visitor* became a weekly guest in a million Catholic homes throughout the United States.

But Father Noll did not stop there. He began publishing books and pamphlets. His instructional course in Catholic doctrine, *Father Smith Instructs Jackson*, was to have a distribution of a mil-

Bishop Noll for years sponsored drives in support of the Shrine of the Immaculate Conception, Washington, D.C.

This new home of the Sunday Visitor was a result of the work of the late Bishop J. F. Noll.

lion and a half copies, not only in English but many foreign languages. Like Monsignor Smith, Father Noll used his facilities to aid needy dioceses, and soon various editions began appearing for dioceses that could never afford to have their own paper, or if they could, certainly not one of the calibre which he produced. He began a magazine, *The Acolyte*, which became *The Priest*. He developed an envelope system for parochial contributions, now in use by many thousands of parishes. Another magazine is now *The Family Digest*.

Even when he became the Bishop of Fort Wayne, the Visitor plant was his immediate concern. He brought his nephew after college into the operation to assist him, and that nephew, Francis A. Fink, was in turn to become a leader in Catholic publishing and a mainstay of the Catholic press in the United States; he held every office in the Catholic Press Association, and during his presidency guided the organization during its greatest period of growth, being instrumental in establishing a permanent national office with a full-time director and other employees. After Bishop Noll died, his successor, Bishop Leo A. Pursley, became publisher and president of the OSV corporation while Fink was to take over the day by day operations of *Our Sunday Visitor*. He directed the growth of the organization, including a new printing plant dedicated in 1961 with the most modern facilities. It is the largest religious publishing operation under one roof in the world. Francis Fink died in December, 1971, and received many posthumous tributes for his contributions to Catholic journalism. He has been succeded by John F. Fink.

Bishop Noll's journalism made him a national figure and his influence extended beyond Fort Wayne through the entire country. He spoke frequently on the radio to national audiences. During the Al Smith campaign, *Our Sunday Visitor*, week after week, answered anti-Catholic charges. He supported all sorts of activities. For years he carried on a crusade and collected monies for the completion of the National Shrine of the Immaculate Conception in Washington, D.C., and that massive structure today is a testimony to his perseverance. He directed fund drives through his paper to erect the gigantic *Christ, Light of the World* statue, which stands before the national headquarters of the U.S. Catholic Conference in Washington, and he preached at its dedication; he was also a key figure in the organization of the National Catholic Welfare Conference. He was on the committee which established the Legion of Decency and was the

Noll speaking before the gigantic statue of Christ at dedication of American Bishops' headquarters.

A testimonial to Bishop Noll's many accomplishments.

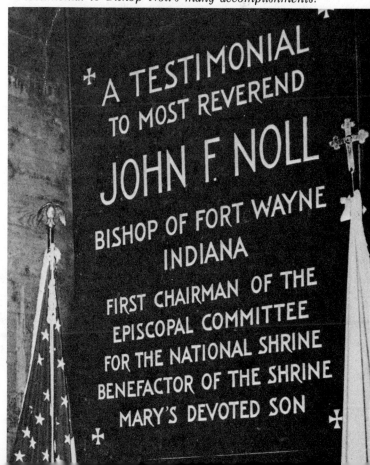

✝ A TESTIMONIAL TO MOST REVEREND JOHN F. NOLL BISHOP OF FORT WAYNE INDIANA FIRST CHAIRMAN OF THE EPISCOPAL COMMITTEE FOR THE NATIONAL SHRINE BENEFACTOR OF THE SHRINE MARY'S DEVOTED SON

Victory Noll, the home of Our Lady of Victory Missionary Sisters, was dedicated by Bishop Noll in July, 1924.

spark for the foundation of the National Organization for Decent Literature (N.O.D.L.). Not to be overlooked is the tremendous help he gave to home mission work, largely through publicity in and profits from *Our Sunday Visitor*. He was steady in his support of the Extension Society and the development of Newman centers. He enabled the newly founded and struggling Victory Noll Sisters to become established in his diocese, helping them to erect a motherhouse there and begin their missions. After he died, July 31, 1956, he was buried at Victory Noll.

There are many things that can be said about Bishop Noll but they would make a book in themselves. On the occasion of his Golden Jubilee to the priesthood, the late Cardinal Stritch of Chicago summed it up: "Bishop Noll loves people because he loves God. . . . He hated ignorance but loved the ignorant. A man of action, he went about doing something to help the ignorant. . . . To help men know the truth about the Church, and to spur the knowing to action for the Church, is the effort of these fifty years."

Another development that had a profound effect on the professionalism of the American Catholic press was the establishment at NCWC in 1919 of a Press Department. One of the functions of this division which survives in the newly created Conference of Catholic Bishops is the operation of a Catholic news service, which gathers news, features, and photographs from correspondents all over the world. This material is furnished to Catholic papers by mail and leased wire. In 1941, *Noticias Catolicas* (since transferred) was estab-

The old home of Our Sunday Visitor was a bit crowded in the mid-forties.

360

lished to service the press of Latin America, and in 1952, a radio division was begun to furnish Catholic programs with a quarter hour of Catholic news each week. Today the NC News Service sends its material to hundreds of publications all over the world and is the main news source for the entire American Catholic press.

In the magazine field, Catholic publications have had a long history. *El Habanero*, a magazine Catholic in tone but published in behalf of Cuban freedom, appeared in New York in 1824. The first fully Catholic magazine, *Metropolitan*, began publishing in Baltimore in 1830, but it was short-lived. That year saw also the first Catholic juvenile publication, *Young Catholic's Guide*, which appeared in Boston. In 1838, the *Children's Catholic Magazine*, began publishing in New York. There were other Catholic publications, all of brief existence. The oldest magazine still in existence is *The Catholic World* (April 1865); *Ave Maria* (May 1865) died in 1970; *Messenger of the Sacred Heart* (1866) departed several years earlier.

Mention has already been made of *The Catholic World* and its founder, Father Isaac Hecker. The publication began with the express purpose of converting America, and Father Hecker intended to attract an intellectual audience by making *The Catholic World* equal in literary quality and appearance to the best secular journals. A glance at the index of *The Catholic World* quickly reveals the high caliber of talent that was attracted to its pages: Orestes Brownson, Agnes Repplier, Cardinal Newman, Alice Meynell, Louis Imogen Guiney, C. C. Martindale, Hilaire Belloc, John Gilmary Shea, are names of some contributors. The magazine also served to introduce new and aspiring authors to the Catholic public. *The Catholic World* never gained a tremendous number of subscribers, but it always had, and still has, a loyal and influential following.

After Father Hecker, its best-known editor was the fiery and crusading Father James M. Gillis. That exceedingly literate Paulist, who could use words with the effect of a sword prick or a sledge hammer, as his fancy chose, gained fame from his hard-hitting editorials and went on to become a leading radio preacher. Father Gillis was afraid of no man. An early supporter of Franklin D. Roosevelt, he turned against that President when America became involved in affairs beyond its borders. He delivered broadsides against Hitler and Mussolini, detested bureaucracy, and had no love for Great Britain. He was a zealot who left little

room for middle ground: one was either an enthusiastic fan or a frustrated critic. Father John Sheerin succeeded Father Gillis and under his direction the magazine had great ecumenical impact.

Father Edward Sorin, founder of Notre Dame University, was also the founder of *Ave Maria*, a magazine that had its ups and downs. In the last few years before its demise it showed tremendous vitality, freshness, and exceptional creativity. The first issue of *Ave Maria* appeared May 1, 1865; it was then a weekly, as it was when it ceased. A printing plant was established to handle the publication. Today that plant, greatly modified and modernized turns out not only magazines but hundreds of thousands of pamphlets, booklets and books a year, plus a great deal of printing for Notre Dame University. An interesting sidelight to *Ave Maria's* history is the fact that one editor, Father Daniel Hudson, served in that capacity for fifty-four years—which should be something of a record in the Catholic press. It is said that, during this half century, Father Hudson did not spend a total ten days away from the Notre Dame campus. Another editor, Father Patrick J. Carroll, managed the publication for almost thirty years. Father John Reedy, a competent editor of broad Church vision, was the last editor. The demise of *Ave Maria* was due to a combination of factors: the normal attrition of a faithful audience, the decline in effectiveness of door-to-door salesmen on which Ave Maria was built, a shift in editorial emphasis without being able to attract sufficient subscriptions from the new audience, rising costs which severely hamper a weekly. Actually, *Ave Maria* itself did not die but was transformed into a new publication called *A.D. 70* which was of short duration.

The Catholic press of the United States has organized itself into a strong cooperative effort expressed through the Catholic Press Association. This trade organization has a national office and full-time staff, and is largely responsible for the tremendous professional strides made by Catholic publications in recent years. The range of publications represented in the association shows the catholicity of the Church, for they cover every interest, age group and taste: men, women, boys, girls, families; young marrieds; children; news, commentary, criticism, scholarship, education, entertainment; devotional, professional. One indication of the strength of the Catholic press is that it has offered assistance to publications beyond the borders of the United States; one program in particular was directed at Latin America which

The difficulty of Catholic publishing is seen in the Sun Herald. Although an excellent publication, it folded in less than a year.

consisted of exchanging personnel and seminar teams from the United States. The Association has had top flight executive directors: James Kane, Roger Caheny and James Doyle. Under Doyle's leadership the CPA began close cooperation with the Associated Church Publishers, a Protestant press association, holding joint conventions and instituting other cooperative activities.

It has been observed that a strong Catholic press is indicative of the maturity of the Church in the United States. This is also shown by the nature of the modern Catholic press which is no longer apologetic and defensive but one that seeks to inform and educate. It also shows its maturity in presenting informed criticism of the Church. The modern American Catholic press is a source of intelligent communication between Catholics and non-Catholics, not in a spirit of combat or competition, but to the end that all men may be one in Christ.

American Converts to the Catholic Church

THE number of adult conversions to the Catholic Church in the United States varies between 125,000 and 150,000 each year. These converts represent a true cross section of America, from the great and mighty to the ordinary man or woman. They came from all faiths, from all professions, from all classes. Most of them find their own way to the Church, and they come as individuals and not as part of a mass movement. A few groups, such as the Paulist Fathers, the Knights of Columbus and the Convert Makers of America, have positive inquiry programs. The Glenmary Fathers and the Missionary Servants of the Blessed Trinity, and others, do mission work in non-Catholic areas, but the average Protestant and non-Church-affiliated American is seldom personally invited to examine the Catholic Faith.

The Church remains dynamic only in proportion to the growth of its missionary concept. The salvation of mankind is the Church's very life, and the fulfillment of this mission was the purpose for which Christ founded His Church. The true Catholic parish is a missionary parish, where clergy and laity are reaching out to all who are not members of that parish. Conversion is both a supernatural mystery and a natural effect; it is the result of the grace of God and the work of man. Systematic conversions result only from unremitting work. They take place only when clergy and laity unceasingly labor to present the proper image of the Church to the public through a broad program of public relations. Inquiry classes, lectures for non-Catholics, advertising and literature, the liturgical life of the parish, and adult education for lay Catholics are all keys to the door of conversion.

In short, the missionary Church is yet to make its impact upon the United States; and this is another way of saying that the Church has not come to full maturity. There are many reasons for this. Historically, the Catholic Church in the United States was on the defensive; it was a minority Church, often under attack, sometimes persecuted. Then with the immigrant wave of the nineteenth century, the Church began to grow numerically strong but was, of necessity, introspective in order to care for the needs of its increasing flock. For many years, there were never sufficient priests to care for the expanding Catholic population. In the early days the Catholic laity belonged to the poorer classes and had little opportunity for education. As a result most Catholics had little understanding of the truths of the Faith, and consequently were not qualified to explain them to others.

The story, therefore, of Catholic converts is a story of individual experiences. Since it is impossible to tell the story of every convert, limitation will be made to only a few of these whose names are well known, people who have had an impact on their times, and who demonstrate that conversions to the Church are truly catholic.

Frances Allen was the daughter of Ethan Allen, the Vermont Revolutionary patriot. Despite the fact that she grew up in an agnostic and anti-Catholic atmosphere, she became a Catholic in 1807. She joined the Hospital Sisters at Hotel Dieu in Montreal, and was the first woman born in New England to enter religious life. The story of Mother Seton has been told previously. Cornelia Connelly, wife of an Episcopalian minister, entered the Church in 1835 with her husband. She founded the Society of the Holy Child of Jesus, while her husband became a priest. Later he returned to Protestantism, and in a famous court trial attempted to force his wife to return to married life. Mother Connelly was supported by the English courts and was allowed to remain at the head of her community.

There have been many conversions of Protestant ministers. Orestes Brownson, one of the most distinguished American converts, was a Unitarian minister before he entered the Church. Brownson was celebrated not only in America but also in Europe as a scholar and writer. He edited *The*

Boston Quarterly Review, famous for its political and social editorials, and after his conversion in 1844, he often used the *Review* for Catholic apologetics. He also wrote some seventy articles for *The Catholic World.* He was the author of numerous books.

Lewis T. Watson is better known as Father Paul James Francis. As an Episcopal priest, he founded the Friars of the Atonement at Graymoor, New York, in 1886. One of the earliest leaders in the ecumenical movement, he began the Church Unity Octave in 1908. The following year he established St. Christopher's Inn at Graymoor, a shelter for homeless men. He caused consternation in the Protestant world that same year when he announced that he and his entire community—friars, Sisters, and tertiaries—were entering the Catholic Church. He was ordained a priest in 1910, and remained as superior of the now Catholic community until his death in 1940.

Harvard-educated Selden Peabody Delany was the rector of the fashionable Church of St. Mary the Virgin in New York City when he was converted to Catholicism. He later became a priest and a prominent Catholic author. Doctor Jesse A. Locke was a Protestant clergyman who became a Catholic and founded the prominent Newman School in New Jersey. James Stone Kent — an Episcopal minister who was president of Kenyon College, Ohio, and Hobart College, New York—was converted, became a prominent Passionist Father, known under his religious name as Father Fidelis.

Teachers, educators and other intellectuals also have been drawn to the Church. One of the earliest was James Roosevelt Bayley, an associate of Washington Irving and the historian, George Bancroft. After his conversion, Bayley became a priest and later Archbishop of Baltimore. Samuel Haldeman, professor at Franklin Institute and at the University of Pennsylvania, was converted in 1843. He was founder and first president of the National Academy of Sciences. Thomas Parker Moon, Professor of history at Columbia University, editor of *Political Science Quarterly,* author, and distinguished member at the Paris Peace Conference of World War I, became a Catholic in 1914. Scholars and intellectuals of our own day who entered the Church include Thomas Merton, who became a Trappist, and Avery Dulles, son of John Foster Dulles, longtime Secretary of State, who became a Jesuit.

Literary figures rank high in the number of important converts over the years. F. Marion Crawford, one of the most famous novelists of his time, was converted in 1880. Joel Chandler Harris, whose "Uncle Remus" stories have delighted millions, entered the Church in 1908. Rose Hawthorne Lathrop, daughter of Nathaniel Hawthorne and wife of George Lathrop of the *Atlantic Monthly,* joined the Church with her husband. Pity for the poor who were afflicted with cancer led her to open a house in New York City where they might find shelter. After the death of her husband, she founded the Dominican Congregation of St. Rose of Lima.

Joyce Kilmer, another convert, was one of America's foremost poets. He died on a French battlefield in World War I. While doing research for a radio program, *The Greatest Story Ever Told,* Fulton Oursler, a distinguished editor and writer, studied himself into the Catholic Church. Oursler's daughter, April, a writer, also became a Catholic. Gretta Palmer, correspondent for the *New Yorker;* Robert G. Anderson, author of the *Cathedral* books; Artemus Ward, famous humorist; and Frances Parkinson Keyes, popular novelist and biographer, are others who have found their way into the Church.

From the field of industry and science, converts include William Henry Goodyear, son of the founder of a vast rubber empire; John Moody, the investment executive and founder of the *Moody Reports;* and many others too numerous to mention. Military conversions would include Admiral William S. Benson, chief of naval operations in World War I; General James Longstreet, one of the leading military figures of the Confederacy; and General William Starke Rosecrans, outstanding field commander of the Civil War. General Creighton Abrams became a Catholic while top military commander in Vietnam.

The law is represented by Andrew Jackson Shipman, who later promoted the publication of the *Catholic Encyclopedia;* William Robinson, instructor at Yale Law School, who later became Dean of the Catholic University Law School; Peter Hardeman Burnett, judge of Oregon Supreme Court, and later first Governor of California. One of the most important converts ever made from the labor movement was John Mitchell, the foremost labor leader of his time, and president of the United Mine Workers. Heyward Broun, founder of the American Newspaper Guild and popular columnist, was another labor convert. Politics can be represented by Stephen A. Douglas, "The Little Giant," who debated Lincoln, or by Senator Robert A. Wagner, of New York, whose labor legislation was a milestone in American industrial progress.

The worlds of sports and the performing arts have been fertile fields for conversions. In sports, two of the best known names are Knute Rockne, famous football coach, and George Herman Ruth, the immortal "Babe." The first family of the theatre—the Barrymores—were Catholics because their mother, Georgiana Drew, was a convert. The dean of theatrical critics, who was also a distinguished theatrical author and historian, George Jean Nathan, became a Catholic shortly before his death. Claire Boothe Luce, author and playwright, was converted when she found strength and hope in the Church after her daughter died in a tragic automobile accident. Joe Mielziner, cited nine times as best theatrical Designer-of-the-Season, and stage designer for hundreds of plays, operas and ballets, is a convert. Fritz Kreisler, distinguished concert violinist, is one of many converts from the art of music.

There have been prominent conversions from Judaism, a change that is often made only at great personal sacrifice. Waldeman Gurian, the respected sociologist and political scientist, joined the Catholic Church. David Goldstein, after he entered the Church, devoted his life to apologetics and an apostolate to the Jews. Max Fischer was converted during his student days in Germany; forced to flee the Hitler terror, he came to the United States where he won fame as a writer. He taught literature and philosophy at the New School for Social Research in New York. Another prominent Jewish convert was Karl Stern. His book on his conversion, *Pillar of Fire*, was a bestseller.

Among the most interesting converts to the Catholic Church are those who come from among the ranks of active enemies of religion and the Church. Martha Moore Avery was a pioneer of Marxism in the United States. An avid Socialist and Marxist long before the Communist Party was organized, she directed the Karl Marx School in Boston. After her conversion in 1903, she worked diligently to expose the errors of socialism and bol-

shevism. Bella Dodd ranked high in the Communist hierarchy in the United States, and she also lectured against communism after her conversion. Louis Budenz was the editor of the Communist *Daily Worker* before his conversion. Dorothy Day, although never a card-carrying Communist, had sympathy for the Red cause. She worked on *The New Masses*, was associated with the International Workers of the World, and various Communist fronts. In 1927, Dorothy Day was received into the Church. She was one of the founders of The Catholic Worker movement and has since devoted her life to service to the poor and an unceasing struggle for social justice.

Another convert from communism was the sensitive and introspective poet and author, Claude McKay, who was born in Jamaica in 1890. McKay came to the United States as a youth and was educated at Tuskegee Institute and Kansas State College. Despite his talent and creativity, the young Negro was unable to find employment in the writing field and had to support himself by traveling about the United States as a waiter and porter. He joined the Communist Party where his talent was recognized, went to Moscow where he met Lenin and Trotsky, and where he wrote for the Communists. Later he became an editor on the *Liberator*, a Communist publication aimed at the American Negro. He was converted in 1944, and became a faculty member of the Bishop Sheil School in Chicago. He died in 1948.

One of the most unexpected converts to the Catholic Church was Colonel Horace Atlee Mann, a native of Tennessee and son of a Methodist minister. Colonel Mann became a prominent Washington attorney and head of the Southern division of the Republican Party. In the 1928 Presidential campaign, Colonel Mann organized the bitter anti-Catholic, anti-Smith movement in the South. The violence and bigotry that developed from that campaign became an American phenomenon. But Colonel Mann and his wife were both received into the Catholic Church in 1933, a year before he died.

THIRTY-FIFTH PRESIDENT 1961-1963

The Sixties—A Pictorial of an Era

The "Mother of a Dynasty," Rose Kennedy has suffered greatly for the fame that belonged to her children. A dynamic woman, she has never shown the sorrow which she has been forced to bear. Three of her sons have died and her daughter was born mentally handicapped. Yet through all of this, she has remained an inspiration to Americans and to the world as a person who can accept the tragedies of life.

Justice Earl Warren swears in the thirty-fifth president of the United States, John Fitzgerald Kennedy. Three years later the Catholic president died at the hands of an assassin in Dallas.

Kennedy and Cardinal Cushing in Rome, the president received gifts from Pope John which included one of the three copies of the encyclical, "Pacem In Terris." Soon these world leaders, John XXIII and Kennedy, would be dead.

Robert F. Kennedy, ". . . a good and simple man . . ."

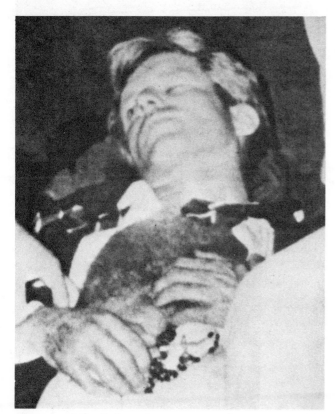

June 6, 1968, Robert Francis Kennedy is assassinated.

A stained glass window portrays John Kennedy's life.

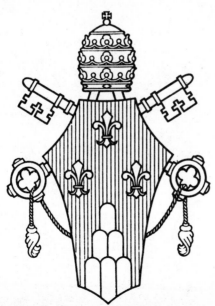

"NO MORE WAR!
WAR NEVER AGAIN!"

His Holiness. Pope Paul VI

United Nations

October 4. 1965

"Multiply bread so that it suffices for the table of mankind."

"Peace I leave with you,
my peace I give to you."

(Jo. 14, 27)

Paulus PP. VI-

-

New York, october 4th, 1965.

Index

Palos, Columbus leaves from, 23
Palou, Fr. Francis, biographer of Junipero Serra, 74
Paris, treaty of, 59; 1863 treaty of, 128
Parran, Dr. Thomas, contributions of, 329
Pegler, Westbrook, columnist, 348
Pennsylvania, Fr. Gallitzen and, 118
Peoria, John Lancaster Spalding made Bishop of, 207
Peralta, Pedro de, succeeds Onate, 62; founds Santa Fe, 62
Perez, Fr. Juan, Columbus and, 22
"Peril", anti-Catholicism and, 357
Perini, Louis, 348
Pesky, Johnny, athlete, 348
Petit, Fr. Benjamin, birth and early life of, 143; at evacuation of Potawatomi, 144; appointed by Brute, 143; death of, 144
Philip II of Spain, appoints de Aviles to colonize Florida, 58
Philippines, Magellan and, 34; Frank Murphy and, 307
Piasecki, Frank, scientist, 329
Pickel, Conrad, 348
Piersall, Jimmy, athlete, 348
Pinta, ship of Columbus, 22
Piscataway, Maryland colonists and, 98
Pius XI, Father Issac Hecker and, 223; science and, 324
Podres, Johnny, athlete, 348
Polaski, Casimir, American Revolution and, 112-113
Polo, Marco, Journal of, 17, 20
Pontifical Academy of Sciences, 324, 329
Potawatomi, inhabitants of, 142; Fr. Benjamin Petit and, 143; evacuation of, 144
Poulton, Fr. Thomas, starts academy at Bohemia Manor, 108
Powderly, Terence V., Knights of Labor and, 294; Cardinal Gibbons and, 295
Powers, Jimmy, television personality, 342, 348
Powers, J. F., author, 340
Price, Fr. Thomas Frederick, early work of, 260; Father Walsh and, 260; Cardinal Gibbons and, 260; "Truth" and, 357
"The Protestant", anti-Catholicism and, 351
Protestant Reformation, 7
Publications (Catholic), Acolyte, 359; A.D. 70, 361; America, 352; Ave Maria, (see Ave Maria); Catholic Advocate, 351; Catholic Herald of Philadelphia, 351; Catholic Journal, 351; Catholic World, (see Catholic World); Central California Register, 354; Children's Catholic Messenger, 361; Cincinnati Telegraph Register, 351; Courier de Boston, establishment of, 350; Daily American Tribune, 351; Diario de las Americas, 352; Draugas, 352; El Habanero, 361; Family Digest, 359; Father Smith Instructs Jackson, pamphlet by Archbishop Noll, 357; Jesuit and Catholic Sentinel, 351; Messenger of the Sacred Heart, 361; Metropolitan, 361; New York Register, 351; Noticias Catolicas, 360-361; Our Sunday Visitor, (see Archbishop Noll); Piolet, 351; Pittsburgh Catholic, 351; Polish Daily News, 352; Priest, 359; The Register (Denver Catholic Register), 354; Shamrock, 350; Shepherd of the Valley, 351; Sun Herald, 351-352; Truth-Teller, 350; United States Catholic Miscellany, 350; Young Catholic's Guide, 361
Puerto Rico, Columbus discovers, 23; conquered by de Leon, 31; Diego Columbus made governor of, 31; de Leon returns to, 31
Purcell, Archbishop John, American Civil War and, 172; succeeds Fenwick, 213; birth and early life of, 213-214; Bishop Flaget and, 213; work of, 214
Puritans, Maryland and, 99
Pursley, Bishop Leo A., president of "Our Sunday Visitor," 359

Quebec, Champlain requests missions in 80; founded by Champlain, 82; early colony of, 83
Quiros, Fr. Luis, meets Don Luis, 55; killed by Don Luis, 55
Quivira, de Padilla and, 48-49

Rafinesque, Constantine, botanist, 329
Rambusch, Harold, artist, 348
Ramirez, Fr. Juan, received at Acoma, 62; missionary work of, 62-63
Raskob, John, Du Pont and, 280; Alfred E. Smith and, 280
Ready, Bishop Michael J., early work of, 215; work in Columbus, Ohio, 216

Reedy, Fr. John, editor of "Ave Maria," 361
Reedy, William, editor, 337
Regenaut, diary of, 84-85
Reid, Christine, authoress, 338
Reilly, John D., work of, 281
Repplier, Agnes, works of, 340; Fr. Isaac Hecker and, 340; "Catholic World" and, 361
"Rerum Novarum," issued by Leo XIII, 296-297; labor movement and, 296-297; Bishop Ireland, and, 297
Revolution, American (see American Revolution)
Rhodes, Mary, founds Sisters of Loretto, 225; Fr. Nerinckz and, 225
Rice, Greg, athlete, 348
Richard, Fr. Gabriel, early life of, 148; during War of 1812; founds University of Michigan, 148; elected to Congress, 148-149; during cholera epidemic, 149; death of, 149, 32; Nicholas Yound and, 211
Rizzuto, Phil, athlete and sportscaster, 348
Robinson, William, conversion of, 364
Rochambeau, Jean de, aide to Washington during American Revolution, 114
Rocky Mountains, La Verendrye at, 129; crossed by Sublette, 134
Rockne, Knute, 348; conversion of, 365
Rosecrans, Sylvester, appointed Bishop of Columbus, Ohio, 215; early life of, 215; work of, 215
Rosecrans, William Starke, American Civil War general, conversion of, 177, 364; military career of, 177; offered vice-residency, 179; Stanton and, 179-180; Horace Greeley and, 179; political career of, 179
Ruth, George Herman (Babe), 348; conversion to Catholicism of, 365
Ryan, Fr. Abram J., American Civil War poet and chaplain, 174; poet, 333

Sadlier, Anna, authoress, 338
Saint Augustine, founding of, 58
Saint Francis Xavier Mission, (see Bohemia Manor)
Saint Ignace, (see Missions)
Saint Lawrence River, Champlain and, 82
Saint Louis, early growth of, 153; de LaSalle and, 95
Saint Sulpice, Priests of, description of, 195; United States and, 195; John Carroll and, 197
San Antonio de Valero (see Alamo)
San Xavier del Bac, 65; architecture of, 67; Fr. Kino and, (see Father Eusebio Kino); Indians and, 67; Apaches and 67
Santa Anna, Antonio de, attack on Alamo by, 144-147
Santa Fe, missions of, 62; de Vargas and, 62; founded by Peralta, 62
Schulle, Edward, 344
Schwab, Charles M., work of, 278
Sebastian, Brother, de Padilla and, 49; reaches Mexico, 49
Segale, Sister Blandina, birth and early life of, 162; at Trinidad, Colorado, 162; Apaches and, 163; work of, 162-163
Segura, Juan de, mission of, 55, Don Luis and, 55; massacre of, 56
Semmes, Raphael, Confederate Naval Captain, 193
Sensenbrenner, Frank J., work of, 281-282
Sequin, Juan, at Alamo, 147
Serra, Fr. Junipero, statue of, 73-74; arrives in Mexico, 74, 76; Palou and, 74; birth and early life of, 74; Galves and, 76; work in California, 76-77; Indians and, 77; death of, 77
Seton, Elizabeth, birth and early life of, 120; in Europe, 120; conversion to Catholicism of, 120; work of, 120; John Carroll and, 122; death of, 122
Setzler, Dr. Frank, contributions of, 329
Shea, John Gilmary, "Catholic World" and, 361
Sheeran, Fr. James, birth and early life of, 175; career of, 176; Union soldiers and, 176; arrest and release of, 176
Sheil, Bishop Bernard, establishes Catholic Youth Organization (CYO), 314
Sheridan, Philip (Union general), birth and early life of, 180; military career of, 180; battle of Cedar Creek and, 180, 183; battle of Five Forks and, 83
Shields, James, birth and early life of, 156; military career of, 156; political career of, 158; American Civil War and, 183; 213
Shipman, Andrew Jackson, conversion to Catholicism of, 364
Siberia, Indian migrations from, 9